EVALUATION ESSENTIALS

EVALUATION ESSENTIALS

Methods for Conducting Sound Evaluation Research

2ND EDITION

BETH OSBORNE DAPONTE, Ph.D.

JOSSEY-BASS
A Wiley Brand

Copyright © 2025 by John Wiley & Sons, Inc. All rights reserved, including rights for text and data mining and training of artificial intelligence technologies or similar technologies.

Published by John Wiley & Sons, Inc., Hoboken, New Jersey.
Published simultaneously in Canada.

No part of this publication may be reproduced, stored in a retrieval system, or transmitted in any form or by any means, electronic, mechanical, photocopying, recording, scanning, or otherwise, except as permitted under Section 107 or 108 of the 1976 United States Copyright Act, without either the prior written permission of the Publisher, or authorization through payment of the appropriate per-copy fee to the Copyright Clearance Center, Inc., 222 Rosewood Drive, Danvers, MA 01923, (978) 750-8400, fax (978) 750-4470, or on the web at www.copyright.com. Requests to the Publisher for permission should be addressed to the Permissions Department, John Wiley & Sons, Inc., 111 River Street, Hoboken, NJ 07030, (201) 748-6011, fax (201) 748-6008, or online at http://www.wiley.com/go/permission.

The manufacturer's authorized representative according to the EU General Product Safety Regulation is Wiley-VCH GmbH, Boschstr. 12, 69469 Weinheim, Germany, e-mail: Product_Safety@wiley.com.

Trademarks: Wiley and the Wiley logo are trademarks or registered trademarks of John Wiley & Sons, Inc. and/or its affiliates in the United States and other countries and may not be used without written permission. All other trademarks are the property of their respective owners. John Wiley & Sons, Inc. is not associated with any product or vendor mentioned in this book.

Limit of Liability/Disclaimer of Warranty: While the publisher and author have used their best efforts in preparing this book, they make no representations or warranties with respect to the accuracy or completeness of the contents of this book and specifically disclaim any implied warranties of merchantability or fitness for a particular purpose. No warranty may be created or extended by sales representatives or written sales materials. The advice and strategies contained herein may not be suitable for your situation. You should consult with a professional where appropriate. Further, readers should be aware that websites listed in this work may have changed or disappeared between when this work was written and when it is read. Neither the publisher nor authors shall be liable for any loss of profit or any other commercial damages, including but not limited to special, incidental, consequential, or other damages.

For general information on our other products and services or for technical support, please contact our Customer Care Department within the United States at (800) 762-2974, outside the United States at (317) 572-3993 or fax (317) 572-4002.

Wiley also publishes its books in a variety of electronic formats. Some content that appears in print may not be available in electronic formats. For more information about Wiley products, visit our web site at www.wiley.com.

Library of Congress Cataloging-in-Publication Data Applied for:

Paperback: 9781394234783

Cover Design: Wiley
Cover Image: © saicle/Shutterstock

Set in 10.5/12.5pt TimesLTStd by Straive, Pondicherry, India

SKY10100657_032125

CONTENTS

Preface	ix
Acknowledgments	x

ONE: INTRODUCTION — 1
Learning Objectives	1
Introduction	2
Size and Importance of Nonprofit Sector	3
The Evaluation Framework	5
Structure of Book	9
Summary	9
Key Terms	10
Discussion Questions	10

TWO: DESCRIBING THE INITIATIVE — 11
Learning Objectives	11
Introduction	12
Reasons to Rigorously Describe the Program	13
The Logistics of Describing the Program	14
Common Mistakes Made Describing Initiative and Programs	16
The Program Is Alive and So Is Its Description	18
Theory of Change	19
The Program Logic Model	25
Analyzing the Program Logic Model	34
Challenges of Multisite Programs	35
Program Implementation Model	36
Examples of Program Descriptions	37
Summary	67
Key Terms	68
Discussion Questions	68

THREE: LAYING THE EVALUATION GROUND WORK — 69

- Learning Objectives — 69
- Evaluation Approaches — 70
- Framing Evaluation Questions — 72
- Insincere Reasons for Evaluation — 75
- High Stakes Evaluation — 75
- Who Will do the Evaluation? — 76
  - External Evaluators — 77
  - Internal Evaluators — 79
  - Independence of the Evaluator — 79
  - External Versus Internal Evaluators — 80
- Confidentiality and Ownership of Evaluations — 81
  - Endorsement and Action on Recommendations — 82
  - Evaluation Policy — 83
- The Evaluation Report — 84
- Summary — 86
- Key Terms — 86
- Discussion Questions — 86

FOUR: CAUSATION — 87

- Learning Objectives — 87
- Introduction — 88
- Necessary and Sufficient — 88
- Setting Cutoff Points and Causal Interpretation — 91
- Intervening Variables — 95
- Types of Causal Effects — 97
  - Lagged Effects — 98
  - Permanency of Effects — 98
  - Functional Form of Impact — 99
  - Spectacular Causes and Effects — 100
- Summary — 101
- Key Terms — 102
- Discussion Questions — 102

FIVE: THE PRISMS OF VALIDITY — 103
- Learning Objectives — 103
- Introduction — 104
- Statistical Conclusion Validity — 105
  - Types of Erroneous Conclusions: Type 1 and Type 2 Errors — 106
  - Threats to Statistical Conclusion Validity — 107
- Internal Validity — 111
  - Threats to Internal Validity — 111
  - Summary — 118
- Construct Validity — 119
  - Threats to Construct Validity — 120
  - Summary — 122
- External Validity — 122
  - Considerations for Determining the External Validity of Studies — 122
  - Summary — 123
- Conclusions — 124
- Key Terms — 124
- Discussion Questions — 124

SIX: ATTRIBUTING OUTCOMES TO THE PROGRAM: QUASI-EXPERIMENTAL DESIGN — 126
- Learning Objectives — 126
- Introduction — 127
- Quasi-Experimental Notation — 127
- Frequently used Designs that do not Show Causation — 128
  - One-Group Posttest-Only — 128
  - Posttest-Only with Nonequivalent Groups — 129
  - Participants' Pretest–Posttest — 130
- Designs that Generally Permit Causal Inferences — 131
  - Untreated Control Group Design with Pretest and Posttest — 131
  - Delayed Treatment Control Group — 137
  - Different Samples from the Same Populations Design — 140
  - Nonequivalent Observations Drawn from One Group — 141

    Equivalent Groups Using Switched Measures 142
    Cohort Designs 144
    Time Series Designs 146
  Summary 148
  Key Terms 149
  Discussion Questions 149

SEVEN: COLLECTING DATA **150**
  Learning Objectives 150
  Introduction 151
  Informal and Loosely Structured Interviews 152
  Focus Groups 154
  Surveys 160
    Survey Instrument Design 161
  Target Populations and Sampling 169
    Informal Sampling Approaches 170
    Formal Sampling Approaches 171
    Best Practices in Administering Surveys to a Purposive Sample 172
    Follow-up for Nonresponse 173
  Secondary Data Sources 173
  Summary 174
  Key Terms 174
  Discussion Questions 175

EIGHT: CONCLUSIONS **176**
  Learning Objectives 176
  Using Evaluation Tools to Write Grant Proposals 177
  Hiring Evaluation Consultants 177
  Writing Recommendations 180
    The Tone of Evaluation Reports 180
    Finalization Process of Evaluation Reports 181
  Conclusions 182
  Discussion Questions 182

Glossary 183

Index 188

PREFACE

In 2008, I wrote the first edition of *Evaluation Essentials*. By then, my evaluation career had included teaching Program Evaluation and working with USA-based nonprofits and foundations to address their evaluation needs and issues.

In the intervening 16 years between the first and second editions of *Evaluation Essentials*, my experience in the evaluation arena grew, and the field evolved. For a few years that deeply influenced me, I worked at the United Nations, directing a small group of evaluators who examined UN initiatives, including peacekeeping operations. While I left that position because of family responsibilities, I continued to work as an evaluator for the UN system, either as a consultant or short-term staff, mostly evaluating projects but also evaluating initiatives as large as the entire UN Accountability System. I also continued my work as an evaluation consultant for US-based entities, including nonprofits and foundations. I started Social Science Consultants, LLC, which allowed me to create teams of evaluators and social scientists to examine initiatives. This gave me broad experience across many countries and cultural contexts, conducting mid-term and final evaluations.

Since 2008, the field of evaluation considerably changed. The demand for evaluative information (and for evaluators) has grown, and organizations often struggle to meet this demand. More entities have developed internal evaluation capacities, which has its benefits and risks. A higher proportion of organizations have evaluators on staff and many who don't have consultants with whom they regularly work to evaluate initiatives.

When I recently taught my graduate-level course in Program Evaluation at Yale University's School of Management, I looked for but was unable to identify a text that guides students and professionals through the various evaluation issues and helps them develop the essential skills that they would need to either work as an evaluator or to wisely hire an evaluator. The first edition of *Evaluation Essentials* seemed dated, and I found myself relying increasingly on my current lectures to convey information and evaluation challenges. I decided that *Evaluation Essentials* needed substantial revising, and fortunately, my publisher, Wiley, agreed.

My hope is that this book will provide a solid background in evaluation for a variety of audiences. Many who struggle with evaluation issues in their daily worklife—including development professionals who use evaluative information for fundraising, education leaders, senior staff in nonprofits, government agencies, and NGOs who want to know how to improve their programming, and funders who struggle with asking reasonable questions about the impact of their investments—can rely on this book to get ideas of how to address the challenges before them. Professors and students can use the book as the basis for a solid course in evaluation. I hope that all audiences find this book a valuable resource for both the present and the future.

Beth Osborne DaPonte Connecticut, USA

ACKNOWLEDGMENTS

This book is the result of many organizations and entities that engaged this evaluator to help them achieve their missions. Each evaluation engagement has broadened my perspective and allowed me to continuously learn. I express my sincere gratitude to my current and past colleagues at the United Nations, including Emily Hampton-Manley, Jessica Guo, Arild Hauge, and Yee Woo Guo. My colleague, Erik Devereux at Social Science Consultants has contributed with his constant encouragement and support. Kevin Gieder, with his enthusiasm for small non-profits to think about about evaluation, supported revising the first edition. My family—Tony Smith, and Noah, Bennett, and Carmela Daponte-Smith—has always been supportive of this effort. The team at Wiley saw the need for this book, gave me the opportunity to revisit *Evaluation Essentials,* and supported me in this revision. I am extremely grateful for the expertise of Nathanael Mcgavin (editor), Palaniyandi Arunpaulraj (production editor), Christina Weyrauch (graphic artist), and others who shepherded this revision.

CHAPTER 1

INTRODUCTION

The role of the program director is to believe, the role of the evaluator is to doubt.

—Carole Weiss

LEARNING OBJECTIVES

After reading this chapter, you should be able to

- Explain the primary and secondary goals of the evaluation
- Describe the steps of the evaluation framework

Evaluation Essentials: Methods for Conducting Sound Evaluation Research, Second Edition. Beth Osborne DaPonte.
© 2025 John Wiley & Sons, Inc. Published 2025 by John Wiley & Sons, Inc.

INTRODUCTION

An executive director of a medium-sized, nonprofit social service agency once told me, *"I know we're doing good—I can see it in our clients' eyes."* I wish that this had been a unique encounter, but I have repeatedly had people responsible for running programs and delivering services—including board members, executive directors, and staff—say some version of the above. Sometimes, there is variation—*"Funders wouldn't fund us if we weren't doing good,"* or from the funders' perspective, *"They must have done something good since they spent all of the money in the way that they said they were going to."* Potential clients may be influenced by the popularity of a program, thinking that people would only flock to impactful programs.

Unfortunately, none of these sentiments tells us what would have occurred to clients if the program hadn't existed. Clients may have been just as successful, or even more successful, if left to their own devices or if they were exposed to a different program. Or, perhaps clients who seemed not to have changed were actually better off, since had it not been for the program, they would have been worse off.

In all fairness, if those who deliver services didn't believe that they are effectively improving people's lives, they might have difficulty devoting themselves to their jobs. In the nonprofit sector, rather than being primarily motivated by wages and compensation, staff are often motivated by their commitment to their organization's mission and belief in the effectiveness of the initiative on which they spend their time and resources.

An evaluator's primary job is to examine rigorously the relevance, impact, efficiency, and sustainability of interventions. Evaluators typically ask questions such as:

- To what extent is the intervention the right way to address the problem it aims to address?
- What is the impact of the intervention on its target population?
- Does the intervention produce unintended consequences?
- To what extent is the intervention being delivered efficiently and how can it be delivered more efficiently?
- Should the intervention be continued and if so, how will it be continued? Who will support it?

By considering these broad questions and interacting with the program designers, current and potential beneficiaries, program governance structures (e.g., boards, trustees, and overseers), and staff, evaluators' insights can result in program improvements for ongoing programs and improvements in program design for initiatives that have not yet started. Note that this set of questions can be asked retrospectively about interventions (e.g., "was the intervention the right way to address the problem?") or prospectively (e.g., "to what extent does stakeholder feedback and a literature review indicate that the planned intervention will be the right way to address the problem?").

An evaluator's secondary job is to encourage program governance, staff, and planners to be more critical of their existing and future initiatives—encourage them to develop a mindset that, rather than assuming that initiatives are effective, instead asks how to make initiatives more effective and whether an initiative should be continued or (gasp!) abandoned. To design the most impactful programs, boards, planners, and staff need to be more critical of the role that their services (or planned services) play (or will play) in their clients' lives. What assumptions are programs making about clients? Conversely, what do clients and potential clients assume about programs?

Although clients' eyes may reflect gratitude, they are not a substitute for rigorous evaluation. For example, they do not reveal whether a program reaches its intended target population or whether clients would have been just as well off without the program. A critical perspective is needed if the efforts are to continually improve over time.

For-profit organizations have metrics for success that typically involve profit margins, stock prices, and return-on-investment. Determining success for nonprofits (in the international sector referred to as nongovernmental organizations or NGOs) is a more nuanced enterprise—success ultimately rests on the degree to which the organization's mission has been accomplished.

In recent years, funders, management, fundraisers, and potential clients want more information on nonprofits' impacts and efficiencies. Competition for resources in the nonprofit sector is fierce. With the proliferation of nonprofit organizations, questions about which are the best, which are worth investing in, and which are strong and resilient enough to be sustainable become extremely important.

SIZE AND IMPORTANCE OF NONPROFIT SECTOR

The demand for evaluation services in recent years has exploded, not only because nearly all nonprofits and governmental organizations have realized that they need to critically examine their initiatives, but also because of the growth of the nonprofit sector. Consider that between 2010 and 2020, in the United States, the number of nonprofits (defined for this purpose as an organization that filed a required 990 form with the IRS) increased from 186,417 to 217,263 organizations. In 2020, these organizations held $5.5 trillion in total assets, nearly $2 trillion in total liabilities, and had total revenues of $2.7 trillion. They spent $2.1 trillion on program services.[1] To put this in perspective, consider that the USA Gross Domestic Product (GDP) in 2020 was nearly $21 trillion. The nonprofit sector's spending on program services accounted for approximately 10% of the nation's GDP.

The nonprofit sector provides services ranging from functions provided by universities, private schools, hospitals, arts and cultural institutions, legal assistance, food assistance, and other safety net and social organizations. Given the magnitude and reach of the nonprofit sector and its importance to the US economy, it is imperative that its entities and funders continue to develop an evaluative mindset. As nonprofits carry out more functions and greater reliance is placed on them, there is increased demand for information about their

---

1 *Source:* Author's analysis of data from the Internal Revenue Service, Statistics of Income Division, Exempt Organizations (Except Private Foundations), November 2023.

ability to accomplish their missions efficiently and their impact on the persons, entities, and/or communities they serve.

In recent years, the role of government versus the nonprofit sector has notably changed. The US government is relying more on nonprofits to provide assistance, sometimes with governmental funding and sometimes without. Government increasingly relies on the nonprofit sector, with its army of volunteers and relatively low-paid staff, to compensate for gaps in governmental programs. This becomes painfully evident during the aftermath of natural disasters, when local food banks and feeding centers run by nonprofits are asked to provide food, the American Red Cross provides shelters, and other nonprofits step up in other ways to serve populations in crisis. But even when there is not an acute emergency, the nonprofit sector is increasingly comprising the safety net for lower-income persons. Rather than providing services directly, federal, state, and local governments increasingly contract with nonprofits to provide services.

With more reliance placed on the nonprofit sector comes the demand for all nonprofit organizations and especially those that compete with other nonprofits for "market share" to show their effectiveness. Government, consumers, and donors would like to know which nonprofits are most effective at providing comparable services. In this respect, evaluation is viewed as essentially a means of providing information to rank programs and organizations. Evaluation reports are used to answer the questions *"which agency should a government contract for a needed service?"* and *"which nonprofits should foundations and individual donors fund?"*

This book is intended to provide leaders, program creators, and program implementers in the nonprofit/NGO/governmental arena with enough knowledge of the evaluation field to empower them to engage with evaluation activities in meaningful ways. Many nonprofit leaders lack training in the nuances of evaluation research. Nonprofit leaders can come to their positions in a variety of ways. For example, the Executive Director of a nonprofit organization that provides guardianship services to the elderly and/or disabled was a noted accountant, but never received any training in evaluation. The same goes for the Executive Director of a local food bank who had been a passionate anti-hunger advocate and the Executive Director of a local library who excelled as a head librarian.

Many influential foundations lack an evaluation policy that would speak to the size of investments that must be evaluated and the types of evaluation activities that would occur when considering whether to fund an initiative. Some leaders and staff of foundations who have decided that evaluation is important lack the background to determine fair criteria by which to judge and reward effective nonprofit organizations and programs.

Working in the background behind service deliverers and funders are people who call themselves evaluators. Many evaluators are primarily trained in fields other than evaluation, such as public health, sociology, economics, statistics, or public policy. They may have had some formal training in evaluation, but they often have moved into evaluation over time and many have acquired only on-the-job training. For this reason, although the majority of evaluators have in common a desire to learn the "truth" about interventions, they bring to the table a divergent set of skills and may place varying emphases on different aspects of programs, policies, and evaluatory practices.

My perspective is aligned with that of Michael Quinn Patton's (1996)—the goal of evaluation is to assist with continuous programmatic improvement and introspection. I readily acknowledge that how to achieve this goal is an art informed by rigorous social science methods. There are tools that the evaluator needs to have mastered and with these tools, the evaluator must create the *least intrusive, least burdensome, and least costly evaluation plan* that will reveal the relevance, impact, efficiency, and sustainability of an initiative. To do so, the evaluator needs to understand the initiative's context and develop knowledge of how others have approached the issue that the initiative aims to address.

THE EVALUATION FRAMEWORK

The evaluative framework for conducting an evaluation that examines an initiative's effects is a 10-step process in which the evaluator and the "evaluand" (the entity, program, or initiative being evaluated) should engage.

1. **Determine the audience and accountability structure for the evaluation activities.**
   Who is the audience for evaluation activities? To whom will the evaluator be reporting? Who will receive reports or memos from the evaluator? Who will endorse the evaluation recommendations? Who will be responsible for ensuring that recommendations are implemented?

   I encourage clients to create an Evaluation Reference Group (ERG) consisting of program administrators, funders, and program beneficiaries. Substantive interactions that the evaluator has with the "client" go through the ERG. The ERG ensures that the evaluation answers relevant and important questions. The ERG includes people who will assist the evaluator in getting access to people and materials during the data collection process and helps bring attention to the evaluation process and final evaluation report. The ERG provides an opportunity for the representatives of the community that the initiative is to benefit to participate in the evaluation process.

2. **Determine the universe of possible evaluation questions.**
   With most initiatives, a nearly infinite set of evaluative questions could be asked. However, there is never enough time or resources to answer them all. When listing the universe of evaluation questions, the evaluator should map out the stakeholders who comprise the audience for each question. Broadly, the questions will pertain to the program's relevance, effectiveness, efficiency, and sustainability.

3. **Rigorously describe the program.**
   The evaluator will describe the initiative by reading its documents, learning the history of the program verbally, and with a group of stakeholders diagramming its *Theory of Change* (ToC) (also known as the *program theory*) and charting out its *program logic model*. These two tools not only force evaluators to become acquainted with the program (theoretically and operationally) but also get the stakeholders in agreement about the program's description and goals. Any evaluation that is done without a thorough understanding of the program can be of no constructive use. For this reason, this book devotes considerable space to describing programs and initiatives.

THE EVALUATION FRAMEWORK

1. Determine the audience and accountability structure for the evaluation activities.
2. Determine the universe of possible evaluation questions.
3. Rigorously describe the program by developing the program theory and using a program logic model.
4. Conduct a literature review around the Theory of Change and to learn about similar initiatives.
5. Revisit and narrow the universe of evaluation questions.
6. Develop the evaluation plan.
7. Carry out the evaluation plan.
8. Report on draft evaluation findings and recommendations to the Evaluation Reference Group.
9. Finalize the evaluation report.
10. An accountability mechanism (e.g., board) endorses the final evaluation report's recommendations and ensures that recommendations are implemented.

4. **Conduct a literature review around the Theory of Change and to learn about similar initiatives.**

    The literature review will inform as to the certainty of the ToC's causal connections actually occurring, once the initiative's activities occur. The literature review will also inform as to the experience of similar programs—their successes, impact, and challenges. The literature review will reveal the measures that other programs have used when considering impact. Essentially, the literature review will allow the evaluator to assess the veracity of the ToC and allow the evaluator to focus data collection efforts on the areas of the ToC that are not certain to occur.

5. **Revisit and narrow the evaluation questions.**

    After rigorously describing the program, the evaluator and ERG should revisit the universe of evaluation questions and narrow them. It is unlikely that any evaluation will have the time and resources to answer all possible questions. Thus, the universe of evaluation should be narrowed according to the resources available for the evaluation, the timeline of the evaluation, the audience for each evaluation question, and the evaluator's access to the information that would allow for the evaluation question to be answered.

The ERG must be involved in narrowing the evaluation questions and developing an understanding of the limitations of the evaluation. The group should be open to the idea that outcome-based evaluation is not the only type of evaluation that could be conducted. Examining the processes in implementing an initiative can also have value. In fact, for unstable programs, process-based rather than outcome-based evaluation will be appropriate.

In narrowing the evaluation questions, thought should be given to who the audience is for each evaluation question and whose interest each question represents. If a group's interest is left out of the list of narrowed questions, the evaluator should encourage the ERG to discuss this omission so that they realize and appreciate the evaluation's focus and direction.

6. **Develop an evaluation plan.**

The evaluation plan, often called an "**Inception Report,**" will cover the evaluation questions that the evaluation will answer and include the data collection and data analysis plan. Without a developed blueprint for the evaluation, there is a risk that the evaluation activities will continue *ad infinitum*. Before the evaluation team proceeds with the evaluation activities, the ERG must provide feedback on the Inception Report and the evaluator should come to consensus with the ERG on how the evaluation will be conducted.

The evaluation plan will include a data collection and data analysis plan. If qualitative data will be collected, the inception report will indicate details such as the number of focus groups and/or interviews that will be conducted, who will be included in focus groups and interviews, and where and when they will occur. The report will include draft interview and focus group protocol. If data collection includes conducting a survey, the inception report will indicate who will be surveyed, when the survey will occur, how data from the survey will be used, and will include a draft survey instrument. The inception report will also identify any secondary (pre-existing) data sources (e.g., surveys conducted by others, census data) that will be relied upon and the analysis approach.

The inception report will include the **quasi-experimental design**(s) that the evaluation will rely upon. The report will show how the data collected and the data analysis techniques proposed will be used to make the argument regarding the program's role in causing any changes that occurred.

The report will also include a timeline for the evaluation activities. This timeline should be reasonable and have built into it time for the ERG to review materials.

It is important that the inception report address the limitations of data collection and of the evaluation, if there are any such limitations. It is better for the ERG to be aware and understand the limitations at the outset rather than after the evaluation activities are complete.

7. **Carry out the evaluation plan.**
    In carrying out the evaluation plan, the ERG should be kept apprised of the unexpected changes to and/or deviations from the plan. It would be wise to have regular meetings with the ERG (e.g., biweekly) to discuss progress.

8. **Report on draft evaluation findings and recommendations to the Evaluation Reference Group.**
    Once the evaluation team has completed data collection, the team should meet with the ERG and present tentative evaluation results and recommendations to it. This meeting and follow-up to it becomes the ERG's opportunity to provide feedback before the report is written. Such a discussion can be very fruitful and can save time (and frustration) in the report finalization process.

9. **Finalize the evaluation report.**
    The evaluator should provide the ERG a written draft evaluation report and give the ERG an opportunity to circulate the draft report among colleagues. The evaluator should ask for feedback on the draft report, especially feedback that corrects (or updates) facts in the report. Remember that errors in the report could impact reliance on recommendations. An important part of the finalization process is bringing attention to the ERG and implementers findings and results in the draft report. Sometimes, there will be an objection to a recommendation included in the draft. The evaluator may decide that there are issues that once raised in a draft report, do not need to be included in the final report.

10. **The Evaluation Reference Group should ensure that an accountability mechanism endorses the final evaluation report's recommendations.**
    After the report is finalized, the evaluator's role in a retrospective evaluation is done. It is then up to the evaluand and/or its governance, with the ERG, to act on the evaluation's recommendations and to communicate the evaluation's results. For example, the ERG could bring the evaluation report to the attention of the organization's board for the endorsement of recommendations and press for there to be a follow-up mechanism on the recommendations. The organization could place the evaluation report on its website, circulate its Executive Summary, and offer a public session regarding the evaluation.

    Separating the evaluation activities into these ten discrete "tasks" allows evaluators to pause and to think about the direction that their activities will take and how they will interact with the evaluand.

    High-quality evaluations can improve ongoing initiatives and inform the field about lessons learned from similar initiatives. When planning initiatives, planners have an obligation to review the evaluations conducted on similar initiatives so that planners can create the most impactful, relevant, and efficient initiatives. Funders have an obligation to support and read evaluation reports so that their resources can be put to the best use. The evaluations of an initiative should eventually become a part of the base of knowledge about a field of initiatives.

STRUCTURE OF BOOK

The remainder of this book is devoted to more fully explaining each of these 10 steps. Regardless of whether you will conduct evaluations yourself or contract with evaluation consultants or firms, these 10 steps must be understood.

The first half of the book focuses on developing the appropriate background for evaluation and the second half addresses the use of quasi-experimentation and data collection in an evaluation context. Unlike many evaluation and economics texts, this one emphasizes that one must rigorously describe the program prior to evaluating it.

Chapter 2 introduces the Program Logic Model and Theory of Change as tools to use when describing the program. The chapter closes with examples of these tools applied to various initiatives, hoping to make you comfortable enough with these tools so that you will be able to apply them to one of your own initiatives.

Chapter 3 discusses the framing of evaluation questions, elaborating upon the pre-evaluation steps that one must consider before embarking on conducting the evaluation activities. Since the ultimate goal of initiatives is to cause positive change, Chapter 4 delves into the meaning of causation in an evaluation context.

To engage in high-quality evaluation activities, one must understand what it means to do valid evaluation research. There are four types of validity and Chapter 5 explains what these are, their importance when conducting literature reviews, and their importance when creating a robust evaluation plan.

Chapter 6 introduces the reader to the quasi-experimental designs used and the trade-offs made between quasi-experimental designs and types of validity. Chapter 7 presents approaches to data collection—interviews, focus groups, surveys, and pre-existing data (archival, administrative, and census data). While the chapter does not substitute for a good course in statistics, it discusses the areas particularly relevant to evaluation research.

Chapter 8 concludes the text, discussing the similarities between grant proposals and evaluation plans. The chapter also includes a template for a Terms of Reference to use when hiring an evaluator or evaluation firm.

SUMMARY

The primary job of the evaluator is to examine the impact of program interventions. The secondary job is to provide a critical perspective to improve programs. The goal of evaluation is to assist with continuous program improvement and introspection. To successfully evaluate a program, the evaluator must follow the steps of the evaluation framework.

KEY TERMS

evaluation
evaluators
formative evaluations
program logic model

program theory
quasi-experimental design
summative evaluations
target population

DISCUSSION QUESTIONS

1. What are the goals of program evaluation?
2. Why is it important to have an evaluation plan?
3. What is the evaluation framework?

CHAPTER 2

DESCRIBING THE INITIATIVE

LEARNING OBJECTIVES

After reading this chapter, you should be able to

- Explain the importance of involving stakeholders
- Draft an initiative's Theory of Change (ToC)
- Draft an initiative's Program Logic Model (PLM)
- Understand why program creators should rigorously describe potential initiatives
- List common mistakes evaluators make when describing an initiative

Evaluation Essentials: Methods for Conducting Sound Evaluation Research, Second Edition.
Beth Osborne DaPonte.
© 2025 John Wiley & Sons, Inc. Published 2025 by John Wiley & Sons, Inc.

INTRODUCTION

Before beginning to evaluate an initiative or program, the evaluator needs to develop a thorough understanding of it. This understanding must be shared by the program's stakeholders—if the evaluator's understanding of an initiative differs from that of the stakeholders, the stakeholders will not use the evaluation results because what was evaluated is unrecognizable to them.

A program's stakeholders typically include any or all of the following groups:

- Program administrator(s)
- Program funders
- The board of directors of the organization offering the program
- Program clients
- Program staff
- Advocates for the program
- Potential recipients of the program's services
- Alumni of the program
- Program partners

Each set of stakeholders' perspectives on the program must be understood and included in order to develop a well-rounded description and shared understanding of the initiative.

Evaluators use two graphical tools to rigorously describe a program: the **Theory of Change** (also known as **program theory**), which is a diagram of the theory behind the program as perceived by the stakeholders; and the **Program Logic Model (PLM),** which models the operation of the program and connects the operations to its goals.

These two models each consider the program in an interrelated but different light. The Theory of Change (ToC) represents the theoretical chain that the program causes, connecting the program's intervention with its ultimate goals. In contrast, the PLM details the program's operations, its available resources, its target population, outcomes, and outcome measures.

When the ToC and PLM both reflect the program's reality, the program benefits. With appropriate modeling, one can clearly see if and where there are opportunities for program improvement and concise ways one may evaluate the program's processes and outcomes. When articulated through these approaches, opportunities for improvement usually emerge.

Spending time and effort on developing an accurate program description pays dividends—the evaluation opportunities and evaluation questions become obvious. Developing a thorough understanding of the program not only makes the evaluation relevant but also allows the evaluator to create the most parsimonious evaluation approach.

Evaluators like the word "*parsimony*"—it comes up often in evaluation. By definition, it means "unusual or excessive frugality; extreme economy or stinginess." In evaluation, "parsimonious" describes the smallest set of questions and narrowest data collection approach that will allow one to determine the relevance, effectiveness, efficiency, and/or sustainability of a program.

Before embarking on an evaluation, the evaluation questions should be whittled down to the most "parsimonious" set. Very poorly planned evaluation studies—such as those that use a ridiculous number of outcome measures, thinking that at least one of them will reflect a positive program result—occur when a thorough understanding of the program has not been developed or when the program is on a fishing expedition to find something positive, regardless of whether it is realistically tied to the program.

Parsimonious program models clarify which evaluatory outcome measures to use, thus allowing the evaluator ultimately to collect and analyze smaller amounts of data, saving time (and money) in the data collection and analysis stages.

REASONS TO RIGOROUSLY DESCRIBE THE PROGRAM

A well-developed program description can be shared with all staff of the program, assuring that all staff share the same vision of the program and that this vision is shared with current and potential clients

A well-articulated program is more likely to attract appropriate clients. When programs are "fuzzy" in their description, they are more likely to attract clients for whom the program is inappropriate. When programs are clear and concise in their descriptions, potential clients are better able to decide whether the services offered are a good fit for their situation.

In terms of public relations, this shared vision means that potential clients, program staff, and other stakeholders all receive and transmit a consistent, clear message about the program's goals and activities. Staff will be unified in setting priorities and determining which aspects of their activities to emphasize, thus decreasing the chances that staff will go astray and that services provided will differ between program personnel.

This is particularly important for multisite programs. In programs that have more than one site, it is easy for differing interpretations of the program to arise. Even when multisite programs started with the same description, over time, local circumstances (e.g, different local leadership, different challenges and opportunities in locales, different populations who are potential clients) could cause some sites to go astray from the original description. For this reason, especially for multisite programs, not only does the program need to have a well-developed program description, but all need to review that description on a regular (e.g., quarterly or semiannually) basis to ensure that the sites are operating as one initiative.

Developing the ToC and PLM increases both the probability of success and attracting money

When stakeholders have developed consensus about the program's description and the program has been rigorously and parsimoniously described in a way that reflects how program stakeholders see it, program personnel will articulate the program precisely and uniformly, which will result in more success in implementation, attracting support, and reaching the program's target population.

When implementers share an understanding of why they are engaging in the program's services or activities, the nuances of the activities become more directed so that goals are achieved. Having a well-articulated program description helps prevent the program from drifting from its purpose. Importantly, the ToC and Program Logic not only describe what the program does, but also show what the program does not do.

Funders appreciate and want to support well-articulated programs that have clear and concise goals and a well-articulated Theories of Change. They want to fund programs that program personnel have carefully thought through. Funders want to see that program designers know precisely what the initiative is and why they are implementing it.

Although funders may require a program description in formats other than the ToC and PLM shown below, having these descriptions in the format used in this chapter allows for ready adaptation to any format needed for a grant proposal. Thus, the organization's development/fundraising personnel should become familiar with how to interpret the initiative's ToC and PLM.

Conversely, nothing will make funders question the credibility of a program or an organization more than if they feel that they need to do the thinking behind the program or if there are many ways to interpret a program. If a funder has a reason to question the program's underlying theory, then it is likely that the funder will not support it. Further, if the funder is the one who brings to the attention of others possible unintended negative consequences of the program, then the funder will question the initiative's credibility.

THE LOGISTICS OF DESCRIBING THE PROGRAM

To describe a program, first read the documents and websites about the initiative. At the start of an evaluation, the evaluator should ask the evaluand/evaluation reference group (ERG) for all documents that give insights about the program. Get background on the initiative's history and how and why the initiative developed. Develop an understanding of the problem that the initiative aims to resolve—the magnitude of the problem, other initiatives that address the same problem, and the politics behind the initiative. Read any media reports that exist about the initiative (e.g., press releases on the program's launch) and/or about the organization that operates the program. For complex programs, the evaluator may want to conduct some informal, informational interviews with a few critical people who may have a deep understanding of the program and its history.

The evaluator should work with the evaluand (the entity or initiative that is being evaluated) in creating an ERG consisting of stakeholders (see box).

EVALUATION REFERENCE GROUP

Throughout the course of evaluation activities, the evaluator needs to engage with a group of stakeholders of the initiative who have agreed to and are ready to provide feedback. With the advice of the evaluator, the program should form an Evaluation Reference Group (ERG) consisting of no more than 15 program stakeholders. The ERG should include people who represent the following groups of stakeholders, to the extent feasible and applicable: funders, organizational senior leadership, program implementers (and on-the-ground-staff), program beneficiaries ("clients" of the program, alumni of the program), program partners, and representatives of the community that the program serves.

The ERG helps steer the evaluation and ensures that the evaluation answers relevant and important questions.

The ERG will be used to draft and finalize the program description, provide feedback on focus group and interview protocol and survey instruments, help the evaluator gain access to materials and people (e.g., focus group participants, interviewees), help increase survey response rates, and review draft evaluation results and recommendations. The ERG will provide comments on the draft reports.

The ERG will bring recommendations to the governing bodies and build awareness about the evaluation activities and the results. All substantive interactions that the evaluator has with the program pertaining to the direction of the evaluation go through the ERG.

While creating the ToC and PLM, the evaluator should develop an understanding of the answers to the following questions:

- What events or circumstances led to the program's creation? Who was involved in its creation?
- How was the perceived need for the program determined?
- How large and dire is the need for the program?
- Is the program modeled on other programs? If so, which ones?
- Why did the program's creators think that it would work in this location at this time?
- Who funds the program?
- How does the program sustain itself?
- How much does it cost to run the program? How have the costs changed over time? Are there any in-kind contributions that defray the costs of the program?
- How does the current program differ from the original plan for the program?
- What proportion of those in need does the program serve?

- How are staff recruited?
- Are there issues with staff retention?
- What sort of training do staff go through?
- What processes exist to ensure that staff adhere to the program's design?
- What do clients expect from the program?
- Do clients stick with the program? Why or why not?
- Are there any apparent unintended effects (positive or negative) of the program?
- Does the program have critics? Who are they? What do they say about the program?

The ERG will be invited to a meeting (the first meeting is usually approximately two hours long) that the evaluator facilitates during which the evaluator drafts a ToC. During the meeting, it will be important to ensure that all voices are heard and that all perspectives are initially reflected. As the meeting proceeds, hopefully, consensus will develop. It is not unusual for the first draft of the ToC to be messy and resemble a bowl of spaghetti.

After the meeting, the evaluator will create a cleaner, draft ToC using computer graphical software (e.g., Power Point). That model will be circulated to the ERG and the ERG will meet again to review and revise and to develop the PLM. The process of revising and meeting will continue until there is consensus on the final description. In my experience, the process has taken anywhere from one to four months. But at the end of the process, not only is there a consensus on the final models, but differences in perspectives have been exposed and resolved. The process results in all ERG members sharing the same vision of the program.

Common Mistakes Made Describing Initiative and Programs

In order for any evaluation reports and recommendations to be used, the evaluation must first start with a program description that is credible and that the audience of the evaluation fully embraces. Evaluation reports and recommendations of a program with a faulty program description will not be seen as credible, recommendations will likely not be implemented, and the evaluation report and other products of it will be buried.

Not spending enough time on program description is the biggest mistake evaluators and program creators make. Insufficient time for program description can occur when the ERG is disinterested in the process, the evaluation timeline has been tightly (and unrealistically) drawn, insufficient resources allow for the evaluator and stakeholders to spend time on the program description, and/or the program (or a funder) has already decided on aspects of the program to overemphasize (or create) so that the predetermined outcomes will seem to be a natural result of the program. The latter often happens when an organization has applied for a grant under an initiative that its current programming doesn't quite fit under, but because of the availability of funding, it "stretches" its programming so it fits under the grant requirements. In its application to the funder and in reporting to the funder, the organization reflects the program not as the program exists, but as the funder expects the program to exist and perform.

The program description must be of **the program as it exists, not of how the program *should* exist**. Sometimes, evaluators and stakeholders are tempted when confronted with a weak program description to revise the program description so it appears to have more potential than it actually has. However, this can result in a description not of an existing program but of a fantasy program.

Evaluators and stakeholders may be so focused on "outcome measures" that they feel they do not have time to develop an appropriate understanding of the program. The pressure to focus on particular outcome measures can be derived from external sources such as organizations that rate all programs working on similar problems according to a single outcome measure, regardless of a particular program's focus. The evaluation then becomes an exercise in producing or explaining outcome measures. This is particularly worrisome when the outcomes being measured are not a focus of the particular program at hand. An evaluation that starts with externally imposed outcome measures that are only tangentially related to the program will not result in recommendations that are relevant to the program. That is, such an evaluation will not lead to program improvement, which would be a wasted opportunity for the evaluation efforts.

If the evaluator has relied on a small number or the same type of stakeholders for program knowledge and perspective, the subset of stakeholders may not have a good understanding of the overall program. Sometimes, the program description may be in the head of one person who is the program's creator. The problem with this is that the program description is one of mono-vision—it represents only one person's perspective and has not been vetted by other stakeholders.

When forming the program description, one must be careful to rely not only on the views of "higher-ups"—for example, administrators and board members—but to include also on-the-ground staff and beneficiaries. Including only higher-ups can result in the description of a fantasy program. The people on the ground—those directly interacting with clients, making personnel decisions, and procuring resources for the program—may have a different view of the program. Further, the program description may not reflect the important views of beneficiaries, clients, and partners of the program.

If an evaluator relies only on written materials about the program to develop an understanding of it, the program likely will not be realistically described. When relying on grant proposals, one should be aware that grant proposals are written to attract money. A disconnect can exist between what was promised to attract funds and how the program actually works or the program's focus. Evaluators should also be wary of many aspects of annual reports, which are often used for development purposes and thus tend to show the program in the most favorable light, again yielding a potential disconnect between the program's image and reality.

It is tempting for an **evaluator to take control of the program description,** especially when the evaluator has experience examining what seem like similar programs and when stakeholders do not have a unified view of the program. There is a subtle but important difference between the evaluator *facilitating* the program description and *creating* the program description. The former allows for the program description to reflect how stakeholders see it, while the latter may result in an ideal, nonexistent program. Evaluators should limit their role to facilitation.

Nothing should be included or excluded from the ToC and PLM without stakeholders' full knowledge and agreement. Although this may produce a model of a weak, infeasible program, the iterative process itself will produce a learning opportunity for the program. If the evaluator does all of the work of describing the program, then the evaluator has robbed stakeholders and program personnel of the opportunity to learn and to better understand their own program. Further, if the evaluator takes too much control of the evaluation process, then the program personnel will never buy-in to the evaluation or evaluatory activities and thus will never be fully vested in the results (including recommendations) of the evaluation.

A program description may stall because of differing stakeholders' views. It may seem that time is being wasted because stakeholders differ on what ought to be included in the description tools. However, a wise evaluator will allow the stakeholders to work it out by incorporating all of their views, giving them an opportunity to delete from the models what seems irrelevant. The program's stakeholders then have the opportunity to create a shared vision of the program.

Developing a shared understanding of the program takes time. Because it is the evaluator's understanding of the program that determines exactly what will be evaluated, it is essential that the evaluator's understanding be precisely on target and that everybody invest in this critical evaluation stage. One evaluates an initiative against its description.

A program will become more effective, focused, and successful when the program's stakeholders all share a detailed understanding of the program and reach a consensus on the logic model and theory. Even subtle discrepancies in the various parties' views of the program can diffuse the program's effectiveness. Once stakeholders share an understanding of the program, the program can and will become more focused. Generally, the more focused a program is, the greater the likelihood that the program will be successful in reaching its goals. The evaluator can act as a mediator between stakeholders but should never take control of the models.

The Program Is Alive and So Is Its Description

Evaluators should think of the PLM, and, to a lesser extent, the ToC, as living documents that perpetually change. A description that is valid at one point in time may not be valid at another time. Because of the fluidity of the environments in which most programs operate, the descriptive models of a program should be periodically revisited (such as every three to six months) to assure that they still apply to the program as it exists at a particular time.

For this reason, it is vital that all program descriptions be dated, allowing one to examine the program's evolution over time. Many organizations do not have a document that describes a program's history and evolution. Such a document enables the organization to keep track of when decisions about the program were made, why they were made, when changes were implemented, and who was administering the program at the time. Understanding the program's history allows for better understanding of the program's current form. It answers the question "How did we get here?"

Many organizations have trouble recounting a program's history—they look for guidance from personnel who may have been with the program over the years. Some with the program history may have left the organization or have unreliable memories. Having the program description dated and retained allows one to see how the program operated in the past, under what assumptions, and under what theory. Keeping track of the program's history can help the program from reverting back to practices that it had abandoned for good reason.

Comparing the current program against past descriptions provides an opportunity to ask questions about why the program has morphed into its current incarnation. There should be good reasons for changes. Programs can go astray from their original design because they want to take advantage of perceived opportunities (e.g., funding opportunities that may exist if the program did something a little differently, such as reaching a new target population, or offering a slightly altered service). Although taking advantage of such opportunities may seem beneficial in the short term, there is the risk that the program could become something that was never intended.

Some programs add on new "components," either in the short term or for the long term. Adding some components may be appropriate, but evaluators should check the degree to which the added components deviate the program from its intended goals and activities, and whether the stakeholders are actually comfortable with the deviation(s) once the deviations become apparent to them in the process of developing the ToC and PLM.

> *Component: an activity or set of activities that is minor or secondary in comparison with the program's main activity/activities. Components are usually added on after a program starts.*

Stakeholders should be conscious of the reasons why and in which respects a program has changed. Sometimes, programs change because they have matured and developed a better sense of what works and what doesn't work. In this sense, we can see that the program is on the same growth trajectory as originally intended. Sometimes, though, programs deviate from their intended path and enter a different trajectory. Left unchecked, they may begin a different orbit, becoming unrecognizable to the program planners. This change may be appropriate but shouldn't be undertaken without deep consideration.

There is no clear place to start when modeling a program. I start with the ToC because my personal approach tends to be theoretical. Other practitioners may feel more comfortable starting with the PLM. The development of both approaches—ToC and PLM—is iterative, meaning that the evaluator and stakeholders should go back and forth on these models as many times as it takes to assure that the results reflect reality, before moving on to measurement.

THEORY OF CHANGE

The ToC should reflect the "if" statements that are relevant to the program. The "if" statements are similar to the following:

> *If we do A, then B will happen, then C will happen, then ... and finally we will observe a change in Y.*

In addition to the general reasons articulated in the previous section, modeling the ToC is an important and necessary step because it allows the program to articulate its vision of how and through which mechanisms the program anticipates the change resulting from its activities. Every program exists because it believes that it causes positive change. Getting stakeholders to display how short-term and (perhaps) long-term change will result from the program's activities reveals the realm in which the program operates. By revealing the chain of the causal process, the ToC potentially reveals weaknesses in connections between the program's activities and short-term and long-term goals.

Getting everybody on board about the program's theoretical underpinnings has value in that it helps stakeholders, and especially program staff, to reflect on exactly what the program theoretically aims to accomplish. Having this explicitly articulated directs staff on how they should consider the services they provide.

Diagramming the Theory of Change Creating an appropriate diagram of the ToC is more an art than a science and can be the most challenging part of developing the evaluation plan. Sometimes, knowing where to begin is not clear, but this ultimately should not matter, because developing the ToC is an iterative process that works best when the evaluator asks prompting questions during the informal interviews, revealing the program's theoretical assumptions. Further, the ToC distinguishes the program's short-term from its long-term goals and reveals the programmatic goals that may exist at different units of analysis.

In drafting the ToC, I find it easiest to start with the program's activities, first considering possible short-term changes, and then long-term changes. Finally, I get the organization to "fill in" the causal chain, by asking what seem like naïve questions, such as "How does B cause C?" Sometimes, implementers have bought into the program's general ideals but they haven't delineated the exact process through which change might occur. Sometimes, when implementers discuss what they expect from an intervention, they gloss over the intermediate steps either because they haven't considered them for some time or have never really thought through the causal chain in any amount of detail. These intermediate steps are important to articulate because they directly relate to the program's probable success in producing the desired changes. The simplest questions can reveal the biggest assumptions that the program makes.

Another aspect of the ToC is the **unit of analysis** of the changes. The unit of analysis is the "thing" that is of interest or affected. Some programs operate at many units of analysis. For example, a program may have individuals as clients but aims to affect families, households, neighborhoods, and municipalities. All of these represent different units of analyses. Some programs not only serve children but also want to affect classrooms, teachers, schools, and curriculum. I knew of one program that worked with individual doctors, but hoped to affect hospitals and even the entire health-care system. One can examine the program's ToC at each unit of analysis, or the unit of analysis can be built into a single program theory. For some programs that operate at many different levels, it may make sense to create more than one ToC, reflecting the different realms in which the program operates.

When considering the issue of the unit of analysis, be wary of incorrectly thinking that the unit of analysis must get broader the further you go down the causal chain. This is not the case. I have seen programs that interact with individuals but aim to affect communities, and I have seen other programs that interact with communities but aim to ultimately affect individuals. Sometimes those who are novices at creating a ToC erroneously think that they must start with individuals and then broaden the program's effects to families, communities, and then, even broader.

There is a fine line between having a causal chain that is detailed enough and having one that is too detailed to be useful. Later in this chapter, in Example 1, union's training programs illustrates this issue.

Even if the ToC that stakeholders articulate seems weak to the evaluator, displaying a weak program theory has merit, in that it exposes flaws in the program's design.

It is the evaluator's responsibility to display the program theory in the leanest way possible, creating a ToC that has no lines that cross. The use of colors is an effective way to show different aspects of causal processes. The ToC should be detailed enough to reveal the steps in the causal chain, but not so detailed that at first glance it seems overwhelming and unintelligible. Words and expressions in the ToC should take on their common meaning rather than some special meaning that only program personnel or people with specific knowledge would use—avoid jargon.

Once the ToC is developed, many of the evaluation questions and assumptions that the program makes become apparent as do many of the questions that one would want a literature review to answer. One can essentially examine the ToC and in planning for the evaluation consider the extent to which the "arrows" in the ToC have actually materialized. The connections in the ToC are essentially assumptions that the program makes. Some of these assumptions will be reasonable and apparent, while some others may be very questionable.

Literature Reviews The links in the ToC should be verified (or shown to be false) by reviewing literature. Long ago, an advisor told me to "read with a purpose." With the ToC in hand, the literature to review becomes apparent. The literature reviewed should include the questions around the links in the causal chain. The literature review should examine the extent to which the literature supports the "arrows"—connections in—the ToC. Ultimately, the literature review should reveal the degree to which the ToC is sound and reasonable.

What is meant by "literature" is reports of evaluations of other programs and initiatives, articles that have appeared in journals, books, websites, etc. The literature review should be pointed and either directly related to the ToC or directly reflect on programs with similar activities or goals. Both the evaluator and the client should become aware of the results of the literature review.

Many implementers, despite spending hours, weeks, months, or years on an initiative, have never reviewed the literature around the initiative. Learning what the literature says about the ToC often comes as a surprise to organizations. It may pleasantly verify their long-held beliefs about an initiative. The results of a literature review can help organizations reconsider an initiative and sometimes adapt it so it or its evolution builds on best practices and becomes more effective. After conducting the literature review, the evaluator should be able to concisely summarize the literature and judge the extent to which the ToC is supported.

The literature review should show which links in the ToC are nearly certain to occur and which links are more tenuous. **When thinking about where to spend evaluation resources and time, those links nearly certain to occur are aspects where one would devote few, if any, evaluation resources beyond the literature review.** Evaluation resources should be devoted to exploring such tenuous links as these are the areas where the program's ToC may be vulnerable. For example, if the ToC was that if B occurs, C would increase and then D would increase and if the literature review shows that if C occurs D will certainly result, then in deciding upon the areas to evaluate, one would not need to reinvent the wheel and show the C–D linkage, as the existing literature will support this certainty.

However, if the literature review shows that the connection between B and C is tenuous, then, the evaluation doesn't need to show that C has caused or will cause D, but instead the evaluation would focus more on examining the B–C link. The evaluation instead would focus on showing that C actually occurred.

Contribution Analysis John Mayne introduced "contribution analysis" to the field of evaluation. "Contribution analysis considers the extent to which observed outcomes are the consequence of the program's activities as opposed to other interventions and/or external factors."[1] Using a contribution analysis lens, after the ToC has been developed and agreed upon, one can consider three important questions:

- What in the ToC is within the initiative's **direct control?** This is the area "where the intervention has fairly direct control of the results, typically at the output level."[2]

- What in the ToC is within the initiative's **direct influence?** This is "where the intervention has direct influence on the expected results …, typically the immediate outcomes and perhaps some intermediate outcomes."[3]

- What in the ToC does the intervention have **indirect influence?** This is "where the intervention has significantly less influence on the expected results due to its lack of direct contact with those involved and/or the significant influence of other factors."[4]

Thinking about the aspects of the ToC that are within the program's direct control, direct influence, and indirect influence allows one to consider which aspects of the ToC will be important to prioritize in an evaluation. Certainly, showing that the program's activities are being implemented and that there is some evidence that those activities are having some short-term effect will be important to an evaluation. The evaluation may devote few resources to areas of indirect influence.

---

1 Mayne, J. (2011). Contribution Analysis: Addressing Cause and Effect." Chapter 3 in. In: *Evaluating the Complex: Attribution, Contribution, and Beyond* (ed. K. Forss, M. Marra, and R. Schwartz). Transaction Publishers.
2 *Ibid.*
3 *Ibid.*
4 *Ibid.*

The Opera Trunk Program Theory of Change Probably the best way to learn how to construct a ToC diagram is to examine some that have already been created. I start with one of my favorite programs, the **Opera Trunk Program.** This program is a favorite because it's focused, small, has clear objectives, and its logic suggests that it has a chance of success (see Figure 2.1).

For background which was gleaned from the program's documentation, website, and two preliminary interviews with implementers from the opera company, the program starts with a city's opera company creating elaborately decorated trunks and filling them with materials associated with an opera. Implementers would bring these trunks to various elementary classrooms in schools that had teachers who indicated willingness to participate in the program. Teachers would use the items in the trunk to introduce their students to a particular opera. The outside of the trunk was decorated to reflect the opera (e.g., the trunk for *Madame Butterfly* had a Japanese motif) and contained various paraphernalia related to the opera—a recording, costumes, materials on the history of the opera's locale, and other meaningful items. Prior to the trunk being delivered, local elementary school teachers who were interested in having their classes participate in the program were invited to participate in a one-day workshop on introducing opera to children and how to integrate opera into existing curricula. The workshop was held on a Saturday, and teachers were not given a stipend for their attendance. This program is what many might consider a "small" program. It does not aim to change the world—its only direct goal is to sustain opera in society by creating an interest in opera among schoolchildren.

The Opera Trunk Program's program ToC (Figure 2.1) suggests that its stakeholders believed that if children were introduced to opera through the trunk and having it integrated into a pre-existing class curriculum (which allowed them to understand opera in a cultural and historical context), then they would develop an increased appreciation of opera, which would increase future opera audiences and ultimately sustain opera in society.

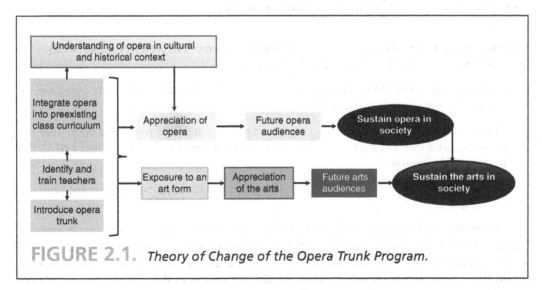

FIGURE 2.1. *Theory of Change of the Opera Trunk Program.*

The program also would have positive *"spillover"* effects onto other art forms. The introduction of opera increases exposure to an art form, thus enhancing children's appreciation of the arts in general, a positive end in and of itself. The spillover effect would extend to building future audiences for the arts (not only opera) and would result in sustaining the arts in society.

Many arts education programs follow a similar ToC where the end goal is both the appreciation of the specific art form and the appreciation of the arts in general. Many children's arts education programs go beyond art appreciation to teach how to create art. When creation is part of the program, then the ToC would likely have the additional goal of inspiring more artists, both on a professional and amateur basis.

In this case, note that the program has not extended its long-term goals to areas such as improving social tolerance, building a cohesive society, etc. Some arts programs do extend their ToC into such areas. The program developers of the Opera Trunk Program didn't see their program as having such grand effects.

Considering contribution analysis, the areas of the program's **direct control** are the implementation of the program—the trunk itself, the integration of opera into the curriculum, and exposure to opera (an art form). The areas of **direct influence** include children understanding opera in context, appreciation of opera, and appreciation of the arts. Whether a child later becomes an audience member later in life is an area of **indirect influence**. Many factors may contribute to one becoming an audience member to opera performances and other art forms in adulthood, and having exposure to opera when a child may be one of many factors.

Stylistic aspects of the ToC to note include that it starts with a very brief description of the activities that interface with beneficiaries. These activities are bracketed to show that the group leads to the next change expected. Arrows show that one thing is expected to lead to another. The arrowhead shows the direction of the expected relationship. The use of colors allows the eye to follow the paths of change. Pink shows the program's effects on opera while blue shows the spillover path—impact on the arts.

Possible Evaluation Questions for the Opera Trunk Program Possible evaluation questions flow from the ToC. For example, one could ask:

- How effective were the workshops held with teachers in increasing their capacities of integrating opera into the curriculum?

- In the short term, do children have a great appreciation of the particular opera that the trunk focused on? Do they understand the opera in the broader historical and social aspects of the period?

- Has the appreciation of other art forms increased in the short term among the children exposed to opera?

Depending on the timing of the evaluation, one would include questions on the sustainability of the appreciation of opera and other art forms, and whether the children later become audience members of the arts. Observing their later ticket-purchasing behavior in adulthood would very likely not be feasible, since the readers of the evaluation would likely want results sooner than, say, a 30-year period.

Literature Review for the Opera Trunk Program The ToC suggests that the literature review should investigate the evidence that exists on the following questions:

- Does introducing opera to schoolchildren increase their appreciation of opera in the short term?
- Does introducing any of the arts at a young age increase their appreciation of other art forms in the short term? Is there evidence of such spillover effects from other programs?
- To what extent does the appreciation of opera or any of the arts at a young age lead them to appreciate opera or any other art form at later ages? Does the appreciation translate into becoming (ticket-buying) audience members at later ages?
- Does integration of opera into the curriculum increase children's understanding of the opera's historical and social context? Does this increased understanding lead to an appreciation of opera?
- Does integrating any art form into a historical and social curriculum lead to greater appreciation of the art form?
- To what degree does audience support drive the sustenance of opera? (e.g., opera companies may be very dependent on foundations and not ticket sales for their sustenance.)

In reviewing the literature on the development of audiences, one might also consider whether children who are brought to sporting events later become paying sports fans.

In the Opera Trunk Program, some of the linkages are more uncertain than others. For example, the degree to which introducing opera to children results in enhanced appreciation of opera is probably uncertain. However, the link between future opera audiences and the sustenance of opera may be so strong that it can be taken off the list of possible questions that an evaluation would examine (beyond the literature review), as it falls into the category of linkages that are so strong that re-examining them would be equivalent to reinventing the wheel. Thus, the literature, rather than primary data collection, can be relied upon to show the linkage.

The ToC also clarifies which linkages would be observed in the near-term rather than the long term. Programs that are offered only on a short time frame typically want evaluation results also on a short time frame, and therefore the evaluations cannot examine long-term impacts. To make the case for a long-term impact, the program must rely on the literature review. Ideally, the literature can be relied upon to make the case that if the short-term impact occurs, the long-term effects will be eventually seen.

THE PROGRAM LOGIC MODEL

Another way of examining a program is through a Program Logic Model. The PLM describes the program at the operational level. Once completed, examination of the PLM will allow one to answer questions such as:

- Does the program have the resources it needs to operate?
- Is the program intense enough to produce the intended outcomes?

- Are the program's goals and outcomes feasible?
- Are the program's assumptions about the environment in which it operates realistic?
- Is the program's reliance on resources realistic? Will the resources it needs to operate be there on a continuous basis?
- Is the program's target population well-specified and within reach?

Similar to the ToC, the PLM reveals the program under a harsh light. It does not address the theoretical underpinnings of the program, focusing instead on the operations of the program.

The version of the PLM that I use and advocate is an adaptation of the W. K. Kellogg Foundation's (1998, 2001) PLM, the difference being that I separate outcomes from outcome measures. What one chooses for outcome measures considers the availability of data, the cost of data collection, and the need for measures that would allow the initiative to be compared with similar initiatives.

The power of the PLM is not evident until all of the columns are completed for a program. Its power becomes apparent when you step back from the program and critically think about the program's logic, its possible weaknesses, how it could be more focused, and the probability of success. Further, a well-constructed PLM, combined with the ToC, will reveal on which basis (outcomes and/or processes) the program should be evaluated. It may also reveal that the program is not stable enough to warrant an evaluation. For example, it could reveal that data on the outcomes that the program desires to impact have not been collected or the cost of collecting such data would be prohibitive.

Columns of the Program Logic Model The PLM has eight columns: Goals, Assumptions, Target Population, Inputs, Activities, Outputs, Outcomes, and Outcome Measures.

The columns should be completed independently of each other. One should not create rows for the PLM. Some novices create rows, start with a goal, and then go across the row, trying to complete each of the columns for a particular goal. Such an approach does not take a holistic view of the program and inevitably leads to repetition (e.g., the target population would be repeated for each goal). Instead, one should complete one column of the PLM and then move to the next (Table 2.1).

The evaluator completes the PLM in collaboration with the ERG and reviewing documents. The worst mistake an evaluator can make in the PLM is to describe a program that is unrecognizable. The ERG ultimately must feel ownership of the product, and for this reason, it is important that the first draft include all of the goals and assumptions the group articulates. This will increase buy-in to the evaluation and evaluation results.

Goal(s) The goal(s) column should reflect the change(s) that the program anticipates will result from its activities. The goal(s) of the program should relate to the ToC. Often, the ToC's ultimate goal, which is listed on the right-hand side of the ToC, is listed in the goals column of the PLM. However, in the PLM many programs will see their goal(s) as the near-term goal, or the goal(s) that are within the program's direct influence. The program may believe that the effects in the program's zone of indirect influence are not the focus of the program, and thus will choose to list in the PLM only those effects of the program that the

TABLE 2.1. Program Logic Model Template

Goal(s)	Assumptions	Target Population	Inputs	Activities	Outputs	Outcomes	Outcome Measures
What the program intends to change or influence, which may include a primary goal and secondary goals, and both long-term and short-term goals	Assumptions upon which the program and its operation are based, usually phrased as statements about the program's environment or human behavior as perceived prior to the implementation of the program	Exactly whom the program is trying to change, usually bound by geography or population characteristics—a program never attempts to change everyone	The money, items, people, and in-kind contributions the program uses to operate—what it takes to run the program	What the program needs to do to engage participants and how it engages participants	Indicators of the program's operation	Aspects of the change that the program may have caused; operationalizations of the goals	Mathematical and/or qualitative measures of the outcomes

program has direct influence over. Typically, the goals will not be the aspects of the ToC that the program has direct control over, since those aspects are typically outputs, and not effects of the program.

Consider a program that has the near-term goal of providing foster teenagers with stable and secure housing situations so they become more confident and directed, with the ultimate goal that the teenagers will transition into well-adjusted, productive adults. In this case, the program may stress in the PLM the short-term goal of increasing in teens their confidence and direction. The ToC would show the long-term goals. (A measurable outcome of the program may be the teen's money management abilities.)

Likewise, a program intended to spur the creation of greengrocers in an inner city may have a primary goal of increasing access to fresh produce for people in isolated neighborhoods, but a secondary goal may be giving farmers direct access to consumers. The ToC for this program would show the paths for affecting both the inner city residents and the farmers. The PLM could include in the goal(s) column:

Primary goal: Increase inner city consumers' access to fresh produce.

Secondary goal: Increase farmers' direct access to consumers.

Working with organizations, I have found a pattern in developing the goals column of the PLMs. When a PLM is first developed, many program administrators seem to want the goals column to be as long as possible and list a multitude of goals. Often, these goals are broader than the program's actual activities; thus, if one were to evaluate the program based on these broad goals and the outcomes and outcome measures that flow from them, the program would appear unsuccessful.

The reason for organizations wanting a long list of goals may have to do with how organizations have historically applied for funding. Many funders have given applicants the impression that their funding application would have a higher likelihood of success if they stressed the larger possible set of outcomes of their programs, possibly overstating the possible impact of the program's activities. Many funding applicants have believed that programs that aim to change the world have a higher chance of being funded. Some program administrators become tied to the goals articulated in funding applications. Thus, when an evaluator interviews personnel for the PLM, the personnel still think in terms of the goals articulated in a grant proposal.

Although I may question some of the goals and ask for clarification on how the program's activities could lead to those goals, I will keep the multitude of articulated goals in the first draft of the PLM. When I later ask program personnel to review the PLM with me, I often find that they are willing to remove some of the goals listed in the first iteration of the PLM.

Conversely, I have seen programs list goals that they believe are somewhat peripheral to the main emphasis of the program—but once the entire program is fully described, it turns out that the peripheral goals are central to the program.

For these reasons, I advise that the first iteration of the PLM include all goals that stakeholders articulate. Developing the PLM is an iterative process, and it often takes much discussion between the evaluator and program personnel before an appropriate and concise PLM emerges. Later drafts of the PLM will offer the opportunity to streamline goals and organize them into long term versus short term and essential versus peripheral.

Assumptions The assumptions column ought to reflect the assumptions the program makes. **All programs make assumptions**. Some assumptions are valid and others, when tested or closely examined, will be shown to be invalid. Some assumptions are not based on data but instead are based on how program creators perceive an aspect of the program. Some assumptions may have been valid at one point in time and have become obsolete.

While all programs make assumptions, most programs, until asked, have not articulated them. Articulating assumptions is useful because it helps one determine how realistic the program is about its environment. The validity of assumptions can reflect on the program's relevance. Sometimes, assumptions reflect what was known about another place, population, or time, and bear no relation to the program's actual current circumstances or target population.

Programs make assumptions about their target population, how activities will result in the desired change, and the environment in which the program operates. Other types of assumptions pertain to the program's inputs (that funding for the program will continue), program's staff (that trained personnel are available), and program's beneficiaries (that people desire the services the program offers). Multisite programs usually assume a shared perspective and similar implementation across all implementers and sites. An evaluation should certainly examine implementation across sites. All programs assume that their efforts are sufficient and intense enough to start the ToC.

Sometimes, the assumptions are negative goal statements. For example, if a program aims to decrease obesity in children by advocating for nutritious foods in schools, then the program is essentially assuming that children are obese because school meals have low nutritional content. The program may also be assuming that contractual agreements between school districts and their food providers allow for healthier food options and that children will eat the nutritious foods and eat less "junk food." All of these are "big" assumptions and the violation of any one of them could jeopardize the effectiveness of the program.

When programs are colossal failures, they fail because of faulty assumptions. If the assumptions had been closely articulated and examined prior to the start of the program, failure may have been avoided. (In contrast, when programs fall short of expectations, it is typically an issue of implementation.)

> *When programs totally fail, they fail because they have made at least one faulty and critical assumption.*

For example, a foundation-sponsored $80 million child-care program targeted at low-income communities failed because it made the following faulty assumptions:

(a) Low-income communities have a supply of buildings that one could inexpensively adapt for child-care uses.

(b) Children in the participating low-income communities would only need part-time care, not full-time care.

(c) There would be a supply of trained child-care professionals willing to work for the wages that child-care occupations offer.

All of these assumptions are "big" assumptions that if violated, threatened the program's chances for success. In this program, all of these assumptions were violated.

When creating the PLM, the evaluator and program administrators should create an exhaustive list of the possible assumptions that the program makes. Once listed, the evaluator should first determine which assumptions are critical—if violated, would risk the entire program. These critical assumptions should certainly be investigated for their veracity. There could be other assumptions that should also be investigated.

Target Population All programs "target" their efforts at a particular population. When one considers the target population, one should be thinking in terms of the "unit of analysis" that the program attempts to influence. The smallest unit of analysis is the individual level. Programs can target a more aggregated unit, such as families, households, neighborhoods, communities, organizations, or systems.

A program can target one unit in hopes that other units will change. For example, a program may work directly with mothers in the hope that opportunities for their families will improve. One should think clearly about which unit of analysis the program directly targets or interacts with, and which unit of analysis the program ultimately hopes to influence. Often but not always, these units are the same.

Often, programs think that they are targeting "everybody" or perhaps every person who lives in a certain geographic zone. A target population such as this can usually be more narrowly specified. Very few programs actually target everybody in the same way. For example, a program that trucked in fresh produce weekly to sell in low-income neighborhoods that lacked local grocers first claimed that it targeted everybody in the neighborhoods. But after reflection, the program appropriately decided that it targeted the people who purchased food in each household. Another target for the program was people who received farmers' market coupons through the WIC program. The third target population was local farmers.

Sometimes, programs do not target individuals but instead may believe that they target organizations or businesses. Even in those cases, they often target certain persons in the entities in hopes that the impact on those individuals will lead to change in their organization or business. For example, rather than target all businesses in an area, a program may target entrepreneurs who started their business within the past year in a particular area.

Often, the target population can be described demographically, and the size of the population can be estimated by using data produced by the census bureau. In the United States, the US Census Bureau produces population estimates for the country, states, counties, municipalities, and census tracks (usually about three thousand people). The US Census Bureau has the information available on its website (www.census.gov).

All evaluations should examine the degree to which a program has achieved its target population. Is the program reaching the people or entities that it aims to reach? Do they stay in the program long enough or receive enough of the program's benefits to be considered "program participants?" In evaluating the program's impact, evaluators need to decide whether the impact should be considered on the population that the program intended to reach (intent-to-treat) versus the population that the program actually reached and participated in the program as the program was intended to be delivered (compliers).

Inputs This column lists the resources that are needed to operate the program. The column should explicitly list the following: monetary funding, in-kind contributions, physical space, characteristics and qualifications of staff, particular expertise of staff, and sometimes the voluntary participation and assistance of others. If the program used something special that was unique to a particular program and cannot easily be replicated, then that should be listed. For example, if the program relies on the media, and someone on the organization's board was able to secure donated ad time on a particular radio station, then that unique "connection" should be listed. Sometimes, programs may have charismatic leaders, or leaders who are extraordinarily competent or unique. Such leaders should be listed as inputs, since they will be difficult, if not impossible to replicate.

Listing the inputs to the program has three advantages. First, listing inputs allows one to objectively consider whether the program has enough resources to operate effectively. Listing the funding, as well as a summary of what the funding supported in terms of personnel and space, quickly gives an idea of the program's capacity to provide services.

Second, listing inputs allows those considering replicating the program to understand what it takes to operate such a program. Those thinking of replicating the program need to see the "special" inputs that are not easily replicable, such as the charismatic, well-connected leader.

Third, listing inputs provide the information needed to do a cost–benefit analysis. In my opinion, you should delay doing an actual cost–benefit analysis until you have determined whether the program has any discernible benefits. A challenge with the cost–benefit analysis is the difficulty of quantifying benefits. Some programs have spin-off and long-term benefits, and quantifying these benefits is an inexact science. For how many generations does one consider the benefits of a program that positively changes the earnings trajectory and life course of a participant? In such a program that shows positive income impacts, should one also consider an estimate of the benefits of the increase in life expectancy that often goes along with increased income? If a program directly influences one person who then becomes a community leader and develops a wider sphere of positive influence, how does one quantify that benefit? If a program increases one's likelihood of graduating from high school or college, should one only consider the difference in the participants' earnings or should one also consider effects on disease rates, mortality rates, and on the educational attainment of subsequent generations?

Sometimes, cost–benefit analyses can be molded to fit particular preconceived ideas. How to quantify the benefits becomes unclear, as do the true costs of the program. Should one consider opportunity costs of participants as costs? For these reasons, I discourage the cost–benefit analyses but encourage the rigorous examination of the benefits and the true costs of a program. However, some funders and some groups that compare programs across the same metrics require a "return on investment" (ROI) calculation. Potential beneficiaries often also want to know the ROI of a program. ROI is a concise (though inexact) measure that is instrumental to fundraising efforts of organizations. When stating the ROI of a program, be very transparent about the assumptions used in the calculation.

Activities This column should briefly list what the program actually does, including the activities that the public may witness as well as the activities that go on behind the scenes. The activities listed in the PLM may be identical to those listed in a program implementation model or workplan, but the PLM may not go into as much detail. The activities column often includes how the program reaches out to the target population (e.g., advertising and partnerships), how clients are recruited (e.g., referrals and screening of potential clients), how staff are trained, how the program reaches the target population, and how the program interacts with its clients. It may also show activities with program partners and follow-up activities with clients.

Outputs Outputs are measures that show that the program is actually operating. Outputs include figures such as the number of clients, numbers of bags of food distributed, number of opera trunks circulated, and number of teachers who participated in the training. Outputs do not reflect any change in beneficiaries, and they do not reflect the achievement of a goal. They simply show that the program is up and running. They are measures of the the program's implementation.

Consider an intergenerational program that gets teenagers together with the elderly to produce visual artwork, believing that the teamwork would allow for greater understanding of the challenges that the other generation faces. In that program, the number of visual art pieces would be an output. However, the change in the intergenerational understanding would be an outcome.

Outputs could be created for each of the program's processes. They should show how the program is intended to be implemented. Thinking about outputs in this way and examining the implementation of the program will reveal whether there are any issues in the program's delivery of services or activities. In evaluating a program, one would examine the outputs delivered versus the outputs indicated in the PLM. One could examine costs per output and compare with similar programs. Costs per output may be a measure of the program's efficiency. For example, how much does it cost to recruit each participant? How much does it cost for services to the participant?

For advocacy programs, an evaluation may emphasize outputs rather than outcomes. In advocacy programs, the ultimate goal is usually to change the targeted population's stance on an issue. In reality, in political advocacy programs, there may be many reasons why politicians vote a particular way on an issue, and many of the reasons may be well outside of the control of the advocacy organization. Holding the organization up to the standard of a changed vote on an issue might be too high (or too low) of a standard, depending on how public opinion on an issue may have shifted.

Outcomes This column should reflect, in words but not quantitative measures, the desired impact of the program. The focus should be on what would have to change in order for the program to be considered successful. Similar to the goals column, the outcomes listed can be near-term or long-term outcomes and include temporary effects of the program versus permanent effects.

Usually, the outcomes relate to the program's goals and to intermediate steps in the ToC. Outcomes differ from goals in that they are usually operationalizations of the goals—the theoretical concept is brought down to the practical realm. For example, a goal of a program targeted to teenage foster children may be to have better prepared adults. The outcomes might include financial literacy, employment opportunities, functional relationships, etc.

Outcome Measures This column should reflect the measures, counts, rates, or indicators used to operationalize the articulated outcomes. An outcome measure could also derive from qualitative data collection—for example, that interviewees express that the program caused the desired change to occur.

There are a number of trade-offs to consider when committing to a particular quantitative outcome measure. Before creating a new, perfect measure, consider whether the types of measures of the concept that are typically used are appropriate for the situation at hand. There are advantages to "borrowing" measures that are already prevalent. Pre-existing measures have usually been field tested. Using a pre-existing measure allows comparisons between programs' outcomes. The value of this cannot be overstated, because programs often want to make statements that suggest that they have been more effective than other programs that they may compete with for clients and funding. For these two important reasons, one should use preexisting outcome measures when appropriate. However, sometimes the preexisting measures do not accurately apply to the program at hand, and, in this case, a new outcome measure might need to be created, understanding that doing so will make the program incomparable with other programs because different measures cannot be directly compared.

Any new outcome measure should have the following attributes. First, it should **exploit data that the program already collects, if relevant**. When new data elements need to be collected for an outcome measure, then there is less likelihood that the new data will be collected right away. Even when there is a commitment to collecting the new information, it may take a while for the data collection system to run reliably and for the correct questions to be asked in order to collect the desired data. Further, if new data need to be collected, then a baseline or pre-intervention measure may not be available.

Second, every outcome measure should have a **clearly defined unit of analysis.** The unit of analysis—the element to which the outcome measure applies—should be clear and explainable. One can readily interpret a unit of analysis of "child" given an age definition. However, the unit of analysis of "family" or "household" may need further explanation.

Third, all outcome measures should be **meaningful to stakeholders.** Stakeholders of the program should be able to readily understand why a particular measure is being used. If the best outcome measure is very complex but a close substitute is simple, then the program should opt for the simpler measure as it will be more transparent to stakeholders.

To save time and resources in the long run, consider developing a one-page sheet on each proposed outcome measure which informs exactly how the measure is to work, starting with a discussion of how the measure is mathematically calculated. For example, is the measure a rate? If so, how are the numerator and denominator of the rate defined? Describe exactly from where the data used in the measure are derived. Do the data come from the program's records? Is the number of residents in the community from census data? Comment on the quality of the data that the measure uses. Are the data reliably kept? Are the data fraught with "measurement error"? Describe whether any primary data collection is needed for the measure. Discuss why data that are already collected are insufficient for the program's purposes, describe measures used by similar programs, and explain why such measures are inappropriate for the program at hand.

The outcome measure sheets are internal documents. They describe exactly how the data will be collected and used. They also give the organization a history of the measure, and in that sense, serve as a blueprint for calculating the measure, which ultimately will allow the measure to retain the same meaning over time. The exercise of developing an outcome sheet prevents the program from changing outcome measures without good reason. Creating such a sheet for each outcome measure may seem like a burdensome task, but it will prevent mistakes that could be costly in terms of time, money, and goodwill.

Analyzing the Program Logic Model

After the PLM has been completed, the evaluator and the ERG should collaboratively review it to see how well, on paper, the program holds together. The essence of the PLM is that it allows one to creatively reflect on the program's chances of success and how that success ought to be measured.

The evaluator and ERG should verify that the PLM's outcome measures relate to the goals. There should be no "orphans" in the PLM—every goal is a candidate for measurement, every activity relates to at least one goal, and if a goal has no activities associated with it, then either the goal should be removed or activities developed. I usually advise removing goals over developing activities, because if the goal were truly important, the program would have already been engaged in related activities.

The review of the PLM considers the following questions:

- How realistic are the program's assumptions?
- Is the target population well specified and an achievable program population?
- To what degree does the achieved program population reflect the target population?
- Does the program have the resources it needs to have the desired impact?
- Are the program's efforts intense enough to produce the desired impact?
- Do the goals of the program relate to the program outcomes?
- Do the outcome measures truly reflect the program's goals and outcomes?
- Does the program have enough resources to attract a well-trained staff?

The PLM shows the program in a very harsh light. Strong, focused programs usually shine under the spotlight of the PLM and weak programs become painfully evident.

I once had the experience of working with three very different food assistance programs over a three-year period. Although the programs were run by three different organizations and had very different activities—a community gardens program, an advocacy effort, and a program that operated a produce truck for low-income, urban neighborhoods—they were bundled together in a grant because a pot of money was suddenly available. Each program approached the creation of the PLM in the same way. At first, they all had very large goals. For example, the truck program believed that it was doing community economic development and the community garden (which was a small plot of land) thought that it was substantively contributing to the community's food resources. Each of the programs was committed to the big goals for about four to six months. As time went on, each of the programs dropped the goals that were tangential to the program and strengthened the activities and measures of the goals that were essential to the programs. That is, over time, each of the programs developed a "leaner and meaner" PLM.

Programs with lean and mean PLMs often have a number of advantages over programs with extensive, broad PLMs. First, outsiders can easily see the program's logic; the program becomes transparent.

Second, program personnel can better define the boundaries of the program—articulating not only what the program is about, but just as importantly, what it is not about. Programs need limits and the PLM is a tool for demarcating these limits. The PLM thus helps the program to develop its own niche and to focus its services and activities there. Programs with broad PLMs have little opportunity for true success, because it is very difficult to be successful when resources and efforts are spread thin.

Third, programs can check in with the PLM before undertaking new activities or changing the program's focus or activities. It is not unusual for programs to lose their focus. Some stakeholders may want to take advantage of dubious opportunities (e.g., more funding may be available if the program changes in what seems like a minor way), or a program may decide to add on temporary components. Before modifying the program, personnel should check the PLM to see how the modification could affect the program's integrity. Further, if an evaluation plan was based on a former version of the PLM, then any modification to the program may make the evaluation plan obsolete.

Challenges of Multisite Programs

Some programs operate at multiple sites. In describing multisite programs, one ought to consider whether on a day-to-day basis the sites are actually offering the same program. Do they really share the same ToC and PLM? Do they really have the same emphasis? If a program has been designed to allow sites the flexibility to respond to local needs, have the sites responded to the same challenges in the same way, or is there so much "flexibility" that the sites should be considered separate and distinct programs? Over time, has the growth trajectory of each site resulted in different programs evolving?

One way of considering these questions is to separately develop ToCs and PLMs for each site—these independent results can then be compared to determine the degree of consistency between sites.

Without adequate oversight, a program's sites can easily evolve differently. This could occur if the sites take advantage of local conditions, respond to local needs, and draw their staff from local labor pools. Some programs encourage their projects to be responsive to local circumstances. When evaluating multisite programs, one first must address the question of whether each site actually represents the same program. For example, Medicaid, a program that provides low-income persons with health insurance, has different eligibility criteria and offers different benefits across states. The WIC program also offers different benefits in each state—for example, ranging from $38 per month per participant in Wisconsin to $76 in New Jersey.[5] When these programs are to be evaluated, one should question whether the differences between the states make a national evaluation of the "WIC program" useful, especially when beneficiaries in one state receive twice the level of benefits as those in another state.

Simply documenting the similarities and differences between the sites that appeared in the program description can provide program directors with valuable information. If differences between the sites have evolved, the program's directors should be made aware of these differences. They may choose to bring all of the projects in line with the original design or, alternatively, to reconsider whether those that vary significantly ought to continue operating under the auspices of the program. In the extreme, having different sites operate under the same program title could dilute the integrity of the program.

PROGRAM IMPLEMENTATION MODEL

Organizations often use program implementation models to describe programs. Such models reflect a sequence of the program's activities, akin to a flowchart. The model starts with the first activities and describes in detail the activities that follow.

Program implementation models can be used to identify opportunities for process-based evaluation. Collecting data on the various steps of the program can assure staff that both public and nonpublic activities are being carried out as intended. One can investigate the areas where the workflow is not occurring as intended. For example, the following questions would be asked:

- Are staff being hired as planned?
- Do staff members possess the qualifications that the program planners envisioned?
- Is the program being marketed properly?
- How much time does it take to process applications to the program?
- Are the services being delivered in a timely manner?

Simple flowcharts of the activities of a program can help pinpoint opportunities to improve the program as designed. They can help identify where the program could become more efficient. However, analysis of program implementation plans and flowcharts cannot help improve programs that have made faulty assumptions. They also do not clarify to stakeholders how the activities connect to the outcomes and goals desired.

---

5 https://www.fns.usda.gov/pd/wic-program. Accessed April 4, 2024.

EXAMPLES OF PROGRAM DESCRIPTIONS

The following examples present various frameworks to address a variety of evaluation challenges that programs present. These programs were selected because they demonstrate common issues that arise. The reader should understand the logic behind how the program description challenge was addressed. The descriptions are a result of reviewing documents, interviewing, and having conversations with program staff, stakeholders, and ERGs.

> **EXAMPLE 1: Training Programs That Fit Under One Umbrella—The Labor Union**
>
> A labor union offers capacity building in three different but related ways. One effort is an ongoing skills development program through which union members can take courses to improve or expand upon their existing skills. For example, a bulldozer operator can participate in training to learn how to operate a crane. The union also offers an apprenticeship program, whereby people with no relevant skills are trained in how to use heavy equipment and the participants apprentice on work sites over a four-year period at reduced pay. Third, the union offers certification tests to persons who already are skilled but have never been certified for the skill (many who come for certification will end up in the apprenticeship program). All three programs come under the rubric of capacity building of members and potential members.
>
> The union is a conduit between employers and workers. Typically, employers will make requests to the union for skilled workers who operate heavy equipment. Employers usually need union members for temporary employment—when construction or destruction is occurring. The employers ask the union for its members to fill temporary positions and depending on the availability of its members, the union does so. Optimally, the union would like to fill every employer's request and have every union member working as much as members would like to work.

Theory of Change of Labor Union's Training Initiatives Figures 2.2–2.5 follow the evolution of the ToC for an initiative of a labor union that offers three types of training. These three "programs" are combined into one ToC because the union thinks of them as different aspects of the same effort. To arrive at the ToC of the training programs, we start with a bare framework (Figure 2.2). By providing training, the union believes that it will see more members that are highly qualified—increases in the number of members certified and the number of certifications held per member. These improvements will in turn lead to more satisfied employers, which will ultimately strengthen the union.

This first draft of the ToC (see Figure 2.2) poorly specifies the theoretical pathway between (a) increased qualifications of union members and employer satisfaction and (b) employer satisfaction and strengthening of the union. The model needs work. While the link between capacity building and having highly qualified members is clear, the links between having highly qualified members and satisfied employers, and then between

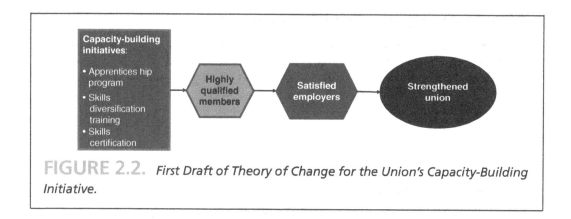

FIGURE 2.2. *First Draft of Theory of Change for the Union's Capacity-Building Initiative.*

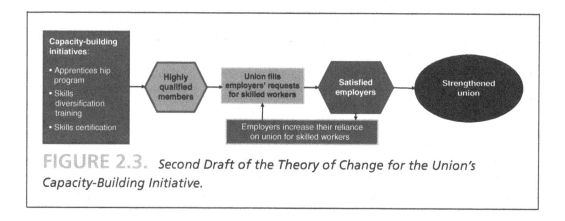

FIGURE 2.3. *Second Draft of the Theory of Change for the Union's Capacity-Building Initiative.*

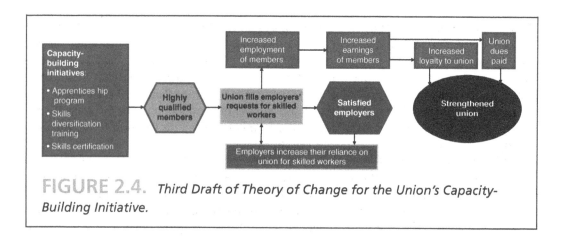

FIGURE 2.4. *Third Draft of Theory of Change for the Union's Capacity-Building Initiative.*

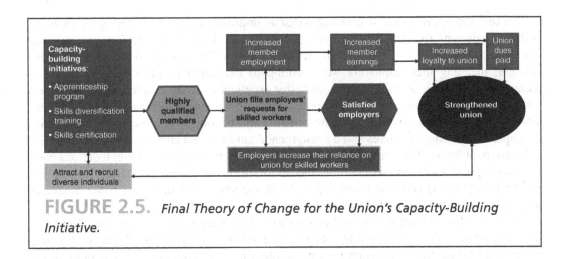

FIGURE 2.5. *Final Theory of Change for the Union's Capacity-Building Initiative.*

satisfied employers and a strengthened do not have enough specificity. In creating a ToC, there is a fine line between too much information and not enough. This draft does not have enough information.

The second draft of the ToC specifies how having more highly qualified members link to employer satisfaction. In this draft (Figure 2.3), the union theorized that if members were more highly qualified, the union would be able to fill a greater proportion of employer's requests for skilled workers, which would lead to higher satisfaction among employers. Satisfied employers will increase their reliance on the union for workers (as opposed to nonunion labor sources) and the more that they rely on the union, the more the union can plan to have members available to them to fulfill requests. Note the circular nature of the boxes pertaining to the union filling request, employers increasing their reliance, and employer satisfaction. In this second draft, increased employer satisfaction somehow leads to a strengthened union.

In developing the third draft (Figure 2.4), the evaluator asked the union's senior staff member to explain how satisfied employers lead to a stronger union. The staff member explained that if employers are more satisfied, then union members are more employable (or that employers are more likely to turn to the union than to nonunion operating engineers when they have job openings). Increased employability means that union members will enjoy increased earnings and job satisfaction—and, thus, will be more loyal to the union. Further, an increase in members' earnings allows the union to increase revenues from its members. Having more resources and more loyal members strengthens the union. By asking for clarification, the senior staff member thought that maybe there was no direct link between satisfied employers and a strengthened union. However, the staff member believed that high employer satisfaction led to more reliance on the union for workers, and having more reliance resulted in the union better able to fill requests for workers (since it was better able to plan for fuller employment of its members) and that this relationship between these two elements was reinforcing. Thus, there is a double-headed arrow showing the linkage.

Further discussion of the ToC revealed that an important reason for offering the capacity building programs (particularly the apprenticeship and skills certification programs) was that the union could attract and diversify its membership. The union believed that if it were stronger, meaning that employers were turning to the union to fill jobs, members had increased loyalty to it, and the union could offer excellent capacity-building initiatives, then nonunion members who may be filling positions (at lower wages, often as freelance or day laborers) would instead want to become certified and become union members. Thus, both the capacity-building initiatives and a strengthened union would attract individuals and thus a diverse population. The union had advertised its apprenticeship program in locations used by diverse populations. In this iteration, the senior union staff member decided that having satisfied employers, combined with more loyal members and being on better financial footing, all contributed to a strengthened union.

The final ToC (Figure 2.5) is well explicated—adding any more would make it too complex, and subtracting anything would not reflect the initiative in its entirety. There is a fine line between a well-explicated program theory and one that is so complex that it is difficult for external audiences to comprehend. External audiences, including potential funders, often do not have the time or interest to decipher complex models of the program theory. This final ToC, in my opinion, successfully explains the complexity of the initiative in a clear, parsimonious way. One can readily understand the union's perspective on its training programs.

Note the stylistic elements of this final ToC.

1. The use of colors (though shown here in black-and-white). The capacity-building initiative is green and the aspects that pertain directly to the effects on the union and its members are in blue. A darker shade of blue is used for the aspects that pertain to the effects on union members. Yellow is used for nonunion members. The ToC uses red for aspects pertaining to employers. The ToC uses black for the goal.

2. A circular, reinforcing aspect. This occurs directly around the union filling employers' requests, satisfied employers, and employers increasing their reliance on the union. It also occurs indirectly around the union being strengthened, attracting (diverse) individuals, and capacity building.

3. No linkages cross.

The ToC directs the evaluator to the literature to read to understand the program's chances of success. Literature on the following questions should be examined:

- What factors are associated with strong unions? This ToC pertains to a union that offers a particular skill set. Can we learn something by examining other labor unions?

- Does increasing the pool of people with certifiable skills in a union cause employers to hire union versus nonunion members? What other factors affect employers' hiring practices?

- What threats to union strength exist?

- What factors are associated with loyalty to one's union? With loyalty to organizations as a whole?

- What leads employers to hire day laborers over union workers?

Reading the literature on the above will help determine the degree to which the program can be successful in the ways that it wants to be. A ToC that is well-proven and strong has a literature that shows that the program will likely have its intended impact when it is implemented properly. If a program has a literature review that suggests that the program will always have the intended effect if implemented well, then evaluation activities would focus heavily on implementation and lightly on other aspects of the ToC. The evaluation activities would show that the theoretical chain of events has been started and rely on the literature review to make the case that the intended results will ensue.

The ToC also tells us what literature should *not* be examined. For example, in this case, one would not review the literature on the effects of job training programs on the unemployed and underemployed because it is not germane to the ToC. There is an enormous literature in the field of labor economics on this question, and before explicating the ToC, an evaluator may have been tempted to put "job training" into a search engine and would inevitably have been overwhelmed by the sheer number of articles and books on the topic. However, the ToC shows that much of this literature would not be relevant to the union's initiative. Having a ToC at hand before conducting a literature review saves time and resources.

The ToC encompasses many levels. While the initiative directly works with individuals, its goal is to impact the organization's strength. The union's activities aim to impact both union members and nonmembers. Employers are regarded as a group.

Considering the areas of direct control, direct influence, and indirect influence, one might say that the area of direct control is the implementation of the training programs. Direct influence would extend to having highly qualified members, filling employers' requests, higher employment and earnings of union members, and more revenues from union dues. One might argue that having satisfied employers and a strengthened union may be areas of direct or indirect influence. Overall, one can easily arrive at the ultimate goal of this program through the initiative using the ToC.

Program Logic Model of the Union's Training Programs The PLM of the labor union's training initiatives (Table 2.2) shows that while the main goal is strengthening the union, there are three important subgoals to note—increasing members' well-being, loyalty to the union, and satisfying employers' needs.

The initiatives are based on a number of assumptions. While perhaps more assumptions could have been listed, the PLM includes the most important or critical assumptions. Violation of any of these assumptions would impact the initiative's impact and/or relevance. For example, if members did not need their well-being improved, then later if one looked at the change in the well-being as evidence of the initiative's success, one would find no substantial change and conclude that the initiative was unsuccessful. Likewise, if members were already fully employed, then an evaluation would show no change in compensation (unless hourly wages had increased).

The initiative has several target populations—it targets union members for broadening skill sets, nonmembers for participation in the apprenticeship programs, nonmembers who may need certification, and current and potential employers. The activities column lists a summary description of what the initiative entails, and the outputs columns are measures that show that the initiative is up and running. Indeed, each of the output measures listed

TABLE 2.2. Program Logic Model for the Labor Union's Capacity-Building Initiative.

Goals	Assumptions	Target Population	Inputs/ Resources	Activities	Outputs	Outcomes	Outcome Measures
Strengthened union **Subgoals:** Improve members' well-being Increase member loyalty to the union Satisfy employers' needs for high-quality workers	Members' well-being needs to be improved Union can improve members' well-being High employer satisfaction strengthens the union Member satisfaction increases loyalty The skills training will meet employers' demand for skilled union members Members want to enhance their skills and need increased employment	All current union members (for broadening certified skills) Union nonmembers • For apprentice program, persons in their early 20s who have a high level of physical coordination and score well on aptitude tests, with an emphasis on women and ethnic/ racial minorities	Funding from union dues amounting to $250K Twelve part-time instructors at a cost of approximately $40K each, $480K total In-kind contributions of workshop equipment and material (valued at approximately $50K)	Outreach to current and potential employers Matching of union members with job requests Advertisement of programs Run seminars and workshops, conducted seasonally Issuing certifications or licenses	Number of classes taught each year Number of students trained per skill area Number of certifications issued Number of applicants to the apprenticeship program Number of apprentices trained Number of apprentices who become active union members	Better-skilled union members Union members are employed for more time Union members have increased annual earnings Employers have higher satisfaction Loyalty to union	Average number of certifications per union member Number of hours worked per member per year Annual earnings from union wages Number of employer requests Proportion of employer requests the union fills Results of employer evaluations/ satisfaction survey Number of union members

Assumptions	Inputs	Activities	Outputs/Indicators
Apprentices will not adversely affect employment opportunities for current members	• For skills certification program, persons with experience using equipment (often foreign immigrants) who are not certified.	Apprenticeships:	Proportion of union members participating in at least one union activity
Apprentices are needed to replace retirees.	Current and potential employers	• Review the applications for the program	Mean number of union activities per year that members participate in
The program will appeal to women and ethnic/racial minorities	For the apprenticeship program,	• Choose apprentices	Number of apprentices who reach journey-person status
Offering certification will decrease low-wage competition with the union	• Jobs and wages paid by the employer	• 6-week pre-apprentice-ship training	Proportion of apprentices who "graduate"
	• Training and support from union members (in-kind contribution)	• Ongoing training sessions at the union for four years	Proportion of union members who are not non-Hispanic white men.
	• Joint labor-management board (in-kind contribution)	• On-the-job training for four years	Survey of members to determine their loyalty to the union, including hours worked outside of union-assigned jobs

pertains only to the operation and not the impact of the initiative. In the example, there are more than one outcome measure per outcome. They represent different prisms of each outcome. One could imagine even more ways of measuring the outcomes listed.

Examining the PLM holistically, one would consider whether the initiative as described seems strong and the extent to which it might be successful. The PLM holds together. One would want to closely examine the assumptions column and perhaps collect preliminary data to determine the extent to which the assumptions are valid. For example, what is the evidence that union members want more certifications? What is the capacity for union members to take on more work? Will having more people go through apprenticeships crowd out work opportunities for current members? Remember, when programs totally fail they usually do so because at least one assumption made was not valid. Some assumptions, for example, "Members' well-being needs to be improved," seem well grounded. However, other assumptions—such as "Members want to enhance their skills" and "Skills training will meet employers' demand for union members"—should be supported with data, perhaps from a needs assessment. In this case, the evaluator would want to carry out needs assessments, which in this case would be a survey of union members to estimate the extent to which they want to enhance their skills and a survey of employers to determine which additional skills they would like union members to possess.

EXAMPLE 2: Partners Working with Different Populations—A Program to Reduce Child Stunting and Wasting in a Developing Country

Three different international organizations with different mandates work in a developing country that has considerable child stunting (short for age) and wasting (weight for height). They collaborated in implementing a program that addressed the issues of household and community food security. Each of the organizations brings expertise working with specific populations.

The program worked on three levels—the policy level, the food production level, and the food usage level. The program worked directly with policymakers to determine which policies needed to be revised or implemented to help communities and households become more food secure. Program staff helped the country's policymakers develop and implement relevant policies (e.g., trade policies, taxation policies, and food subsidies). The program worked directly with households and small farmers to help them adopt crops that would provide more protein, introduced them to techniques that would be beneficial to poultry production, and introduced fish farming to some landholders. The program also had trained nutritionists who held in remote communities demonstration workshops with parents of infants and toddlers. The parents would bring their children to the sessions and learn how to make nutritious foods such as porridge. The young children were fed porridge and other nutritious foods at the community sessions.

Theory of Change of a Joint Program to Reduce Child Stunting and Wasting The evaluation of the Joint Program began with the evaluation team (an international and a local evaluator) meeting with representatives of the three organizations and creating the ToC. Like many programs, the program was implemented before a ToC and comprehensive PLM was created. These models were not developed until the program was nearly finished. The ToC went through three substantial iterations. Figure 2.6 displays the final ToC.

The ToC shows these three levels—policy, household, and farmers. It also highlights the important intermediate goals of the initiative using a hexagon (increased availability of nutritious food to households) and an oval (food security). Thinking about an evaluation plan, the organizations did not want to follow children for years to see if the program impacted their heights and weights. The assumptions, proven by the literature, were that if households had a greater quantity of nutritious foods available to them and knew how to best use the foods, their food security would increase, their children's nutritional levels and health would improve, and child stunting and wasting would decrease. Because the two ovals in the ToC past food security are extremely likely to occur once households are food secure, one would not devote evaluation resources to showing the subsequent effects.

Program Logic Model of Program to Reduce Child Stunting and Wasting The PLM shown in Table 2.3 shows that the program has primary and secondary goals. While the ToC explicitly lists the primary goal of decreasing child stunting and wasting, the secondary

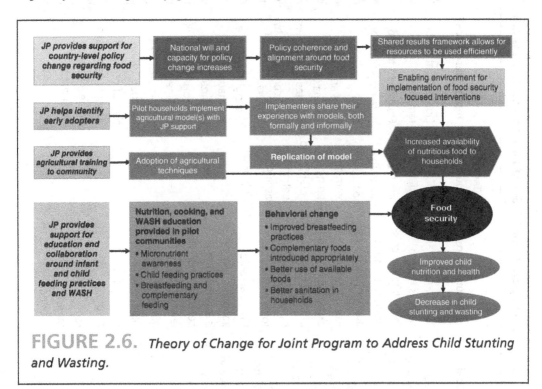

FIGURE 2.6. *Theory of Change for Joint Program to Address Child Stunting and Wasting.*

TABLE 2.3. Program Logic Model of Initiative to Address Child Stunting and Child Wasting.

Goals	Assumptions	Target Population	Inputs/Resources	Activities	Outputs	Outcomes	Outcome Measures
Primary Decrease in child stunting and wasting **Secondary** Improved community food security Improved nutritional intake of infants and children	Teaching small area farmers how to farm different crops will result in them adopting the crops Farmers want to expand the breadth of their crops Farmers are willing to try new crops Financial risk of adopting new crops is less than the potential financial reward of the new crops Farmers have the time for the program Farmers have land to devote to fish farming	Small area farmers Parents of infants and toddlers in communities with high levels of child stunting and wasting Policymakers	Eight educators for farmers Equipment to lend to farmers for new crops Seeds and small banana trees donated for farmers Land contributed by farmers Oversight by staff at international organization (approximately ½ of the time of a professional staff member, 1/8 the time of one staff member from each of the 3 partner organizations)	Identify local areas that would benefit from program Meet with local officials for approval for program Identify farmers for program Train farmers on new crops Continue monitoring and training farmers as crops grow Collect data for program Identify communities with high rates of child stunting for program	Number of farmers identified Amount of seeds and seedlings distributed Number of farmers who participate in program Number of nutrition education sessions held Number of infants and toddlers and mothers and fathers that attended nutrition education sessions	New, more nutritious crops are developed Parents feed their infants and toddlers more nutritious foods A greater quantity of nutritious food is available in rural communities with high levels of stunting and wasting	Kilos of the following brought to market by local farmers: • Bananas • Fish • Kale • Yams • Chicken • Eggs (dozens) • Spinach • Rice (higher protein strains) Survey of and interviews with parents on changes in feeding practices

Parents are unaware of how to prepare nutritious foods for their child(ren)	Approval of local officials	Advertise nutrition education sessions in community	Number of meetings with policymakers	New, more nutritious crops are developed
Parents have access to the foods their child(ren) need	Location to hold community meetings with farmers and with parents of infants/toddlers	Carry out nutrition education sessions		Parents feed their infants and toddlers more nutritious foods
Parents are interested in adopting new foods	One dietician (full-time for 1 year) supplied by international organization	Measure and monitor children's growth at nutrition education sessions		A greater quantity of nutritious food is available in rural communities with high levels of stunting and wasting
Improvements of policies would result in more food available to rural communities with stunting and wasting	Items and food used for nutrition education (e.g., scale, logs, flip-charts, bananas, protein powder)	Meet with policymakers about taxation and trade policies		For infants and toddlers, before and 1 year after intervention, anthropometric measures: • Height-for-age • Height-for-weight • Weight-for-age

goals of community food security and improved nutritional intake of infants and children are implicitly included. Many of the assumptions the PLM lists are critical to the program. For example, the program could not be successful if farmers were not willing to try and adopt new crops. In planning the program, one could have asked farmers about their willingness to adopt new crops. Would there need to be a base income guaranteed in order for farmers to try new crops for one season? Program planners could test the assumptions when planning the program to ensure that the program is built on solid information.

The program has three distinct target populations—parents of infants and toddlers, small area (community) farmers, and policymakers. The PLM lists the resources it takes to operate the program and the program's activities.

The outcomes are at the construct level. There are two broad outcomes—new, more nutritious crops are developed and parents feed their infants and toddlers more nutritious foods. There are a number of ways to measure each of these outcomes. The PLM lists the possible ways that the program will be used. Once a literature review is completed around the ToC and it becomes more apparent how others have measured these constructs, the evaluator may modify the outcome measures to allow for greater comparability with other initiatives. Combining the ToC and the PLM, one can readily determine what the initiative is about and how it intends to operate.

EXAMPLE 3: Targeting Organizations—A Funder's Nonprofit Capitalization Initiative

A foundation created a program where it identified small human service nonprofits that faced financial risks which jeopardized their futures. The foundation aimed to stabilize these organizations. One challenge for these organizations (and others like them) is that while they are often reimbursed for their services by governmental agencies, other organizations, and/or participants, the reimbursement rates are not high enough to cover capital expenses that the nonprofits incur (e.g., for upgrading computer systems, replacing roofs, and consultants to get new initiatives started). Further, the organizations do not include the funding of capital expenses in their annual budgets, so when needed, the organizations do not have financial reserves to pay for inevitably needed improvements. The improvements cannot be deferred forever. Deferring improvements can lead to the organizations providing suboptimal services to their communities, becoming inefficient, becoming unattractive to funders, becoming financially vulnerable, and/or not able to take advantage of opportunities that may arise. If such an organization chooses to make needed improvements, it may draw on a line of credit and find paying it off very difficult—the debt can destabilize the organization.

To address the problem of undercapitalization, the foundation sponsored a pilot capitalization initiative. It carefully selected nonprofits in a city to participate in the initative. The foundation provided these organizations with consultants for capacity development. The consultants helped the organizations create sustainable business plans and budgets and helped them develop a targeted capitalization request. The foundation ultimately funded most of the requests with substantial grants.

Theory of Change of Nonprofit Capitalization Initiative The ToC is from the funder's perspective. It shows that while the initiative's ultimate goal is that the organizations reliably meet their community's current and future human service needs, before they can do that, they need to be stable and healthy. By increasing the organizations' financial capacities, the organizations become better able to manage risks and threats, which will contribute to their stability and "health." They also will invest in their own capacities and needs, which will make them better able to take advantage of opportunities that arise (which will improve their "health").

The blue in the ToC (Figure 2.7) shows the foundation's activities and the red boxes show the short-term change in the organizations that is expected to result. The green boxes show the longer-term change that is expected to result, and the black oval shows the ultimate goal of the initiative.

Another ToC could have been developed at the grantee level. That is, each organization could have developed a ToC that would show how it believes the capitalization grant would result in the organization being better able to meet the community's current and future needs. In this case, one can imagine that the ToC would start with the grant, and then, for example, lead to the funding of a development position, which would lead to more assets, which would stabilize the organization.

Program Logic Model of a Foundation's Capitalization Initiative The goal of the initiative's PLM (Table 2.4), at the direction of the ERG, is a combination of the nonprofits becoming stable and serving their communities' needs reliably.

Some assumptions listed pertain to the need for the initiative—a lack of funding from reimbursements and insufficient private donations. The target population is succinctly listed and described. One activity is that the initiative's staff and consultants identify nonprofits that

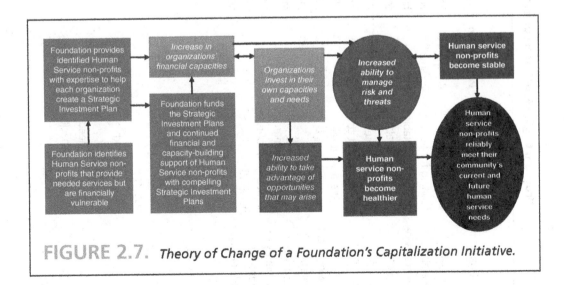

FIGURE 2.7. *Theory of Change of a Foundation's Capitalization Initiative.*

TABLE 2.4. Program Logic Model of a Funder's Nonprofit Capitalization Initiative.

Goals	Assumptions	Target Population	Resources	Activities	Outputs	Outcomes	Outcome Measures
Financially vulnerable human service nonprofits become stable and thrive, allowing them to reliably meet their community's current and future needs	Government funding for human services is unstable and unpredictable • Reimbursement rates do not cover the true, total cost of services Many small- to mid-sized human service nonprofits have little ability to innovate or fund desired business model changes due to limited financial capacities and resources. • The staff and boards of nonprofits need financial capacity development	A cohort of 25 small- to medium-sized vulnerable nonprofits in Fictitious County that serve critical needs	Total: $15 million invested by foundation, to support direct grants to organizations, technical assistance, program management, and evaluation over a 5-year period	The Foundation's grants committee and board approves the program Finalize program design The initiative's staff and consultants identify nonprofits that would benefit from the initiative. The program provides training to 40 organizations on capitalization. Of the 40, 30 are awarded planning grants and 25 are awarded grants to create their Strategic Investment Plans	Number of organizations that received preliminary training Number of applications received for the planning grants Number of organizations that received planning grants and created Strategic Investment Plans Number of consulting hours provided Number of cohort meetings Number of organizations that receive funding of their Strategic Investment Plans Amount of Strategic Investment Plan funding committed and used	Increase in organizations' financial capacities Operational and balance sheet health of organizations Organizations reliably meet their community's needs Organizations have an increased ability to adapt/pivot Improved business practices	Change in financial capacities of organizations (interviews with staff and board) Unrestricted net income of organizations Unrestricted liquid capital available to organization Change in funds raised Case study of organizations navigating acute threats Human resource turnover rates, particularly in senior positions

- Without external support, human service nonprofits cannot develop the internal capabilities to strengthen their financial management
- Being in a cohort of organizations provides peer support for organizational changes

- The program trains and oversees consultants that provide the organizations with expertise
- The Foundation assesses the Strategic Investment Plans of organizations and awards capital grants
- Annual formative evaluation of the program by external consultant
- Implementation and ongoing coaching of organizations by consultants

- Case study of organizations improving business practices
- Case study of meeting community's needs (e.g., decrease in waitlists, stability or increase in proportion of those in need served)

would benefit from the program. This should alert one that the initiative has not been provided to all nonprofits in need—the initiative was only available to organizations that were prescreened. This could become relevant when thinking of applying the results of an evaluation of this initiative to other areas or nonprofits or thinking about scaling up the initiative. The nonprofits included in this initiative are likely not representative of all nonprofits in need.

The resources used for the initiative are clearly shown. The outputs show that the initiative operated—organizations participated in preliminary training, they applied for the planning grants, they created Strategic Investment Plans, the plans were funded, and the organizations used the funds.

The program's outcomes range from very short-term outcomes (e.g., operational and balance sheet health) to longer-term outcomes (reliably meeting communities' needs). Not all of the outcome measures are quantitative measures—some are case studies and they will utilize, in addition to quantitative financial measures, analysis of interviews, and possibly focus group data.

EXAMPLE 4: Comprehensive Charity Services

A large, well-respected charity provides for its region's low-income population free food (a food pantry), clothing (a "closet" with donated clothing), tuition assistance for summer camps and college, and emergency funds (e.g., to help avoid eviction, and repair vehicles). The charity also had a social worker on staff and offered, when needed, a caseworker to clients. The charity operates in a very high-income small town and is fortunate to have available to it a pool of capable volunteers, mostly who were highly educated spouses and parents of school-aged children who did not otherwise work and had ample time to volunteer. Coalescing around the charity was a way that the volunteers and donors, particularly those who did not have roots in the community, made friends and networked in it.

Theory of Change of a Comprehensive Charity The charity's ERG (consisting of the Executive Director, Finance Director, Social Worker, Volunteer Director, and Director of Programs) believed that the charity made the community stronger and more cohesive. While the organization existed to provide resources to persons in need, it also aimed to impact persons who give time and/or money to the organization. The ToC (Figure 2.8) shows how the charity sees itself impacting the three populations. Not all charities will see themselves

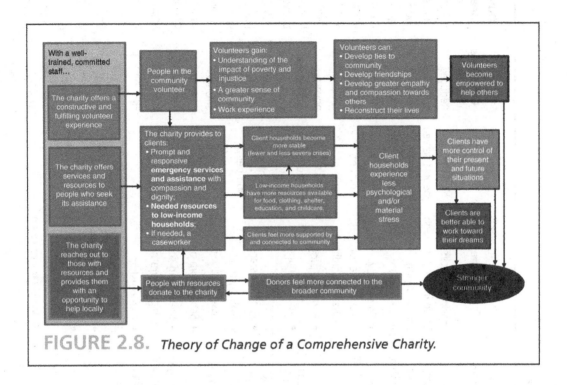

FIGURE 2.8. *Theory of Change of a Comprehensive Charity.*

as having a substantial impact on volunteers and donors. In that case, the middle thread of the charity might be a reasonable approximation of such organizations' ToC.

The zone of direct control is the first box—creating a constructive and fulfilling volunteer experience, offering services and resources to people who want it, and reaching out to persons and entities with resources for donations. The charity also directly controls the services and resources it provides to clients. The zone of direct influence includes, for volunteers, that people actually volunteer and what the volunteers gain. Beyond that, the ToC extends into areas of indirect influence. For donors, the zone of direct influence is where they actually donate to the charity. Beyond that one gets into a zone of indirect influence. For clients, the zone of direct influence extends to the household experiencing less stress and beyond that, the path is one of indirect influence. Overall, much of this ToC is in the zone of indirect influence. Certainly, one would question whether the charity can "cause" a stronger community to be formed. While it may result in more people feeling a connection to the community (particularly the volunteers), there could be a number of other factors that make a community stronger.

TABLE 2.5. Program Logic Model of a Comprehensive Charity.

Goals	Assumptions	Target Population	Resources	Activities	Outputs	Outcomes	Outcome Measures
Overall: A stronger, more cohesive, and harmonized community **For clients:** Less psychological and/or material stress **For volunteers:** Greater understanding of the impact of poverty and injustice Stronger emotional ties to the community	The government's social safety net is insufficient Offering help to people in crisis can prevent a crisis from escalating People will want to volunteer their time to the Charity The affluent and business community in the region will donate money and items to the Charity Many in the region do not recognize the negative impact of poverty and injustice Without the Charity's activities addressing periodic need, short-term crises could have a negative domino effect on people and families	People in need in the region who may need assistance and/or case management The affluent in the region Persons who feel that they have something to give to the community (e.g., educational experience, wisdom, time)	Personal and business cash contributions and grants that total approximately $5 million per year Noncash contributions that total approximately $10 million in value A staff of 17.5 FTE Subsidized use of the grounds and facilities of the church campus where the program is located	Provide services to those in need through the following mechanisms: • Emergency Assistance for shelter & utilities • Furniture program • Ad hoc financial assistance • Food assistance • Holiday food assistance • Scholarship program • Mentoring scholarship program • Campership program • Clothing assistance • Baby basics (layette program) • Holiday toy program	Number of people served by type of service provided Amount/value of services provided Number of volunteers Number of donors Leadership opportunities	Reduced household chaos & stress amongst clients Greater poverty awareness and sensitivity among volunteers Stronger community ties for volunteers and donors Improved graduation rates and reduced indebtedness for scholarship recipients	Greater household food security (as measured using USDA short form 30-day food security questions) Index of household stress as determined by a survey of clients Volunteer survey responses Interviews with donors Graduation rates of scholarship recipients

| For donors: Provide an opportunity to donate for local impact. Stronger emotional ties to community | Without the Charity's resource augmentation initiatives, the lives of those in need would be more stressful and less hopeful. Children of the Charity's clients who go to college need financial assistance and mentoring Being provided a layette improves bonding and family harmony between a family and a newborn Children of low-income households benefit from a summer day camp experience. | People in need in the region who may need assistance and/or case management The affluent in the region Persons who feel that they have something to give to the community (e.g., educational experience, wisdom, time) | A volunteer fundraising group that organizes fundraising events Volunteers Support from the church's parish | Provide the community with a meaningful volunteer experience Train volunteers Attract and retain donors Attract and empower community leadership |

Program Logic Model of a Comprehensive Charity

> **EXAMPLE 5: First Impressions Are Not Always Correct—Addressing Medical Needs of Unsheltered Homeless Individuals**
>
> When teaching my graduate-level course on evaluation, a "client" for one of my class's team of students was a program run out of a hospital that provided free medical care where the unsheltered homeless population was situated. Reading the documents and website on the program, one would logically conclude that the program's purpose was to provide the homeless population with free medical care. However, a closer look at the program showed that first impressions were deceiving.

The initiative's ToC (Figures 2.9 and 2.10) and PLM (Table 2.6) reveal that the program had four goals: (1) to provide the unsheltered homeless population with access to health-care services; (2) to train service leaders, focusing on medical workers, in how to treat the homeless; (3) to inspire service leaders, focusing on medical personnel, to serve the homeless; and (4) to create a new model for medical service, medical service delivery, and training for the benefit of the homeless population. The first goal is consistent with first impressions of the program. The other goals, though, are not the same as providing health care. Instead, they pertain to affecting how the health-care system treats and provides care to the homeless population.

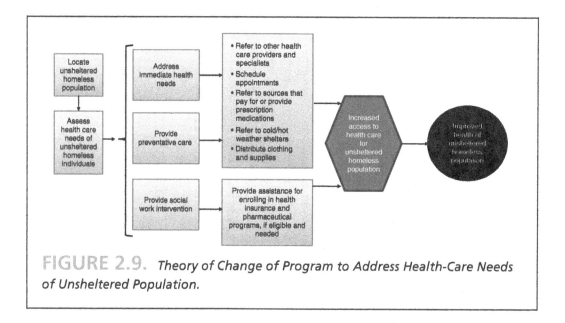

FIGURE 2.9. *Theory of Change of Program to Address Health-Care Needs of Unsheltered Population.*

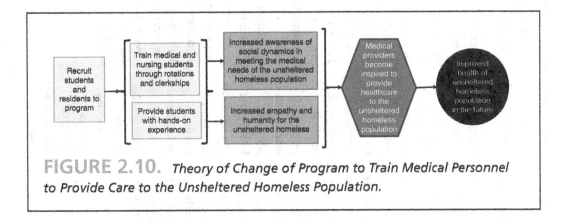

FIGURE 2.10. *Theory of Change of Program to Train Medical Personnel to Provide Care to the Unsheltered Homeless Population.*

If the evaluation students had stopped describing the program after the first impression and based an evaluation plan on that—examining the degree to which the unsheltered homeless population had an increase in interactions with medical personnel and the effects on the unsheltered homeless of the interactions—the evaluation would have not focused on the important aspect of the program's goals that pertain to training medical personnel on how to best provide care to unsheltered homeless individuals. In fact, the more interaction the students had with the program, the more they came to believe that the medical care the unsheltered homeless individuals received was somewhat incidental to the program.

The program's real aim was to change the way the health-care system interacted with unsheltered homeless individuals. Training medical personnel (most of whom were medical and nursing students) to provide care to the unsheltered homeless was a way to decrease barriers to service delivery, increase empathy for the population, and make them an important constituency throughout the trainees' entire medical careers. The program's ultimate hope was that "graduates" of the program would be inspired to replicate the program in the geographic areas where they would be practicing later in their careers.

The second (training) and third (inspiring) goals of the program rest on the assumption that health-care workers want to be involved in providing health care to the unsheltered homeless population. Implicit in that assumption is the assumption that unsheltered homeless individuals have different health-care needs and that health-care workers will improve their skills in treating the population through the program activities.

The PLM shows the multifaceted aspect of the program—providing the unsheltered homeless population with medical services, training medical personnel, and creation of a new model to serve the unsheltered homeless. Creating two independent Theories of Change captured the program's different aspects. One ToC relates to how the program improves the health status of unsheltered homeless individuals. In evaluation terms, this part of the program is not very interesting. It should be of little surprise that if medical services are provided to a previously underserved population, the health status of those served will improve. This ToC suggests that evaluators should limit themselves to considering whether the program actually located the unsheltered population and then whether the trainees were

TABLE 2.6. Program Logic Model for Program That Addresses Providing Health Care to Unsheltered Homeless Population.

Goals	Assumptions	Target Population	Inputs	Activities	Outputs	Outcomes	Outcome Measures
Provide the unsheltered homeless population with access to health-care services	There is a significant unsheltered homeless population without access to health-care services. Better access to health care will make people healthier	Unsheltered homeless population in [CITY], focusing on the neighborhoods of [...]	Administrators, (e.g., physicians, nurses, other clinicians), program managers, volunteers, outreach workers, case managers. Funding from federal, state, and local governments, private foundations, and from individual contributions. In-kind contributions of office equipment, medical supplies, pharmaceuticals, vans, office supplies, computer systems, and PDAs.	Locate unsheltered homeless population. Perform health-care assessment on unsheltered homeless patient. Address patients' immediate health-care needs & provide preventative care, arrange for referrals and schedule appointments for patient to see other health-care providers	Number of unduplicated homeless who receive care through program	Improvements in the overall health conditions of the unsheltered homeless population	Quantitative score of health-care status of unsheltered homeless participating in program
Train service leaders, with a specific focus on medical personnel, in providing services to the homeless	Health-care workers want to be involved in providing health care to the homeless	Medical and nursing students and residents who are passionate about serving the poor			Number of health-care "visits" by program with homeless	Increased number of medical personnel inspired to provide health care to the homeless	Survey of program participants and graduates—analysis of questions on empathy for unsheltered homeless, inspiration to serve unsheltered homeless
Inspire service leaders to work with the homeless, with a specific focus on medical personnel	There is a need for a model of serving the unsheltered homeless population	Medical and nursing students and residents who are required to participate in the program as part of their training			Number of medical personnel trained to provide health care to the homeless	Number of medical graduates of program who replicate the program where they practice medicine later in their careers	

Create a new model for medical service delivery and training for the homeless	There is a need to inspire and train service leaders	Other service providers with the capability of providing these services to areas and populations in need	Access to the sponsoring hospital's resources (e.g., support services, human resources, security, and insurance coverage of administrators	Provide social work interventions	Follow-up with participants post-graduation from medical program regarding their professional interactions with unsheltered homeless population
	There is a need to develop a model for training health-care workers in homeless issues and the specific challenges of providing services to the homeless	Other service leaders: non-medical school students, volunteers, outreach workers, health-care administrators, civic leaders, community leaders	Medical schools from which students are sent	Refer to cold weather shelters	
				Provide assistance in signing up for free or subsidized insurance, if eligible	
	Treating the homeless presents unique challenges		Cold weather facilities	Recruit residents and students	
			Reimbursement for services provided	Train medical students through rotations and train nursing students through clerkships	
			Material donation items (new white socks, underwear, boots, sleeping bags, and blankets) that are distributed to homeless	Provide all students with opportunities to observe training and treatment	
				Provide residents with hands-on experience in medical, dental, and podiatric care	

able to provide the population with medical care that they wouldn't have otherwise had access to. However, it would not be necessary to examine whether providing health care improves health, because a literature review would support that known linkage.

The other aspect of the program—its effects on those it trains—presents more of an evaluation challenge. Here, there is a jump in the theory between people being trained in providing health care to the unsheltered homeless population and being inspired to provide unsheltered homeless individuals with care in the future. The jump between providing and inspiring may be reasonable, but the connection will not happen with certainty or even near-certainty. The evaluation will likely concentrate on this theoretical linkage. To consider the program integrity and interest of the trainees, evaluators should track the number of people who enter and the number who complete the program. Evaluators could also check to see whether participants retain their knowledge of issues that impact the unsheltered homeless population and whether they are committed to providing them with care later in their careers. For example, are the medical students planning upon graduation to practice in areas with large numbers of unsheltered homeless individuals? Will they volunteer time to doing so?

If one were to think of the program more narrowly, which is how program administrators actually regarded the program, and restrict it to a program that aimed to train medical personnel to provide care to unsheltered homeless individuals population, then only the bold-faced text would remain in the PLM. Further, only the second ToC would be relevant.

If the program were so narrowed it is likely it would become more effective. Everybody involved would be clear on what the program's goal and the program's activities and stakeholders would stress the training aspect. Would it be ethical to narrow it as such? Yes. Unsheltered homeless individuals would be receiving care that they likely would not otherwise receive. Albeit, the care provided would be directly from students who are supervised by professors and mentors and not directly from experienced medical professionals. But without the program, it is likely that the population would not have received any benefits at the location where they are found, which is not a medical facility.

Though both ToCs have the ultimate goal of improving the health of the unsheltered homeless population, the first (Figure 2.9) pertains to the effects of providing direct care while the second (Figure 2.10) has a longer-term and arguably potentially broader effect (Table 2.5).

EXAMPLE 6: Trickling Down Information—Children's Health Insurance Outreach Program

A very different example of a program that operates at the community level comes from a child advocacy coalition. This program aimed to increase enrollment in the state's Child Health Insurance Program (CHIP), a program that offers health insurance for children in low-income families at little or no cost. A child advocacy coalition (CAC) assumed, based on national studies, that many children in the community were eligible for but not participating in the health insurance program. The coalition assumed that the national data applied to the local situation, although it did not have any data at the local level to support this assumption.

> To increase enrollment in the CHIP program, the advocacy coalition created "community collaboratives," small groups of nonprofit organizations that operate at the neighborhood level. Organizations that would belong to a "community collaborative" would include local churches, local offices of other need-based programs, food pantries, emergency feeding sites, schools, and so on. The coalition thought that if it shared information about CHIP with these small groups of nonprofit organizations that work at the neighborhood level, the nonprofit organizations would proceed to share that information with the people that they serve and the information would eventually reach parents and guardians of uninsured low-income children. The program also entailed the coalition working directly with families who requested assistance through the CHIP application process, answering questions, and helping them appeal any negative enrollment decisions.

The ToC (Figure 2.11) shows that the coalition believed that if CHIP information was shared with the community collaboratives, then this would increase community awareness of CHIP, leading to increased individual or parental awareness of CHIP, thus increasing the perception and knowledge of the program's benefits. Also, increasing community awareness of the program (and how to enroll in the program) would decrease potential barriers to enrolling children in the program. Together, these improvements in awareness of and access to CHIP would increase the number of eligible children enrolled in the program. Having health insurance increases access to care, which in turn increases the use of health-care services, which finally means that health needs are met and preventive care is used on a regular basis.

This ToC mixes the community level with the family level. The coalition essentially believed that creating higher community awareness "trickles down" to families. They also believed that the community collaboratives ultimately result in healthier children.

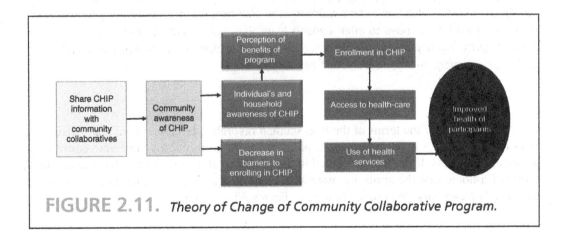

FIGURE 2.11. *Theory of Change of Community Collaborative Program.*

The literature that evaluators ought to review should pertain to the following questions:

- Does increased community awareness trickle down to needy families?

- Does decreasing barriers to program enrollment (not necessarily only health insurance programs, but also for other types of means-tested programs, such as SNAP, WIC, or housing assistance) ultimately result in an increase in program enrollment?

- Does increasing the perceived benefits of a program result in increased program enrollment?

- Does health insurance status affect utilization of health-care services? Does it affect utilization of preventive care?

- To what degree does enrollment in governmental health insurance programs increase the proportion of people actually insured (or have the new enrollees simply gone from private insurance to public insurance)?

Literature that does not directly pertain to these questions should not be examined.

When deciding what to emphasize in the evaluation, if the literature on the second half of the ToC (links between health insurance and utilization of services and health) is very strong, then one does not need to form evaluation questions that will again prove what is already known. Instead, the evaluation should focus on what is theoretically unknown—the link between providing community organizations with information and that information trickling down to the household and/or individual level. The evaluation would also examine whether individuals act of the information and enroll in the program.

EXAMPLE 7: A Program That Failed Because of Faulty Assumptions—Rehabilitating Housing

A city agency, through a public–private partnership, aimed to increase the rehabilitation of dilapidated homes by the city's low-income residents. The agency sponsored the Housing Recovery Program, which was intended to offer residents loans that had, according to the agency, very favorable terms. Agency personnel were concerned about the program because participation fell well below the program's capacity and had decreased over time.

Many aspects of the terms of the loan seemed favorable, but there were many disincentives to participating in the program. Applicants had to go through a very time-consuming application process. If the loan pertained to the purchase of a house rather than the rehabilitation of a home that the applicant already owned, by the time the program processed the applicant's paperwork, the house could have been sold to another buyer.

The program required that any rehabilitation project comply with the Americans with Disabilities Act, even though nearly all homes in the low-income targeted areas were quite old. The unintended consequence of this specification was that it greatly increased construction costs—all doorways would have to be widened, bathrooms would have to meet ADA standards, and the house would have to be ADA accessible. The specifications seemed far-reaching, especially in a city with many houses built on hills where it was not uncommon to have to climb flights of stairs to get to a house.

Other possible reasons for the lack of applicants to the program included potentially unsuccessful marketing efforts. Further, the basis of the program was to improve the housing stock in low-income areas. It is difficult to convince people that taking on personal debt, even under favorable terms, in order to have the best house in a poor neighborhood is a wise financial move.

Delving into the details of the program by creating a PLM for it (Table 2.7) and examining some basic data on the terms of the loans and the number of applicants, the reason for the decline in applicants became readily apparent. The PLM shows that a major assumption of the program is that it will offer loans at favorable terms. Being government-run, the program was less able than private lenders to respond to a decrease in interest rates and a loosening in the availability of home equity lines of credit. At the time, interest rates had decreased and home equity lines of credit were readily available. The loan terms offered by the program, coupled with the specifications and regulations it imposed on applicants, made the program unattractive.

This program provides an excellent example of the fact that when programs truly fail, they usually do so because of incorrect or off-base assumptions that they have made about the environment in which they operate. Well-designed programs are based on realistic, accurate, well-thought-out assumptions about their environments. Programs that fail usually are designed poorly. Even if implemented well, programs that make faulty assumptions usually cannot succeed.

In this case, the program seemed to be implemented well. The program administrators appeared to be doing everything right—they worked well with community groups, processed applications quickly, and took advantage of all opportunities for the program. However, outside of the administrators' control was the faulty basis for the program.

Evaluators provide a great service when they are involved in the design of programs. An experienced and good evaluator should be able to draw out the assumptions of a program and critically examine them. The program should try to provide as much evidence as possible to ensure that the assumptions it makes are realistic. Creating a rigorous description of a program prior to its execution and noting the possible pitfalls (which are typically the assumptions made) can prevent the implementation of programs that are bound to fail. It can allow for corrections to be made prior to implementation.

TABLE 2.7. Program Logic Model of Housing Recovery Program.

Goals	Assumptions	Target Population	Inputs	Activities	Outputs	Outcomes	Outcome Measures
Stimulate the rehabilitation of deteriorated residential buildings	Individuals want to buy and live in homes in the city	All residential properties at least 20 years old within the city limits	Agency staff: • Director of housing (5% FTE) • Program manager (20% FTE) • Program officer (20% FTE) • Program assistant (20% FTE) • Budget officer (10% FTE) • Rehabilitation officers (45% FTE) • Credit counselors (as needed)	Build public awareness of the program by sponsoring print ads on buses, mailing program brochures, and giving promotional presentations to neighborhood groups, realtors, and community organizations	Number of applicants	Improvement in the housing stock of the city	Number of properties cited for blight in city
Promote home ownership in targeted city neighborhoods	Individuals want to buy and/or rehabilitate houses older than 20 years and in need of repair	Individuals with houses in need of substantial repair who want to refinance to pay for the rehabilitation of the house		Screen applicants and when appropriate, provide combination mortgages and remodeling loans	Number of loans provided	Increase in the city's tax rolls	Number of program properties that are categorized as blighted
Return vacant and underused properties to tax rolls	Private sellers are willing to wait for buyers to go through the Housing Recovery Program (HRP)	Individuals who will purchase dilapidated properties		Secure program funding from multiple sources, for example, Federal Community Development Block Grants, Federal Home Investment Partnerships Program, the state's Department of Community and Economic Development, and the municipal bond market		Increased property values of HRP participating houses	Number of condemned houses
Eliminate vacant and underused housing	House rehabilitations will not occur without HRP Housing stock will remain vacant and underused without HRP					Decrease in vacant and condemned houses	Assessed value of properties
Diversify the income mix of neighborhoods	HRP offers competitive interest rates Individuals will accept HRP rehabilitation guidelines Applicants exist who meet HRP requirements					Increase in the income mix of neighborhoods	

Funding:
- Federal ($1.15 million)
- State ($200K)
- Agency ($1.7 million)
- Banks
- Realtors (account for 20% of referrals to HRP)
- Agency office space
- City cable feature on HRP
- Lead inspectors
- Code inspectors
- Program website hosted by agency

Determine where house is located and determine the structure of the loan

Assure that program's regulations are being applied appropriately to the rehabilitation project

- Borrowers are willing to go through the application process
- A market exists for the agency's financial instruments/tax-exempt bonds
- HRP funding from HUD and the State remains constant
- Available housing stock meets HRP regulations
- Public awareness of HRP exists
- Contractors are approved and willing to rehabilitate the houses
- Homeowners will reside in rehabilitated houses
- Homeowners will repay agency when they sell or transfer title of their house

EXAMPLE 8: Spillover Effects—Prenatal Care Program

A state wanted to decrease the health-care costs its Medicaid and Child Health Insurance program incurred as a result of premature births. So, it sponsored a program aimed to improve the health of pregnant women who lived in low-income areas of the state's five largest cities, which in this state, each had populations of less than 130,000 persons. The program was delivered through existing community health centers.

Program activities started with staff assessing the needs and capabilities of clients, and then developing a care plan for the clients. The target population column of the PLM shows that the program aims to assist pregnant and postpartum women and their children under three. In order to participate in the program, the household income of the women cannot exceed 185% of the federal poverty threshold.

The program provided wraparound services to eligible pregnant women, aiming to improve their health and that of their babies not only through direct health interventions but also by improving the family's financial security. The key to the program's success was that the program must accurately assess a mother's social and financial security and be able to directly respond to her needs. If the first assessment was inaccurate, then the program would fail its clients.

According to the ToC (Figure 2.12), if the program develops the client care plan, the women will receive appropriate services and referrals, increasing their use of services. This would lead to increased awareness of health issues, which will further improve the chances that they will make health a higher priority for themselves and their families which will improve birth outcomes. Increased use of services will also directly impact birth outcomes, which will result in cost savings for the health-care system.

The ToC also includes the program's hoped for spillover effects. Perhaps because the program was run out of community health centers, the program's designers were very tied to the idea that the program would have an effect on the community at large. However, the program had no activities that pertained to the community at large. For the program to have an impact on the community, the program was making big assumptions—that pregnant women would amplify their knowledge awareness to their communities, and that the program was impacting enough people to have an impact on communities. These aspects were only hopes and dreams.

The evaluation of this program focused on birth outcomes. The evaluation showed that compared with the births of women who were enrolled in Medicaid and with all women in the state, despite the target population being at higher risk of premature and/or low weight births, the birth outcomes were more positive than those of either of these "control" populations. The literature was relied on to arrive at estimates of cost savings.

The ToC would have been clearer and more relevant to the program if it did not include the community aspect. But sometimes, clients do not want the cleanest ToC or PLM. They want or need to include spillover effects, no matter how unrealistic their achievement may be.

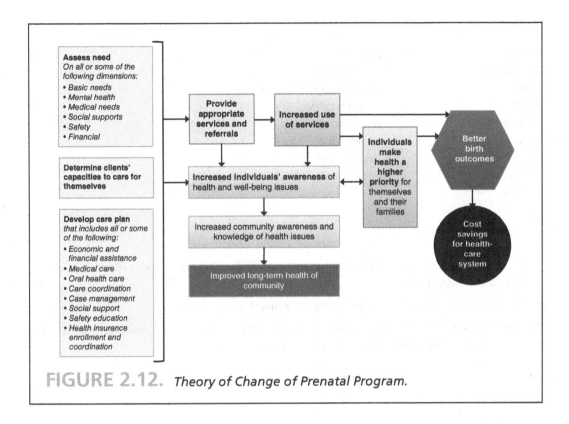

FIGURE 2.12. *Theory of Change of Prenatal Program.*

SUMMARY

Before evaluating a program, the evaluator needs to thoroughly understand it. Involving stakeholders to reach a description of the program is essential—if stakeholders don't recognize the program, they will not put the evaluation to use. By using these models to describe a program, one can clearly see the opportunities for improvement and concise ways to evaluate the program's processes and outcomes.

Program creators would do their due diligence if, before implementing a program or asking for it to be funded, they create (or work with an evaluator in creating) the program's ToC and PLM. Creators would see, on paper, the program's prospects of having the desired effects. Program creators should also do (or have the evaluator do) a thorough review of the literature. Carrying out the program description and review of the literature for prospective initiatives can prevent weak programs from being implemented.

When evaluating a program, one is evaluating against the ToC and PLM. The ToC and PLM guide all evaluation activities.

KEY TERMS

activities
assumptions
goals
inputs
iterative process
operationalize
outcome measures
outcomes
outputs

parsimony
primary goals
Program Logic Model (PLM)
program theory
secondary goals
stakeholders
target population
unit of analysis

DISCUSSION QUESTIONS

1. What are the common mistakes evaluators make when describing a program? How can you avoid making these mistakes?

2. Using one of the examples, create five interview questions to ask an ERG.

3. Examining the outcomes of one of the examples, critique the outcomes measures provided. Are there better or other outcome measures that should be used?

CHAPTER 3

LAYING THE EVALUATION GROUND WORK

LEARNING OBJECTIVES

After reading this chapter, you should be able to

- Describe summative and formative evaluations
- Understand the importance of choosing evaluation questions
- Be familiar with the advantages and challenges of the three types of evaluators
- Be familiar with the inception report

Evaluation Essentials: Methods for Conducting Sound Evaluation Research, Second Edition.
Beth Osborne DaPonte.
© 2025 John Wiley & Sons, Inc. Published 2025 by John Wiley & Sons, Inc.

EVALUATION APPROACHES

There are essentially two approaches to evaluation: **formative evaluation** and **summative evaluation.** Both approaches examine the program in reference to its Theory of Change (ToC) and Program Logic Model (PLM) but at different stages of the program, for different audiences and for different reasons. While both approaches usually result in reports that are often referred to as *the evaluation,* the approaches serve different purposes.

Evaluators conduct **formative evaluations** before an initiative ends, since their purpose is to improve an ongoing initiative. Formative evaluations produce information and recommendations that are fed back to decision-makers who can then use the information to improve the program. A formative evaluation may also be referred to as a midterm evaluation or a real-time evaluation.

During a program's existence, depending on the length of the program's implementation, more than one formative evaluation may be done. For example, if a program is a four-year initiative, a formative evaluation may be conducted after year one *and* after year two. A formative evaluation will focus on the degree to which the program is being implemented as intended and examine preliminary, short-term outcomes (if such outcomes could be expected within the timeframe of the formative evaluation). For example, if a formative evaluation takes place after the first year of the program's implementation, only evidence of the outcomes that would be expected within a one-year period would be considered. A formative evaluation will ask whether there is any evidence to suggest that the ToC has been activated. A formative evaluation's primary audience is program implementers, though funders may also be interested in how the program is going. Rather than a finalized report, findings from a formative evaluation may be expressed in a presentation (e.g., Power Point) to stakeholders. Since the audience of the formative evaluation is usually internal, an organization may not want or need to devote resources to having a finalized report that could be circulated to external persons created. This is especially the case for real-time evaluations, which are usually done with light data collection and turnaround results in a short period of time (e.g., six weeks).

In contrast, **summative evaluations** are usually done after the program has been completed. Sometimes, summative evaluations are done in the waning months of the program because the program (and the evaluator) may lose access to staff, partners, and beneficiaries after the program has ended. The information produced is not used to improve the program (since the program has or will soon end) but may be used in the literature review of other programs. Summative evaluation can be used for organizational learning and examining the initiative's effects and efficiency.

While summative evaluations focus on an initiative's effectiveness and efficiency, they also include descriptions, observations, and quantitative measures of the initiative's implementation. They usually take the form of polished evaluation reports—research is done on the intervention, a report is written, and the report is disseminated to the relevant stakeholders (such as funders, program administrators, and boards of directors).

Pilot programs should always have a summative evaluation commissioned, since the purpose of a pilot program is to learn the effectiveness of a "new" approach and, hopefully, inform the field of the experiences with the results of the new approach.

The inclusion of a summative evaluation in the literature review done by the creators of subsequent initiatives could allow the creators to avoid identified weaknesses and address potential challenges. It could also give others a benchmark measure for the effectiveness of similar programs. For these reasons, it is important that all summative evaluations be made public, regardless of whether they are "positive" or "negative" evaluations. (Positive evaluations show that the program was effective, efficient, and relevant, whereas negative evaluations do not.) Unfortunately, program implementers and funders often bury negative summative evaluations and flaunt positive evaluations. This gives the creators of subsequent initiatives a biased view of the success of an approach, since many negative evaluations may not be accessible to persons conducting literature reviews.

The distinguishing feature between formative and summative evaluations is how the program or organization learns from the evaluation. Formative evaluation is used for making "data-driven decisions," which have the appearance of being impartial and dispassionate. Summative evaluations are not used for ongoing programmatic learning.

A program need not be stable in order to utilize the formative evaluation. In fact, formative evaluations conducted early on in a program's implementation are often used when there remains flexibility in the program's design, when program personnel aim for continuous improvement, and/or when decision-making about the program's design or implementation are on the horizon. In contrast, if a summative evaluation is claiming that an initiative caused an effect, then the initiative should have been stable (otherwise, what is it that caused the effect?).

Evaluations tend to make program personnel very nervous. Program staff often feel that the evaluator will judge not only the program but also their work—to a great extent, they are correct. The ramification of this becomes that the staff then tries to present the program in the best light—for example, they spruce up the facilities, may put in extra effort when the evaluator is present, may discourage clients who are not a good example of the program's strength from attending when the evaluator will be present, may make available for interviews only the best staff. If these strategies occur, the evaluator will get a biased view of the program and perhaps not ultimately be considering the program as it operated, but considering some special, fantasy version of it.

Evaluator joke:

Evaluator to program director:

"Hello, I'm your evaluator and I'm here to help you improve your program."

Program director to evaluator:

"It's very nice to meet you."

While in theory, summative and formative approaches to evaluation have clear distinctions, in practice, the world is a bit different. What was intended to be a summative evaluation may take on the role of a formative evaluation if, for example, the program was shown to be very successful and funders decided to extend to scale-up the program. Or, a midterm evaluation may show such poor results that the program is put on a temporary hold or ends.

Another somewhat superficial distinction is drawn between process-based and outcome-based evaluations. Process evaluations focus on the "how" of program delivery—and outcome evaluations emphasize the change in "clients" or "participants" that result from the program's activities. However, for some programs, especially for advocacy-type programs, the processes *are* the outcomes-- having contact with the targeted population (such as legislators or policymakers) may be the short-term goal of the program. It may be inappropriate, for example, to hold advocacy programs up to the standard of a changed vote on an issue. Even for programs that are not advocacy programs, "outcome-based evaluations" should include analysis of the processes implemented to "cause" the outcomes.

FRAMING EVALUATION QUESTIONS

Once the program has been described through its ToC and PLM, the evaluator, in conjunction with the Evaluation Reference Group (ERG), must plan the evaluation activities. Before starting data collection and the labor-intensive activities that evaluation can entail, the evaluator must determine the questions an evaluation will answer. Otherwise, the evaluation will have no end. The evaluator and ERG must come to terms over the scope of the evaluation and formulate concise evaluation questions.

Asking too many questions exhausts everybody involved in the evaluation activities. Because of time and money constraints, no evaluation will answer all questions of interest. Before collecting data, the questions must be narrowed down to the most parsimonious (smallest) set. Many novice evaluators plan to ask a large quantity of evaluation questions about all aspects of the program, but the answers they get are frequently not informative. The most pertinent questions have not been asked, the answers to these questions are buried under the pile of material produced by the evaluation, and the sheer number of questions asked in surveys and interviews exhausts respondents and results in unreliable data. Not asking the correct set of evaluation questions not only wastes monetary resources, but perhaps more importantly, can waste the goodwill, buy-in, and time of everyone involved in the evaluation. Further, unless stakeholders see that the evaluation answers questions important to them, the evaluation report and process will fail because stakeholders will find it "off the mark" and "irrelevant." If an evaluation is seen as irrelevant, then the results of the evaluation will not be used and time and resources would have been wasted.

In my course on Program Evaluation, I pair evaluation graduate students with nonprofit organizations that serve as course clients. The students must create an appropriate evaluation plan for one of the nonprofit's programs by the end of the semester. At the beginning of the semester, when discussing the issue of how to decide upon evaluation questions, the students tend to think that this part of developing the evaluation plan will be simple. They quickly want to move on to the "real" part of the evaluation.

However, even three months into the semester, after reviewing materials, interviewing clients and having described the program, often, the students still struggle with exactly what the evaluation questions should be (and sometimes remain unsure of the program description).

It is rarely obvious exactly what questions the evaluation should aim to answer. In Chapter 2, I recommend that not only should evaluations show the extent to which the program was implemented as intended, evaluations should stress the links in the ToC that remain uncertain, with few evaluation resources devoted to proving that the ToC's certain links occurred. But narrowing the universe of possible questions to the smallest, most parsimonious set of questions is not only an issue of focusing on the uncertain links in the ToC.

Each possible evaluation question has a constituency group or groups. Typically, funders want to know whether resources are being utilized wisely and whether they should decrease or increase funding to it. Program directors want to know whether their efforts produce intended effects, and program personnel typically ask whether their efforts are appropriate—how they might be more effective the degree to which they are reaching the right people. Current clients want to know how the program is likely to affect them and potential clients want to know how the program compares with other programs.

Thus, the prioritization and whittling process also is a process of knowing which questions satisfy the interests of various stakeholders and balancing that with the questions that can be answered using a sound evaluation approach that is feasible considering the money and time being spent on evaluation. In the best of all possible worlds, the evaluator would find answers to all pertinent questions about the program and satisfy the needs of all stakeholders. Unfortunately, there are rarely enough resources for such a comprehensive evaluation. So, evaluators and the ERG must prioritize evaluation questions—consider which are essential and which are not absolutely necessary to answer.

Some questions may be politically necessary to answer—the sustainability of a program may depend on the results of the evaluation. For example, a Board of Education may not include the funding for a program in a budget unless an evaluation shows that the program is having a desired, specific impact on students.

The prioritization of possible evaluation questions may depend on the clout of the stakeholder who advocates for the question, the amount of time it would take to answer the question, the resources needed to answer the question, and how central the question is to the program's mission. Further, organizations usually have an idea of which processes and outcomes must be included in the evaluation rubric. After the evaluator, with input from the ERG, identifies the universe of stakeholders (see box in Chapter 2 on the ERG for a list of possible stakeholders), the evaluator should elicit input from all of the stakeholder groups, to the extent possible, about their expectations for the evaluation. To conserve resources, if the ERG includes representatives from all relevant stakeholder groups, the discussion about the evaluation questions can be held with the ERG as a whole. However, if some members of the ERG dominate the conversation and essentially silence the voices of some stakeholders, the evaluator should conduct initial informal (individual or group) interviews with persons who represent each type of stakeholder. These informal interviews with stakeholders will help clarify which evaluation questions are important, and which are not.

How should you select representatives of the groups of stakeholders? Some people, such as the program funder, executive director, and program administrator, certainly should be contacted and interviewed and it is likely that their input could be obtained through a discussion with the ERG. There exist other groups, such as program clients and alumni who may not be represented in the ERG or whose voices in an ERG meeting may not be heard.

These groups are too large to allow for individual interviews of all. The evaluator should carefully consider how to select interviewees from these groups. One method is to randomly choose individuals and another approach is to choose individuals from the program's extremes—those who have benefited and those who seem not to have benefited; some who seemed pleased with the program, versus those who are not, and so on. Evaluators should elicit from stakeholders their expectations regarding the evaluation, with a goal of forming appropriate evaluation questions.

The universe of evaluation question typically includes but is not limited to the following in Table 3.1.

TABLE 3.1. Typical Evaluation Questions.

Formative (midterm) evaluation	Summative (end) evaluation
How is the program being conducted?	How was the program conducted?
To what extent is the program reaching the target population?	Who participated in the program? How does this compare to the initial target population?
How are clients interacting with the program? Is this as intended?	How did clients interact with the program? Was this as intended?
Are there any preliminary outcomes being produced? What are they?	What outcomes did the program produce? How did clients benefit (or not)?
Are there differences in the preliminary effects being produced by type of participant?	Did the program work equally as well for various types of participants?
Is the program a/the reason for the preliminary outcomes?	To what degree can one attribute the outcomes of the program?
Is the program operating efficiently?	Were program operations efficient? What was the cost of implementing the program (Per client? Per session?)
What is the program costing to date?	Was the program worth the resources used? What is the return-on-investment?
Compared with similar programs, are the findings to date similar or unusual? Why?	How do the program's effects rate when compared with similar programs?
Is there any evidence that the Theory of Change has been activated? Does the ToC need to be reconsidered or revised?	Given the evidence the evaluation produced, should the ToC be modified? If so, how?

Answering these questions requires a rigorous evaluation approach. Staff cannot be relied upon to answer these typical evaluation questions—they are often optimistic about the impact of their efforts and look for positive evidence (and overlook negative evidence). Staff cannot be impartial about the degree to which the program implementation adhered to plans. Customer satisfaction surveys also will not answer these questions. Such "surveys," which typically elicit responses from clients passively (e.g., survey boxes or QR codes that clients could access if they take the initiative) often only receive responses from clients at the extremes of satisfaction—either very pleased or very disappointed. Although responses to such surveys may reveal kinks in the process of service delivery, such surveys cannot reveal any long-term program impacts, and clients usually do not know how to gauge whether the program is successful or being implemented as intended.

INSINCERE REASONS FOR EVALUATION

Sometimes, decision-makers commission evaluations for reasons other than program improvement. Evaluation can be used to delay decision-making *("let's first evaluate the program before making a decision")*. Decision-makers may commission an evaluation to support a decision that they have already made but haven't yet publicly announced. In such evaluations, the evaluator is swayed to examine aspects of the program that will support the decisions. The evaluation will be used to give legitimacy to the decision.

Evaluation may also be used as a way of ducking responsibility for a decision. For example, administrators may know that there are not enough funds to support all of an organization's programs and call for an evaluation to provide dispassionate evidence on which programs to cut. The decision-makers can thus blame the evaluation results for the decisions.

An evaluation may be used as a way to glorify a program, or to provide a public relations opportunity. In this case, those ordering the evaluation may bear pressure on the evaluator to research only the potentially positive attributes of the program and to produce a positive evaluation.

All of these circumstances have the potential to create an uncomfortable environment for an earnest evaluator. Therefore, from the beginning, the evaluator must develop a thorough understanding of the perspectives that stakeholders hold regarding the evaluation and the specific questions that they want the evaluation to answer.

HIGH STAKES EVALUATION

Increasingly, outcome-based evaluation is being used as the basis for making important decisions—such as distributing funds, ranking organizations, rewarding staff, and even rewarding schools and other organizations. High stakes evaluations occur when evaluation is relied upon to make important decisions about a program's survival. They may also be used when to make decisions about staff compensation.

Usually, high stakes evaluation entails some form of high stakes testing, which occurs when results are used to make decisions with large ramifications. The following is the American Evaluation Association's position on high stakes testing on pre-K–12 students:

High stakes testing leads to under-serving or mis-serving all students, especially the most needy and vulnerable, thereby violating the principle of "do no harm." The American Evaluation Association opposes the use of tests as the sole or primary criterion for making decisions with serious negative consequences for students, educators, and schools. The AEA supports systems of assessment and accountability that help education.

—American Evaluation Association (source: https://www.eval.org/Policy-Advocacy/Policy-Statements/High-Stakes-Testing.)

The essential worry regarding high stakes testing is that putting too much emphasis on a test or evaluation result can lead to distorted behavior around the evaluation activities and tests associated with it. A weak evaluation can result because the evaluation becomes entirely outcome-based, and unless those outcome measures perfectly reflect the goals of the program, the reliance on high stakes testing will not improve the program. For example, if the outcome is intended to be improvements in a student's mathematical ability, then the test needs to perfectly measure the theoretical construct of "mathematical ability." The evaluation may not cover important processes that contribute to the result. For example, relying on mathematics scores may ignore the importance of school attendance and issues that impact school attendance. Or, if the goal of public schools is to make students better prepared for their future role of engaged, voting citizens, tests given around mathematics and language arts are poor operationalizations of the construct of potential engaged citizenry.

If people believe that critical decisions will be based on the results of a test, then behavior around the test may be distorted. For example, teachers may start "teaching to the test"—that is, teaching students only material that will be on the test and teaching students how to take tests—rather than teaching a comprehensive curriculum, which may include topics not specifically on the test. Other examples of distorted behavior include encouraging people who may not do well on the test to be absent on the testing day and encouraging test-takers to somehow behave differently for the test (such as to eat sugared cereal for breakfast if the test is given in the morning, which has been suggested to improve test performance). Also, taking prep courses for tests distorts the effectiveness of the test in measuring the desired construct (e.g., mathematical ability) rather than the construct of one's familiarity with the test itself.

WHO WILL DO THE EVALUATION?

There are essentially three different types of evaluators:

1. External evaluators (or firms) with whom the organization:
    a. has no previous relationship or
    b. has previously worked and

2. Internal evaluators (or a department) that the organization employs.

These three types of relationships each have pros and cons.

External Evaluators

External evaluators, hired on a contractual basis, have the appearance of impartiality, and because of this, consumers of their evaluation reports may place greater credence in the reports' results and recommendations than in those of reports written by an in-house evaluator.

To identify an external evaluator, an organization may issue a Request for Proposals (RFP) and open the evaluation activities for competitive bidding. The RFP usually indicates the scope of the evaluation, the time period, and the funding available for the evaluation. When posted on the American Evaluation Association's website, professional evaluators will become aware of the opportunity. Before contracting with the evaluator, the organization should understand the evaluation approach to which the evaluator subscribes.

When hiring a new external evaluator, the organization or program should enable the evaluator to develop an understanding of the organization and initiative, the personalities involved, the culture of the organization, and the context of the program. The organization will need to help the evaluator develop this understanding, which can take some time, but this can be shortened if the evaluator chosen has experience working with similar programs, organizations, or in the same (or similar) communities.

The organization will need to open itself up to an "outsider," and therefore place trust in this outsider. For this reason, an organization is wise to request references from any potential evaluator, and the organization should inquire not only about the quality of past work but also the quality of the relationship that an organization developed with the evaluator. It is neither unreasonable nor uncommon for an evaluator to sign a nondisclosure agreement with the organization.

Because of the trust factor and the start-up costs incurred when contracting with a new evaluator, an organization often develops a relationship with an outside evaluator and becomes a repeat client of the evaluator. After the first contract, the outside evaluator will have gained valuable knowledge about the organization and *if all goes well,* the organization grows comfortable with the evaluator, who will then be the prime candidate for the organization's future RFPs. Some organizations may choose to bypass opening future RFPs up to competitive bidding because they already have an evaluator with whom they are comfortable. In this way, such an external evaluator will have the "inside track" to a future RFP. In this case, there is a risk that the external evaluator will segue into a role close to that of the internal evaluator, although the external evaluator is never formally on the staff of the organization.

But note the caveat "if all goes well." Usually, "if all goes well" to the evaluator means that the evaluator constructively critiqued the program, pointed out areas where the program could improve, and performed analyses within their realm of expertise. However, "if all goes well" to many organizations means that the evaluator was relatively uncritical of the program and provided a positive evaluation-- the evaluator acted as a cheerleader rather than an impartial evaluator of the program.

Judging an evaluator's past performance on the basis of whether the evaluation was "positive" may lead to a bias toward contracting with evaluators who are not as critical as they ought to be about a program. A client may prefer, in the short term, an evaluator who doesn't reveal blemishes in a particularly harsh light, even when they ought to be. Unless an evaluator has a steady source of clients, the evaluator may be reluctant to provide a negative evaluation, even of a program in need of substantial modification.

I witnessed an instance where a very influential foundation funded a multimillion-dollar large-scale pilot project to make available high-quality child care in low-income communities. Embedded in the grant were funds for an outside evaluator. At midcourse presentations of the project, the evaluator glossed over the most basic of critical flaws in the program—that it simply did not attract participants, and many families who did enter the program did not stay with it for the expected amount of time. Evaluators who point out critical flaws early on provide the program with opportunities for improvement. Withholding such information can doom a program, and in this case, the program never did achieve a reasonable level of participation. Some believed that because the "outside evaluator" worked for a university that was also a recipient of the foundation's generosity, the evaluator was very reluctant to reveal that the program's design and implementation was weak. The strong ties between the evaluator, university, and foundation may have jeopardized the presumed impartial role of the evaluator.

Another example is a firm that was a subcontractor for a large, Washington, DC, "beltway bandit" (a term used to describe some firms in the Washington, DC area that provide consulting services to governmental entities). Beltway Bandit was trying to develop a reputation and expertise in a particular field. Beltway Bandit hired a smaller, local firm to conduct focus groups and interviews with beneficiaries of a multisite education program. Most sites could provide a list of the beneficiaries, allowing the small firm to randomly select beneficiaries to interview. However, two sites were unable to provide a list of beneficiaries. The sites had not even kept track of who was participating in the program. The small firm brought this to Beltway Bandit's attention. However, Beltway Bandit was reluctant to provide a negative evaluation of the program seemingly because it was competing for an even larger, second evaluation contract and the persons who were the decision-makers for the second contract were responsible for the first program's oversight. Beltway Bandit believed that a negative evaluation of the first program would jeopardize the awarding of a subsequent contract. The small firm was unwilling to write a report that did not address the glaring lack of implementation for the two sites and parted ways with Beltway Bandit.

Thus, while the great positive of external evaluators is their potential ability to be impartial, in practice, unless an organization has a strong commitment to impartiality and encourages the evaluator to have independence and to be frank, the evaluator may find future opportunities rosier if a report is positive about an initiative.

One strategy to ensure impartiality of external evaluators is for the funder, not the organization, to hire and supervise the external evaluator. Consider a foundation that provides grants to organizations in various fields. The foundation could have external evaluators with whom it works, either on a contractual basis or who are staff of the foundation. The foundation would assign to initiatives it wants to evaluate a specific evaluator, and this would be a condition of the organization receiving the grant. This structure assures the independence of an external evaluator.

Internal Evaluators

Internal evaluators (or evaluation departments) are employed by the same organization that implements the program. Benefits of an internal evaluator include the evaluator's familiarity with the organization and sometimes even with a particular program, reducing the amount of time that it takes to get to know the program. The internal evaluator may also have access to organizational documents—access that an external evaluator may not have—giving the internal evaluator a better understanding of the organizational history and a particular program's context. The organization has a degree of trust with the internal evaluator. An internal evaluator may have a better understanding of the personalities in the organization, and how, for example, the personalities affect the program's degree of success. For example, an administrator's personal charisma may influence the success of a program.

Conversely, it may be socially or politically difficult for an internal evaluator to be frank about problematic programs. For example, consider a program where an internal evaluator finds that a program is not being implemented as intended, possibly due to an administrator's negligence. This evaluator may find it difficult to highlight such problems. In the case of a weak program, an internal evaluator may put too much weight on outside forces, and in the case of a strong program, he may give too much credit to a program. An internal evaluator may be biased and should take precautions against such biases.

Because of the above social and political ramifications of evaluation activities, internal evaluators must be protected within the organization, both for their sake and for the sake of the credibility of evaluation function. They must be assured that their job security is unrelated to the results of an evaluation and that their compensation is only related to the *quality* of their evaluation activities, not the *results* of them.

The biggest strike against using an internal evaluator is the appearance of partiality. If the evaluation report will have an external audience, then using an internal evaluator will not be the best option since the internal evaluator may be seen as being positively biased to the organization. If the appearance of impartiality is essential, then an external evaluator must be used. However, if evaluations will ultimately be used primarily for the internal purposes of program improvement, then an organization may use an internal evaluator.

Independence of the Evaluator

To protect the independence of an internal evaluator, the evaluator must not report to program implementers. The organizational structure should allow for the internal evaluator to be independent of implementers—the implementers cannot have the opportunity to impact an evaluator's career. Optimally, the internal evaluator would report directly to the organization's governing body (e.g., board of directors, trustees, General Assembly). The evaluation function may be part of the oversight function (in the UN, the Inspection and Evaluation Division is a part of the Office of Internal Oversight Services, which also holds the Audit Division and the Investigations Division) or could be a part of the Monitoring, Evaluation, and Learning function (MEL).

If reporting to the governing body is not an option, then a second best option would be for the organization to have an evaluation department that is separate from departments that implement programs that are evaluated. But in this case, both implementers and evaluators would then be reporting to the Executive Director. This is not ideal because the Executive Director is ultimately responsible for both implementation and evaluation. The Executive Director could be tempted to either explicitly or implicitly pressure the evaluation department to produce positive evaluation reports.

External Versus Internal Evaluators

There are pros and cons of both external and internal evaluators. To determine which is best for a situation, first determine why the evaluation is needed.

> **To determine whether the evaluation function is structured in a way that allows it to speak the truth about an initiative, consider the following:**
>
> - **Did the evaluator play an active role in the initiative's creation or did the evaluator simply create the program description for the initiative's creators and revise it as the creators examined the logic?** If the former, the evaluator may be compromised.
> - **To whom does the evaluator function report?** If the evaluator reports to the initiative's implementers or anyone responsible for the implementation of the initiative (including the executive director), then the evaluator may be compromised—suffer financially or reputationally if the findings negatively reflect on the implementers. If an internal evaluation function, the head of the office should have a reporting line to the governing body rather than those responsible for implementation. If external, the evaluator should not be hired by implementers, but instead by the governing body or funder.
> - **If an external evaluator reports to a funder, would the evaluator curry favor if the initiative were shown to be more effective than it actually is?**
> - **For external evaluators, how financially dependent is the evaluator on the evaluation contract?**

Small nonprofits usually do not have the funds to employ an in-house evaluator. Large organizations that operate a wide assortment of programs and use evaluation primarily for internal purposes would be wise to develop in-house evaluation capabilities, either by hiring employees with evaluation expertise or by training the current employees in evaluation.

If an organization sponsors evaluation activities to satisfy an external audience, then an external evaluator is most appropriate. However, if an organization embarks on evaluation for continuous improvement, if funds allow, and if the organization is large enough, then it may consider having an evaluator on staff or developing a long-term relationship with an external evaluator.

If an organization chooses to use external evaluators, then the organization should get evaluation expertise on its side so it can make the best contracting decisions. Sometimes, organizations issue RFPs with the evaluation approach lightly describe and rely on the evaluators who submit proposals to determine how the evaluation will be conducted. The risk in relying upon those who submit proposals to do the thinking for the organization is that the deliverable the organization receives may not ultimately be satisfactory with respect to the evaluation questions asked, methods used, and focus. Alternatively, an organization can design the evaluation plan itself, providing it has some evaluation expertise on either staff or retained, and then issue an RFP for evaluators to carry out the plan. An organization must decide whether it wants to be hands-on in the design of the evaluation or whether it wants to leave that up to those who submit proposals. I advise organizations to work with an experienced evaluator in constructing evaluation plans, and then issue an RFP for the evaluation plan to be carried out (see Chapter 8).

CONFIDENTIALITY AND OWNERSHIP OF EVALUATIONS

Before embarking on an evaluation, an organization or client and evaluator ought to consider the confidentiality of the evaluation and intellectual property rights. It is best at the outset if these issues are settled and made explicit.

Regarding the ownership of reports and data collected for analyses, normally, *the entity that pays the bill "owns" the evaluation and the data collected for it, stripped of identifying information.*

When a funder provides an organization with a grant that includes funds for an evaluation, the organization normally owns the report and any data—stripped of information that would allow the identification of the person(s) who provided the information or feedback—that result from the evaluation. For example, if the evaluator conducted a survey, the organization would own the survey instrument (questionnaire), aggregated survey results, and also the individual-level survey results, providing that they could be stripped of any information that would allow one to determine the identity of the person who provided the information. The organization would be responsible for distributing the report and any other results of the evaluation to the funder. The evaluator could only distribute the report to the organization and has no contractual relationship with the funder.

In contrast, a funder may directly hire (or have on staff) an evaluator who conducts an evaluation of a program that the funder directly sponsors. In this case, the funder owns the report and is responsible for distributing it.

I can think of no case where the evaluator owns the report or the data. Unfortunately, I am aware of cases where evaluators believe that they own the data or reports. Such situations can quickly deteriorate and have legal consequences. For example, I know of two different cases where two different international organizations hired evaluators who carried out, in the scope of the evaluations they were conducting, international surveys with hard-to-reach populations. Neither international organization had built into the contract with the evaluator who would own the survey data collected. While the survey results were included in each evaluator's report, both evaluators refused to turn over the data to the respective international organizations. In fact, both used the survey data as the basis to get subsequent contracts. In both cases, the organizations were unable conduct further analyses of the data themselves and had to hire the original evaluators for further analyses.

> **Availability of negative evaluation reports**
>
> *No funder likes it to be widely known that it wasted significant amounts of money and human capital on an unsuccessful program. There are exceptions, though, where a funder showed courage.*
>
> *After the failure of the Heinz Endowments' "Early Childhood Initiative"—which cost the foundation over $20 million—the foundation, not satisfied with the initial evaluation of the program, hired Rand Corporation researchers to thoroughly investigate reasons for the initiative's failure. The Heinz Endowments made the monograph written on the initiative's failure publicly available (see Gill, Dembosky, and Caulkins. 2002. A "Noble Bet" in Early Care and Education. https://www.rand.org/content/dam/rand/pubs/monograph_reports/2005/MR1544.1.pdf).*

An evaluator cannot take it upon themself to distribute an evaluation report. However, there could be situations where the evaluator uncovered egregious wrongdoing and the evaluator might be covered by whistle-blower protection laws.

Implementers and funders are often reluctant to make negative evaluations available to the public for a variety of reasons, including reputational risk. When conducting a literature review, one should be aware of the "availability bias" and do one's best to obtain a representative sample of evaluation reports. One strategy is to directly contact the implementers of similar programs and converse about the evaluation activities that may have occurred. If approved by the client, an offer could be made that the client would allow other organizations access to the evaluation report being developed in exchange for other organizations sharing their evaluations (including negative evaluations).

Endorsement and Action on Recommendations

Evaluation reports typically include recommendations. Formative evaluations include recommendations for immediate improvements and summative evaluations often include recommendations for actions to be taken at the organizational level.

To give the recommendations more power, there should be a process where the recommendations are endorsed. If the evaluation goes to a governing body, then the governing body could have a session where it discusses the evaluation report and its recommendations and votes on endorsing the recommendations. When the governing body does so, it is saying that the Executive Director must implement the recommendations.

For example, in the United Nations, evaluation reports go to a committee of the General Assembly. The evaluators typically present the report and its recommendations to the committee (e.g., Fifth Committee) and the committee will vote on whether to endorse the recommendations. If the committee endorses the recommendations, the Secretary General then must see to it that the recommendations are implemented. There is follow-up on the recommendations. The evaluators occasionally check the status of the recommendations. The evaluators subsequently report to the committee on the status of each recommendation (whether it was implemented and can be "closed," whether its implementation has been started but not completed, and whether the recommendation's implementation has not even begun).

At the nonprofit level, a report and its recommendations could go to the board of directors. The board would include in a meeting a discussion of the report and vote on endorsing the evaluation's recommendations. For example, a recommendation may be that the program needs to meet with community leaders about recruitment for the program. To give the recommendation "teeth" and to ensure its follow-up, the board would vote to endorse the recommendation. Program implementers would report subsequently to the board (perhaps in the form of a memo) on how and when they interacted with community leaders about the program's recruitment.

Evaluation Policy

To increase transparency, organizations often create evaluation policies. Entities of the US Government are bound by the Foundations for Evidence-Based Policy Making Act of 2018, "Evidence Act", Pub. L. No. 115-435, 132 Stat. 5529 (2019). The law requires all US governmental entities to have an evaluation policy. At a minimum, the policies must incorporate the evaluation standards that the US government's Office of Management and Budget refers to in a subsequent memo—see OMB memo dated March 10, 2020, with a subject of "Phase 4 Implementation of the Foundations for Evidence-Based Policymaking" (M-20-12.pdf (whitehouse.gov). The memo goes into detail about exactly what federal agencies should include in their evaluation policies.

Similarly, the United Nations has an evaluation policy. The Secretary General ordered (see UN document ST/AI/2021/3) each UN entity to have an evaluation policy.

Many, though not enough, funders have evaluation policies. Many large funders (e.g., the Gates Foundation) have a commitment to evaluation and make that clear by having an evaluation policy.

At a minimum, an evaluation policy should cover the following:

(a) **Which initiatives will be subject to being evaluated**. This would consider the importance of the initiative to the organization. Importance could consider factors such as the cost of the initiative, the partnerships the initiative relies upon, the reputational risk to the organization if the initiative was not to deliver promising results, and the longevity of the initiative.

(b) **Who will carry out the evaluation function and their relationship to the organization.** The policy could describe the responsibilities of internal evaluators and under which circumstances the organization will contract with the external evaluators.

(c) **How the independence of the evaluation function will be secured.** The policy could specify that the evaluation function will report to the governing body.

(d) **The endorsement and follow-up on recommendations.** Who will have the responsibility for endorsing recommendations from evaluations? How will recommendations from evaluations be followed-up on. Who will be responsible for tracking the implementation of recommendations? What are the consequences for not implementing recommendations that the governing body endorsed?

(e) **The protection of human subjects and data.**

(f) **The distribution and availability of evaluation reports and products.** This aspect would cover which reports and products will be made available to the public, and how they will be made available. For example, the policy could specify that all summative evaluation reports will be made available on the organization's website.

THE EVALUATION REPORT

Evaluation reports usually have similar outlines. The outline below is the one that I typically use for both midterm and summative evaluations. What exactly is included is dependent on the particular initiative and circumstances.

Executive Summary

(a) Introduction
   Include a brief history of the program and the evaluation process; Evaluation questions

(b) Methodology

(c) Summary of findings

(d) Conclusions

(e) Recommendations

Report

I. Introduction
   Brief history of program, description of the problem the program addresses, where the program sits in the organization, and evaluation process.

II. Description of program
   a. Context of the program
      Information about the community the program serves, where the program sits in the organization, perhaps include its importance to the community, what differentiates the program from other programs.
   b. Theory of Change
      Present the ToC graphic and in the text, walk the reader through the ToC.
   c. Program Logic Model
      Present the PLM and in writing, walk the reader through the PLM. Discuss the program's goals, assumptions, target population, activities, inputs/resources, outputs, outcomes, and outcome measures. In this discussion, cover how the program actually operates and why the particular outcome measures were selected.
   d. Summary of Program Description
      Remarks on program's stability, anything else that would be relevant and allow the reader to understand the program.

III. Evaluation Questions and Process
   Present the evaluation questions upon which the evaluation focuses. Discuss how the questions were selected? Whose interests do the questions represent? What is the time period that the evaluation covers?
   How did the ERG interact with the evaluator?

IV. Literature Review
   Summarize the literature surrounding the program and its ToC. Discuss prior and/or other efforts to address the problem that the program addresses.

V. Methodology
   a. Data collection
      How were data collected? Over what time period? From whom? Discuss sampling approaches implemented. If there was a survey conducted, refer the reader to the survey instrument which should be included in an appendix to the report. If interviews and focus groups were conducted, include in the appendix the interview and focus group protocol. What secondary data were used? What is the potential bias in the data used?
      What were the response rates to surveys?
   b. Data analysis
      How were data analyzed? What software was used? What statistical tests were done? Discuss sources of uncertainty.

VI. Findings
   a. Program implementation and processes
      Intensity of program, how beneficiaries interact with program, verification (or not) of the program's assumptions with respect to implementation.
   b. Lead the reader through the answers to the evaluation questions.

VII. Conclusions
   This is the only section where the evaluator can give an overview of the results of the findings and put the findings into context. The implications of the findings should be discussed. The findings should be linked to what was found in the literature review. The evaluator can opine, discuss how the evaluation results compare with the results of evaluations of similar programs, and discuss the risks to the organization if the recommendations are not followed.

VIII. Recommendations
   Each recommendation should be based on a finding (some evaluations refer to the numbered paragraphs or sections of the report that support the recommendation). Each recommendation should refer to an actor that has the responsibility for implementing the recommendation.
   The recommendations should be organized. One should distinguish critical recommendations (those which, if not implemented, would be serious consequences for the program and/or organization) from important recommendations and opportunities for improvement.

IX. Appendices
   a. Data collection tools, names and positions of ERG members, etc.

SUMMARY

There are two approaches to evaluation: summative and formative. Summative evaluations are usually done after the program has been completed and are used to determine the program's effectiveness. Formative evaluations produce information that decision-makers use to improve the program.

It is vitally important to determine the appropriate evaluation questions. The evaluator and the stakeholders must agree on the scope and depth of the evaluation by agreeing on the questions. Without agreement, the evaluation will not be impactful because the stakeholders will find it irrelevant.

There are three types of evaluators an organization can choose to perform an evaluation: an external evaluator new to the organization, an external evaluator with prior experience with the organization, and an internal evaluator.

For an evaluation to be impactful, there should be a mechanism that endorses the evaluation's recommendations and a follow-up mechanism that oversees the extent to which the recommendations have been implemented.

KEY TERMS

evaluation reports
external evaluators
formative evaluation
high stakes testing
internal evaluators
outcome evaluation
parsimony
process evaluation
publication bias
summative evaluation

DISCUSSION QUESTIONS

1. Describe the difference between summative and formative evaluations.
2. What are the drawbacks of having too many evaluation questions? How can you drill down to the most important questions?
3. For each of the typical evaluation questions listed,
    a. What follow-up questions could be asked?
    b. Map which stakeholder groups would be most interested in each of the questions.
4. What are the pros and cons of using an external evaluator? An internal evaluator?

CHAPTER 4

CAUSATION

LEARNING OBJECTIVES

After reading this chapter, you should be able to

- Define necessary and sufficient causation
- Describe how definitions of variables can greatly impact conclusions drawn
- Understand the importance of intervening variables
- Describe how anticipating the effects of a program will affect data collection
- Articulate the advantages and disadvantages of continuous versus categorical variables

Evaluation Essentials: Methods for Conducting Sound Evaluation Research, Second Edition.
Beth Osborne DaPonte.
© 2025 John Wiley & Sons, Inc. Published 2025 by John Wiley & Sons, Inc.

INTRODUCTION

What does it mean to say that a program is effective? Usually, it means that the program *caused* a positive change to occur. Those who design programs or interventions do so because they believe that, ultimately, the intervention will produce, or *cause* a change. But what does it mean to cause a change?

Program evaluation differs from statistics in one critical way—causation. Ultimately, programs are based on the belief that the program will cause a positive change to occur. Evaluations, especially summative, outcome-based evaluation, are done to examine whether a program or policy *causes* a change and the magnitude of the change. If an intervention does not cause a change, then there exists no justification for the intervention.

In contrast, statisticians examine data to investigate whether the null hypothesis—the intervention is associated with no positive change—can be rejected. When the null hypothesis can be rejected, it may seem likely that the intervention is associated with change, but statisticians cannot fully determine whether the intervention caused the change beyond a reasonable doubt. While statistical analysis skirts the edges of causation, summative program evaluation is often done specifically to investigate whether a causal relationship exists between an intervention and outcome(s).

Cause can be interpreted in many ways. In this chapter, we consider the meaning of causation and its various theoretical forms. The chapter's goal is to peel away at various forms of causation. We start with two aspects of causation: necessary and sufficient.

NECESSARY AND SUFFICIENT

Evaluators consider an intervention necessary and sufficient in the following ways:

- Is the program **necessary** for the change in the outcome to occur? That is, could the change have occurred without the program?

- Is going through the program **sufficient** for seeing a change occur? Do all people who go through the program change? Is going through the program guaranteed to result in a positive change?

Consider the change or outcome that stakeholders desire a program to produce. In the case of a substance abuse program, the intended outcome could be reduced (or no) use of harmful substances; in the case of an opera appreciation program the intended outcome could be a positive change in one's regard of opera; in the case of a "dress for success" program, the intended outcome could be an improvement in one's employment prospects; or in a math tutoring program, a change in one's understanding of mathematical concepts. Each of these programs aims to produce a desired outcome—they want to cause a change.

We would say that **the program is *necessary* for the change if the desired outcome could *only* occur if the intervention caused it to occur;** thus **the change would be seen *only* in cases that had gone through the program**. This is the definition of a causally necessary program.

Very few programs live up to this stringent view of causation. Clearly, people can develop an appreciation for opera without going through an opera appreciation program, students can understand mathematics without a math tutoring program, and people can have good employment prospects without a dress for success program. Often, there are many ways for the desired outcome to be achieved, the program being just one of the ways. People may have characteristics that allow them to possess the desired outcome even in the absence of the intervention. Or, they may have gone through another program, or have acquired information in a variety of ways, none of which have anything to do with the program being evaluated. Labor market conditions may have changed so that everybody becomes more employable, not only those who completed an employment or "dress for success" program. So, making the case that a program is necessary becomes difficult, and a sound quasi-experimental design (Chapter 5) is needed to make the causal connection.

With respect to the concept of *sufficient*, one would say that a program is *sufficient* to produce the desired outcome in situations where one is guaranteed to have the outcome if one went through the program. All who go through the program have the outcome. If there are cases where program participants do not have the outcome, then the program *is not sufficient*. If a program is sufficient to produce an outcome, then going through a program will assure that the outcome occurs, even though the outcome can occur in the absence of the program. If a program is sufficient, nonparticipants could also display the outcome. Sufficient only pertains to participants.

If a program is **necessary and sufficient**, then the outcome can *only* be produced by the program or intervention, and, if one went through the program, the outcome would *always* be produced. Given this definition, it is clear why few, if any, interventions live up to this level of causation. I can think of no program where (a) the outcome could *only* be produced by the program, (b) there does not exist a single case when the outcome exists without having gone through the program, and (c) the program will certainly produce the outcome in all of its participants.

A two-by-two matrix illustrates the concepts of necessary and sufficient. In the cells of the matrix are the number of observations that display the outcome. Consider three different scenarios: necessary but not sufficient, sufficient but not necessary, and necessary and sufficient.

Case 1: The Program is Necessary But Not Sufficient

In the case where the program is *necessary*, then one will never observe the outcome among nonparticipants of the program (Table 4.1). Therefore, all nonparticipants, whatever the number, will fall into the *no program/no outcome cell*. Among program participants, the program will be enough to produce the outcome for some, but not for others. Therefore, some participants will fall into the *yes program/no outcome* cell, while others will fall into the *yes program/yes outcome* cell. That the *no program/yes outcome* cell has zero observations suggests that the program may be necessary to produce the outcome.

Case 2: Program Is Sufficient, But Not Necessary

If a program is *sufficient* to produce the outcome, then all program participants will display the outcome (Table 4.2). Hence, all participants belong in the *yes program/yes outcome* cell and the number zero belongs in the *yes program/no outcome* cell. There will never

TABLE 4.1. The Program is Necessary but Not Sufficient.

	Is the outcome observed?	
Did one go through the program?	No	Yes
No	All nonparticipants	Zero
Yes	Some participants	Some participants

TABLE 4.2. A Program that is Sufficient but Not Necessary.

	Is the outcome observed?	
Did one go through the program?	No	Yes
No	Some nonparticipants	Some nonparticipants
Yes	Zero	All participants

be a case where a participant does not possess the outcome. Among nonparticipants, the outcome may or may not be exhibited, because the relationship only considers sufficiency, not necessity. Therefore, some cases of nonparticipants will fall into the *no/no* cell, while others will fall into the *no/yes* cell.

Case 3: The Program Is Necessary and Sufficient

In the ***necessary and sufficient*** program, one will observe zeros in the *no program/yes outcome* cell and the *yes program/no outcome* cell (Table 4.3). That is, considering the participation status rows separately, nonparticipants will never exhibit the outcome because the program is necessary, and participants will always display the outcome because the program is sufficient. Zeros in the other two cells complete the matrix.

The above cases are gross but useful simplifications of how one can interpret the relationship between participation and outcomes. Complications arise, even in this grossly simplified display of data. Using this neat two-by-two matrix requires concise definitions of program participation, program nonparticipation, and the presence of observed outcomes. In this scheme, one is either a participant or a nonparticipant, and the outcome is either present or absent. Participation and outcome are dichotomous variables—they have two (dichotomous) categories—yes or no. The real world, though, is not generally dichotomous. Often, data are nuanced, variables are continuous rather than discrete, and we need to make decisions about definitions.

TABLE 4.3. **A Program that has a "Necessary and Sufficient" Relationship with the Outcome.**

	Is the outcome observed?	
Did one go through the program?	**No**	**Yes**
No	All nonparticipants	Zero
Yes	Zero	All participants

SETTING CUTOFF POINTS AND CAUSAL INTERPRETATION

The definitions of variables can ultimately impact the causal conclusions drawn. For example, defining who is and is not a program participant seems trivial at a first glance—those who went through the program are participants, and those who did not are nonparticipants. However, there is a grey area. How to classify someone who started the program but didn't finish it? Is a program participant defined as someone who completed every aspect of the program? At what level of participation does one become defined as a participant? Or consider someone who went through 90% of the program. By nonparticipant, do we mean someone who received all aspects of the program, or only most aspects?

Likewise, defining whether an outcome is present or absent requires careful consideration. At what level of the outcome measure has the desired outcome occurred? If there was a positive change in the outcome measure, but it does not meet the arbitrary threshold that may have been set at the start of the program, is the outcome still present?

To illustrate the importance of the decisions surrounding the classification of data, consider the fictional data in Table 4.4 on the number of minutes parents spend reading with a child and the child's test scores. A fictional program aims to increase children's reading ability by encouraging parents to read with their children. The thinking is that by increasing the amount of time that parents read with their children, a child's language proficiency would increase. (Although the example provided pertains to parent reading and test scores, the same data could also apply to a program where data was recorded on the number of hours of program sessions attended and increase in monthly income. In such a case, one would be interested in the relationship between the program attendance and the change in monthly income.)

In this example, we explore the causal relationship between the intervention (parental time) and the outcome (a child's test scores). We see that children whose parents do not read with them have scores ranging from 280 to 340 and those with parents who spend 20 minutes have scores ranging from 500 to 600. On the surface, there seems to be a causal connection.

Next, we split the intervention and the outcome into categories. At first, we define a "low" amount of reading time as anything less than 10 minutes, and a "high" amount of time as 10 minutes or more. Likewise, we define a "low" test score as anything less than 400 and

TABLE 4.4. Fictional Data.

Time (minutes) spent reading with child at end of program	Test score
0	280
0	300
0	320
0	340
5	350
5	370
5	375
5	380
10	400
10	415
10	420
10	440
15	450
15	450
15	460
15	480
20	500
20	550
20	600

a "high" test score as 400 and above. When we classify cases according to these definitions, we get the "matrix shown in Table 4.5.

The figures in the cells of this matrix suggest that whenever there is a low amount of time spent with a child, the test score is low, and whenever there is a high amount of time spent with the child, the test score is high. There are no cases where a child who spends a low amount of time with a parent receives a high score, and where a child who spends a high amount of time receives a low score. This fact suggests that reading with a child may have a *necessary and sufficient* relationship with test scores. That is, in order for a child to have a high test score, the parent must read to the child, and if the parent does not, the child is doomed to low test scores.

The interpretation of the data can change simply by changing the definitions of the categories used. To demonstrate, in the next case, we use the same data but define a low amount of time as 10 minutes or less and keep the same definition of a low test score—any score less than 400. When we modify only the definition of the amount of time spent, the matrix in Table 4.6 results.

TABLE 4.5. Cutoffs Suggest a Necessary and Sufficient Relationship.

	Test score	
Time spent reading with child	Low (<400)	High (400+)
Low (<10 minutes)	7	0
High (10+ minutes)	0	11

TABLE 4.6. Cutoffs Suggest a Sufficient but Not Necessary Relationship.

	Test score	
Time spent reading with child	Low (<400)	High (400+)
Low (10 minutes or less)	7	4
High (more than 10 minutes)	0	7

The results of this categorization make it appear as if reading with a child for a longer amount of time is sufficient to produce high test scores—but isn't necessary. There are cases where a parent spent a low amount of time with the child and the child scored highly on the test.

In this next case, we modify the definition of a high test score to be at least 500, and the definition of a high amount of time remains at more than 10 minutes. When we do this, then the matrix in Table 4.7 results, and it appears that reading with a child is necessary but not sufficient for high test scores.

These three simple examples demonstrate that changing the cut points of variables in an analysis can change the interpretation of the effectiveness of the program. When one performs a linear regression using the data, one sees that the variable "time spent reading with a child" accounts for 90% of the variation in test scores and that for every additional minute spent reading, the test score increases by nearly 11 points. However, when we think of the possible causal relationship between reading time and test scores, we draw different conclusions, depending on how we divide the continuous data into categories.

In order to avoid arbitrary conclusions, the cut points of categories of variables must be carefully considered. When converting continuous data into categorical data, one should be able to substantively and theoretically justify the boundaries of the categories.

TABLE 4.7. **Cutoffs Suggest a Necessary but Not Sufficient Relationship.**

	Test score	
Time spent reading with child	Low (<500)	High (500+)
Low (10 minutes or less)	11	0
High (> 10 minutes)	3	4

If the boundaries are determined arbitrarily and there is no substantive justification for the categories, then what the data reveal and the conclusions made will also be arbitrary. Decisions made about the definitions of categories have ramifications throughout the remainder of the analysis and the conclusions drawn from the data analysis. In the above simplified case, we see how we could come to different conclusions about the nature of the causal relationship between variables and outcomes.

It may seem that the solution, then, is to keep the data in its continuous form. Statistically that might make sense, but in program evaluation, we usually want to comment on the effectiveness of a program on participants versus comparable nonparticipants. Participation is usually defined as dichotomous—either one does or does not participate. Or, one could separate participation into three categories—did not participate at all, participated somewhat, and fully participated. Participation in a program will almost always be considered as categorical and not continuous. Ultimately, one wants to succinctly remark on the degree to which participating in a program helps participants.

On the outcome side, the question in summative evaluation is often whether the participants show success as opposed to not showing any success or being partially successful. Often, programs have set a measure of what success means. Unfortunately, these measures are often arbitrarily set—typically, round numbers are used.

Many funders' grant applications require that applicant programs set "targets," which are sometimes called "benchmarks." The program then is held to these targets, and success is defined as whether the program meets the targets. There are many problems with this approach. First, applicants sometimes think that setting grandiose targets in the application will result in a higher probability of funding, set the targets too high. The naïve funder may reward this type of "pie in the sky" target setting—but if the program's success is measured against this high threshold, it may ultimately be deemed unsuccessful.

Conversely, a few applicants will set their thresholds too low, knowing that the program's success will ultimately be judged against these thresholds. This is likely to be the case only among applicants who feel secure in their chances of receiving funding—such as repeat grantees or grantees who may have a monopoly on satisfying a foundation's funding priority.

Sometimes, measures of success are set by people who have little expertise in the field. For example, I once saw business executives define success for a preschool program. This essentially results in arbitrary (and unrealistic) targets.

My preference is that programs aim for continuous improvement in their processes, with the expectation that if the program's Theory of Change (ToC) is sound and logic tight, improved processes will result in better outcomes. In the best of all worlds, targets would not be set a *priori*. However, knowing that many funders want set targets, my preference would be for targets to be based on the program's past experiences. In the case of new programs, it might be impossible to set realistic targets. One may turn to the documented performance of similar programs.

When it comes to data collection, it is important to consider the limitation of data collected in categories rather than in a format that allows for continuous variables to be created and analyzed. If data on program effects are collected in terms of categories, it is possible that even if the intervention had an effect, the effect may not be observable because participants did not change their behavior enough to warrant moving into the next category. The effect occurred within a category. Depending on the size of the category, the effect could still be significant, but not large enough to move from one category to the next.

For example, an evaluator may decide to collect income information categorically and may be interested in determining if households that participate in an antipoverty intervention move out of poverty. In this case, income data may be collected to reflect whether the household is below poverty, between 100 and 185 percent of the poverty threshold, between 185 and 250 percent of the poverty threshold, or over 250%.

A participating household may have seen its income increase, but not to the extent that the household moved from one category to the next. With the categorical data, the program may seem to have no effect. However, if the data were collected continuously (where households were asked the dollar amount of income rather than their income category), then in the analysis, one could examine increases in income, rather than whether a participant moved from one category to the next. That is, collecting data in categories often restricts the analysis and can mask real changes that participants may have experienced. Collecting data in their rawest, noncategorical form allows for more flexibility in the analysis, which may uncover some unanticipated effects.

In summary, the causal connection between two variables can depend on the definitions used to create categories, and more often than not, evaluating programs becomes an exercise in examining the relationship between categorical variables. Evaluators should be able to justify the definitions of the categories created.

INTERVENING VARIABLES

Another aspect of causation concerns how the presence or absence of other factors influences the relationship observed between the cause and effect of interest. The observed relationship between X (cause) and Y (effect) may be influenced by whether other factors are present. (X is the independent variable and Y is the dependent variable—what is being explained.) Some other factors may dampen or amplify the magnitude of the observed relationship between the cause and the effect.

Let us consider cases where the cause is denoted as X, the effect as Y, and an intervening variable as I. The three variables form a triangle. Different relationships between X and I, X and Y, and I and Y will result in various erroneous conclusions about the true relationship between X and Y. Consider the following three cases.

Case 1. Overestimating a Program's Effectiveness Because of the Presence of an Intervening Variable. In this case, X actually is positively related to Y—when X increases Y also increases, and conversely, when X decreases Y also decreases (Figure 4.1). However, X also has a positive relationship with I, an intervening variable that has an independent, positive relationship with Y. Thus, when X increases, I increases, and an increase in I results in an increase in Y, independent of X's increase in Y.

If the evaluator does not take into account the independent impact of I, the evaluator will erroneously over-state the magnitude of the effect that X has on Y. In the simplest case, the ultimate effect on Y will be additive—it will be the sum of X's effect on Y and X's effect on I, which then influences Y. However, one cannot assume that the two independent effects are simply additive—they could be multiplicative, or have some other functional form or relationship. The important point here is that unless one takes into account I, the effect of the program on the outcome will be overestimated. One would be attributing too much effectiveness to the program. If the program were to be implemented in a place or with a population where I was not present, then it might seem that the program was not as effective (and implementers might be blamed for the reduced impact). But, in fact, the program's effectiveness remained the same, what differed was the presence of I.

Case 2. Underestimating a Program's Effectiveness Because of the Presence of an Intervening Variable. As in the first case, X is positively correlated with Y (Figure 4.2). However, X is negatively correlated with I—when X increases, I decreases, and I positively affects Y. The net result here, if you only examine X and Y without considering the dampening effect of I, is that you would underestimate the impact of X on Y. In an extreme case, it would seem that there is no relationship between X and Y, when, in fact, there is. This case is also known as drawing a false negative conclusion. In the extreme, you could erroneously conclude that X does not impact Y because the effect of I on Y negates the impact of X on Y.

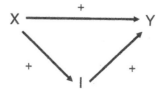

FIGURE 4.1. *Overestimating the Program's Effectiveness Because of the Presence of an Intervening Variable.*

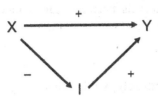

FIGURE 4.2. *Underestimating a Program's Effectiveness Because of the Presence of an Intervening Variable.*

FIGURE 4.3. *Misestimating the Relationship Between X and Y.*

Case 3. Misestimating a Relationship Between X and Y. One may erroneously interpret a situation as X causes Y, when in fact what happens is that X causes I, which in turn causes Y (Figure 4.3). In this case, there may seem to be a correlation between X and Y only when I is present. But when I is absent, there is no relationship between X and Y. If one observes X and Y only in the presence of I, then it would be easy to misinterpret the relationship between X and Y. If the program has only operated in circumstances where I is present, then it will seem that the program is effective. However, if the program is implemented in an environment where I is not present, then it is likely that the program will fail.

Intervening variables are important to consider because their presence or absence can cloud the true relationship a program has with its outcomes. If the program purely causes a change to occur, then it must do so in the absence of intervening variables.

TYPES OF CAUSAL EFFECTS

Another aspect of causation pertains to the type of effect or outcome one anticipates the program will cause. We can think of this in terms of how long it takes for the outcome to appear, the sustenance of the intervention's effect on the outcome, and the functional form of the effect. All three aspects of the effect should be considered prior to collecting data on effects. The type of effect that you anticipate will relate to the length of time that data are collected and the length of intervals between data collection. There exist a number of scenarios about which evaluators need to be cautious.

Lagged Effects

Some effects may appear immediately, while others may take some time to appear or be lagged. Before starting with data collection, one should consider how much time it would take for the effect to appear. If an effect will take time to appear and the evaluator collects data too soon, then even if the program ultimately impacts participants, the data will suggest that it has no impact. The effect will appear after the data have been collected and the evaluation of the intervention will suggest that it has been ineffective.

Lagged effects are difficult to attribute to the intervention. With lagged effects, it is more difficult to make the argument that the intervention caused the outcome and that the events or influences that occurred between the intervention and the outcome did not cause (entirely or partially) the outcome (Figure 4.4).

Permanency of Effects

Similarly, some effects are long lasting, while others may be short-lived. If an effect is short lived, then one must collect evidence of the outcome before the effect wears off. Evaluators refer to impacts that wear off as **discontinuous** (e.g., people who go through a smoking

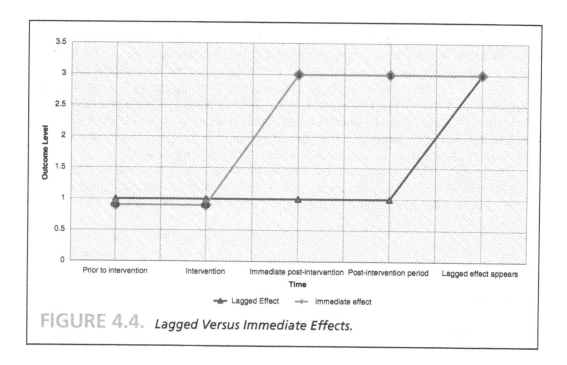

FIGURE 4.4. *Lagged Versus Immediate Effects.*

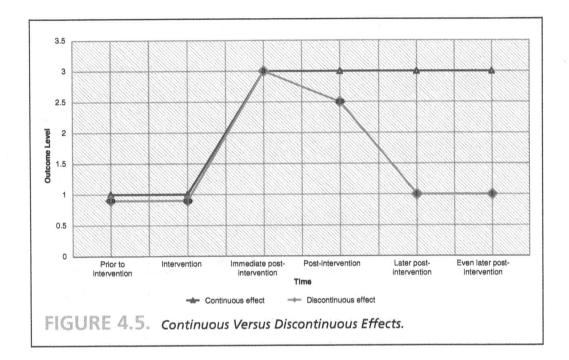

FIGURE 4.5. *Continuous Versus Discontinuous Effects.*

cessation program and reduce smoking for a length of time, but then return to smoking). Conversely, effects that last forever are referred to as **continuous effects.** Usually, programs that provide skills training have continuous effects, although the skills may atrophy to some degree if not used after the program. Figure 4.5 shows one way that the difference between continuous and discontinuous effects could be manifested. Of course, the timing and the way that the effect dissipates can vary from what the figure suggests.

Functional Form of Impact

Some effects may exhibit themselves as a change in slope of an existing trend, a change in intercept of the trend, or a change in the functional form of the trend (Figure 4.6). For example, a tutoring program may modify the pace at which children learn, which would be exhibited by an increase in the slope of the functional form. Conversely, some programs aim to decrease the rate of change—consider programs aimed at slowing the aging process or decrease the proportion of ex-convicts who are re-arrested.

If a program shows a change in intercept, there is a one-time change in the outcome level and following, participants have the same rate of change that they had prior to the intervention. The outcome level would be at the higher level. Consider a program that aimed to provide tutoring to students struggling to understand particular mathematics concepts. Tutoring would be provided to help them catch-up to classmates. This program would show a change in the intercept of increase in skills, and thereafter the students would increase their

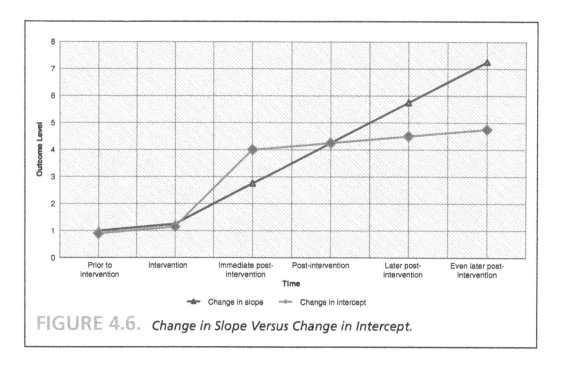

FIGURE 4.6. *Change in Slope Versus Change in Intercept.*

math skills at the same rate as prior to the program. The program may not affect the students' overall pace of learning.

Figure 4.6 contrasts a situation where program participants showed a change in slope with a change in the intercept. With a change in slope, the rate of increase has changed—in the example, the program caused the rate of increase to be higher. The second line demonstrates a change in intercept. The slopes before and following the intervention are equivalent. The program only caused a change in the line's intercept.

Finally, an effect may be manifested in the change of a functional form of the effect. Consider a program where the outcome shows a seasonal trend. For example, food insecurity tends to increase in winter months. An outcome of a program addressing food insecurity could be a reduction in the seasonal swings of food security. Figure 4.7 illustrates an example of a change in food seasonality. Note that one needs many measures prior to the intervention to determine the pattern of seasonality. There are other ways that the change in functional form can manifest itself.

Spectacular Causes and Effects

Another aspect of causation to consider is **spectacular causes** and **spectacular effects.** It is possible that small degrees of the causal variable or small doses of the program or intervention can produce very large effects. Conversely, it is also possible that large doses of the cause can produce small effects. Sometimes, planners think that intense interventions will produce large effects. This is not necessarily the case. There may be a "tipping point," below

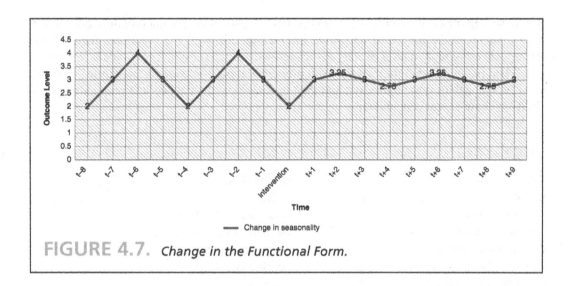

FIGURE 4.7. *Change in the Functional Form.*

which the intervention will seem to have no effect, a threshold at which the intervention will seem to have a great effect, and above which the intervention may seem to have no additional effect. One should be aware of the possibility of a tipping point situation and create data collection approaches that will be sensitive enough to detect the existence of such a situation.

The evaluator must anticipate how the effects of the program will be manifested, since this will have an impact on the type of data collected, the length of time prior to and after the intervention that data are collected, and the intervals of data collection. Therefore, it is critically important that when planning data collection activities, the evaluator considers the timing and type of effect anticipated from the intervention.

SUMMARY

This chapter has shown that the issue of causation must be carefully considered prior to data collection. What does it mean to say that the intervention has caused a change in the outcome?

Getting to know a program through its program description (ToC and Program Logic Model (PLM)) is essential before tackling the question of what type of effect one would anticipate from the intervention and the influence of possible intervening variables. The literature review should shed light on the hypothesized causal relationship.

Classifying data greatly impacts conclusions. Changing the boundary of a category can alter the interpretation of data significantly. How the evaluator anticipates the effects of the program will be manifested has an impact on the type of data collected, the length of time the collection goes on, and the intervals at which the data will be collected. Collecting data in their rawest, noncategorical form allows for more flexibility in later analyses.

While having more data collection points before and after an intervention allows for determination of the degree to which the intervention changed the functional form of the effect, collecting more data is usually associated with higher cost and respondent fatigue.

When planning a program and considering evaluation, be aware of the various types of causal relationships that might exist and the ramifications of a data collection plan on one's ability to draw causal conclusions.

KEY TERMS

categorical data
causation
continuous data
continuous effects
discontinuous effects
false negative conclusion
false positive conclusion
intervening variable

lagged effects
necessary
necessary and sufficient
permanency of effects
spectacular causes
spectacular effects
sufficient
targets (benchmarks)

DISCUSSION QUESTIONS

1. Why is it necessary for evaluators to posit the causal relationship between the intervention and outcome(s) prior to data collection?

2. Create your own example of how changing the boundaries of categories using the same raw data can significantly alter your conclusions.

3. Provide your own examples of:
   a. A lagged effect?
   b. A continuous effect?
   c. A discontinuous effect?
   d. An immediate effect?
   e. A continuous effect?
   f. A discontinuous effect?
   g. A spectacular effect?

CHAPTER 5

THE PRISMS OF VALIDITY

LEARNING OBJECTIVES

After reading this chapter, you should be able to

- Understand the four types of validity
- Define "threats to validity"
- Describe the common threats to each type of validity and how to best minimize or negate them

Evaluation Essentials: Methods for Conducting Sound Evaluation Research, Second Edition.
Beth Osborne DaPonte.
© 2025 John Wiley & Sons, Inc. Published 2025 by John Wiley & Sons, Inc.

INTRODUCTION

When evaluators plan an evaluation or read an evaluation report, they consider the strength of the research through four related but distinct prisms—the four types of validity. Validity refers to the extent to which there has been an approximation of truth—if the research is valid in all respects, then the conclusions that are reached through it are legitimate and generalizable.

In their seminal 1979 book, *Quasi-Experimentation: Design and Analysis Issues for Field Settings,* Cook and Campbell distinguished four types of validity:

- construct validity,
- internal validity,
- statistical conclusion validity, and
- external validity.

This chapter discusses each type of validity and their common "threats" in the context of program evaluation. Threats to validity are events or circumstances that have the potential to invalidate evaluation research in a certain respect. There may not be anything that the evaluator can do to avoid the threat, but one should be aware of the threat(s) that exists and may potentially jeopardize the evaluation's findings, perhaps in an immeasurable way. Threats to validity can be so serious as to invalidate the study's conclusions—for example, evaluators cannot claim that theoretical constructs have been operationalized appropriately, that the intervention has produced results, and/or that the results obtained are not simply an anomaly found in one instance but are not generalizable to other populations.

The best evaluations take the threats into account and have been structured to minimize their impact. Because of the real-world constraints on research (e.g., money, time, and access to particular populations), when designing an evaluation, evaluators must make trade-offs between the types of threats and validity. An evaluator may introduce a less serious threat to the validity to the research in order to reduce or avoid a more serious threat. When planning an evaluation, the evaluator must create an evaluation design that is as robust as possible to threats to validity. To do that, the evaluator must learn the threats to validity and be able to assess their application to the evaluation being designed.

The threats directly relate to the issue of causation and the choice of the quasi-experimental design (presented in the next chapter). Once one knows which threats to validity are present and need to be balanced, it usually becomes fairly obvious which quasi-experimental designs are applicable and which design is the best, given the circumstances.

In brief:

- **Construct validity** refers to the degree to which the theoretical constructs have been well specified and both the cause and effect constructs have been appropriately operationalized.

- **Internal validity** pertains to the degree to which the study has shown that a causal relationship between the intervention and outcomes exists.

- **Statistical conclusion validity** refers to the appropriateness of the statistical techniques used for the analysis.
- **External validity** refers to the generalizability of the relationship found in one evaluation or study to other people, places, and contexts.

In general, the priority evaluators would give to the types of validity is internal, construct, statistical conclusion, and then external. Certainly, if a relationship has not been shown to exist, there is no reason to generalize the relationship.

However, priority between the types of validity may be reordered, depending on the reasons for evaluation. For example, if the evaluation is being done to better understand theories behind human behavior (rather than to understand if particular interventions have intended consequences), then the priority might be construct, internal, external, and statistical conclusion.

Beyond program description issues, there are four sets of questions about a program's impact that the evaluator must answer:

- Is there a relationship between the intervention and the observed outcome? Is program participation related to observed outcome measures?
- Given that there is a relationship, is this relationship causal? Did the program *cause* the outcome measure to change?
- Given that the relationship is plausibly causal, what are the particular cause and effect constructs involved in the relationship? What causal construct does the program represent? What effect construct does the outcome measure represent?
- Given that there is probably a causal relationship between the cause and effect constructs, how generalizable is this relationship across other types of people, other settings, and time periods?

Each set of questions pertains to a type of validity. The first set pertains to statistical conclusion validity, the second set to internal validity, the third set to construct validity, and the fourth set to external validity.

Each type of validity has particular threats. There are more possible threats to each type of validity than discussed here. Those threats are well explicated in Chapter 2 of Cook and Campbell's *Quasi-Experimentation*. I discuss here only those that commonly surface.

STATISTICAL CONCLUSION VALIDITY

Evaluators often use quantitative analyses and statistical tests to determine whether a presumed cause (e.g., the initiative or program) and effect (outcome) covary. In the simplest form, the cause and effect could either positively or negatively covary. If they positively covary, than an increase in the cause would be associated with an increase in the effect and if they negatively covary, an increase in the cause would be associated with an observed decrease in the effect.

The existence of a covarying relationship does not imply a one-to-one relationship between the causal variable and the effect variable. Covarying relationships can have different strengths. Some may positively covary, but weakly, meaning that an increase in the causal variable is associated with a very small increase in the effect variable. In other relationships, a slight increase in the causal variable is associated with a very large increase in the effect variable. Or, the relationship may be one where the covariance is found only in a small minority of cases, but in that small minority, the impact seems substantial.

Three groups of questions, posed by Cook and Campbell (1979, p. 39), are at the heart of statistical conclusion validity:

1. Is the evaluation designed so that it can detect covariation between the intervention and outcomes? Does the sample size available for study allow for the sensible use of statistical analysis? If the number of cases available to study is too small to apply appropriate statistical techniques, one cannot draw conclusions about the strength of the statistical relationship. If a large number of interviews were conducted, can they be coded to allow for quantitative analysis? Can data be collected and organized so that statistical analyses are appropriate?

2. If covariation can be detected, then does any evidence exist that suggests that the cause and effect actually do covary? If so, what type of evidence exists?

3. If there is evidence, how strongly do the intervention and outcomes covary? Will there always be a change in outcome for those who have been touched by the intervention, or will the change in outcomes only be present among some participants? Will there be a large or a small change? How much of the intervention (intensity) does a participant need to receive in order to see a change? Does the intervention work for everybody, or do pre-existing conditions need to have been present?

In the simplest of forms, evaluators are testing the null hypothesis that there is no difference in outcomes between program participants and nonparticipants. That is, if a program has an effect, one would reject the null hypothesis. Statistical tests would show that the outcomes differ between participants and nonparticipants and that the participants show (more) improvement than nonparticipants.

Types of Erroneous Conclusions: Type 1 and Type 2 Errors

There are two types of errors one can make about the nature of the relationship between the program and its outcomes:

- **Type I error** occurs when one concludes that the outcomes of the various treatment groups differ, when in reality, they do not. In this case, *one erroneously concludes that the program had an impact* when in fact, it's ineffective.

- **Type II error** occurs when one concludes that the outcomes of the various treatment groups do not differ, when in fact, they do. In this case, *one erroneously concludes that an effective program did not have an impact.*

Take a situation where the evaluator concluded that the program is effective, but in fact, the program is ineffective. This evaluator would be making a Type I error. The converse can also occur, where the evaluator concludes that the program has no effect, when in fact, it does. If an erroneous conclusion of no impact has been made, then a Type II error has occurred.

Funders and management should particularly take note of the impact of these two types of errors on their work. Type I error would lead to funding or enabling ineffective programs and Type II error can result in missing opportunities to fund or support effective programs. It is likely that funders would particularly like to avoid Type I error.

Threats to Statistical Conclusion Validity

When the following situations occur, there is a higher chance of making either a Type I or Type II error. These situations are known as *threats to statistical conclusion validity*.

Small Sample Sizes Small sample sizes are associated with an increase in the amount of variance—a measure of uncertainty—around a statistic. The smaller the sample size, the larger the variance. Until the sample size hits a minimum of approximately fifty units, statistics on the population may be too unreliable and real relationships cannot be statistically detected. Thus, the small sample size has introduced a threat to the statistical validity of the evaluation.

Small sample sizes occur in a few ways. Sometimes, programs serve a small number of clients at a time. For example, at a given time, a local child-care center serves a total of 31 children across four different age categories—infants, toddlers, early preschool, and late preschool. Clearly, especially when broken down by age category, this number is too small to yield reliable statistics.

One typical approach to increasing the sample size is to combine client data from a number of time periods. For example, rather than only examining data on the 31 children in a child-care center in a year, one might combine the data from children in the center this year, last year, and the previous year. If the center serves 31 children per year, then the number of children whose data one can analyze increases to 93, a sample size that could allow for many types of statistical analyses. However, if this sample was broken down by age category, it is likely to be too small to avoid the threat to statistical validity.

However, it is important to be careful when combining data across time periods. Combining data is reasonable only when the program and the circumstances of the program have not changed during the period. If changes have occurred, then it would be inappropriate to combine different time periods. Therefore, combine data across different time periods only when both the program and the program's environment have been stable.

Another way that small sample size becomes an issue is when breaking the sample down into subpopulations. Often, it is desirable to see the intervention's effects on men versus women, or on an urban population versus suburban and rural populations, or on various racial or ethnic groups, or on various levels of educational achievement. Even if disaggregating by gender and using a sample of one hundred, then the sample could break down to approximately 50 men and 50 women. When running analyses on smaller categories, the sample size in each of the cells will decrease even more. In this case, we started with a reasonable sample size of 100, but the answers that we wanted involved breaking the sample down into finer categories with smaller sample sizes. If analyses will be done to draw conclusions about subpopulations, then the sample size in each subpopulation needs to be sufficiently large and the initial sample size may need to be increased to allow for such analyses.

Returning to the child-care center example, assume that combining the most recent two years of data is reasonable, but because of programmatic and staffing changes, combining data from more than two years ago is inappropriate. This leaves us with a sample of 62 children. For many questions involving children, one would disaggregate analyses by age groups. In this sample of 62 children, we have 16 infants (2 classes each with 8 infants), 20 toddlers (2 classes each with 10 toddlers), and 26 three- and four-year-olds (2 classes each with 13 children). These are very small sample sizes once disaggregated by age. It may not make sense to report "outcomes" because the statistics may vary from year to year—different children will be in the classes at any given time, there may be idiosyncrasies in data collection, and so on.

Another way that small sample size often results is when a data sample is taken from a larger population. A researcher may have anticipated a survey response rate that was higher than that achieved, with a resulting sample size that is relatively small. One solution to this situation would be to take another sample, and survey this newly selected sample. However, having survey responses from two different points in time might be an issue. Further, the opportunity to take another sample may not exist. For example, one may plan on surveying 100 randomly selected "graduates" from a program that served 400 people, but it's possible that only 40 will respond to the survey (a 40 percent response rate). This sample may be too small to provide statistical reliability.

To avoid this situation, the evaluator can create a larger sample to begin with, or alternatively, take initial actions that will increase the response rate. Between these two alternatives, the latter is the better approach. It is best to avoid low response rates, because the people who respond to the survey may be systematically different from those who did not respond. Differences between the respondents and nonrespondents could result in a biased achieved sample. Respondents may be biased in an unknown way and drawing conclusions about the program's effectiveness based on the responses of a survey that had a low response rate could lead to erroneous conclusions.

One approach to deal with this situation is to take a small sample of survey nonrespondents and then continue to follow up with them until they ultimately respond. This is known as sampling for nonresponse follow-up; this sample is intended to represent all nonrespondents. One could examine whether the responses of the respondents and the very limited sample of nonrespondents differ.

Creating a survey process that will yield a higher response rate will reduce potential bias in the surveyed population. Techniques known to increase response rates include:

- giving people notice of a survey or interview;
- having someone whom the sampled person respects encourages participation in the survey;

- keeping the survey as short as possible;
- design questions so they are easy to answer;
- pretesting the survey instrument and rectifying glitches in the survey;
- incentivize responding (e.g., pay people to respond); and
- providing respondents with information on the sponsorship of the survey and assurances of confidentiality and anonymity (if appropriate).

Incentivizing responses often decreases differences between respondents and nonrespondents. For example, giving people cash, checks, or vouchers in exchange for their responses helps increase the response rate. A modest stipend shows that the evaluator respects the respondent's time and acknowledges that providing information is burdensome. Whenever possible, evaluators should offer modest incentives to respondents (e.g., grocery store gift certificates, a meal at focus groups). It has been shown that giving people a certain, modest stipend is more effective in increasing the response rates than giving them a "chance" to receive a larger benefit, such as a place in a drawing for a prize.

Measurement Error Most measures have a degree of imprecision or "noise," known as measurement error. Any data that evaluators use—survey data, administrative data, interviews, observations, and focus groups—can have measurement error. Measurement error encompasses the difference between the "true" level of an indicator and what the data reveal. In the best case, the measurement error is unbiased—that is, it is not skewed high or low. In the worst case, the measurement is biased and the evaluator does not know the direction or the magnitude of the bias.

Such errors can derive from many sources. For example, if a survey question is not written clearly enough to be interpreted identically by all respondents, then respondents will provide different responses, not because their situations differ, but because their interpretations of the questions differ. If some provide a response that is higher than their true level while others give a response that is lower, then the measurement error, while it can be large, could be unbiased. However, if respondents tend to provide higher levels of responses than their situation calls for, then the measure would be biased. Questions that ask about situations that are not current tend to have measurement error, simply because of a hazier recall of past situations and feelings than current situations.

Another source of measurement error results from questions that respondents do not have precise knowledge of the answer—for example, exactly how much they spend on utilities per month, birth dates of distant family members. Respondents may "estimate" their response by rounding (e.g., rounding to the nearest 10 dollars, reporting the first of the month of birth as the birth date.)

Every measure may have some degree of inherent error. Measurement error threatens statistical conclusion validity because it increases the variance of a measure. When the variance of a measure increases, there is a higher risk that one will make a Type II error—erroneously concluding that there is no effect, when there is.

When evaluating particularly important measures or issues, there are ways to mitigate the threat of low reliability of measures. For very important measures, it could be important not to rely on simply one question to collect information but to ask supplementary questions that either support or refute the first response. For example, if asking about whether a program changed participants' knowledge about a subject (such as drug awareness programs, contraception and abstinence programs, and training programs), one would want to include questions that would affirm what that knowledge base is or was. Further, if asking about attitudes, one might decide to ask supporting questions that would verify that the person actually holds the attitude that she expresses (e.g., who they voted for in the last election, media sources consumed).

Pretesting a survey instrument (or questionnaire) safeguards against low question reliability. When pretesting, the surveyor does a post-survey interview to ask the respondent about how they interpreted questions, inconsistent responses, and how the respondent interpreted those questions. Another way of pretesting is to ask the respondent to think aloud while completing the survey with the survey designer present in the room (or remotely), with the survey designer getting immediate feedback on how questions are being interpreted. The survey draft should be pretested until the process has worked out all of the kinks in the survey instrument.

Unreliable Treatment Implementation Implementing a treatment unreliably poses a serious threat to statistical conclusion validity. When different implementations of treatment occur, then the variance of the treatment increases, further increasing the likelihood of Type II errors. That is, when the treatment is implemented differently across participants, then one is more likely to conclude erroneously that the treatment had no effect, when in fact it did.

There is one exception to this. In an instance where a treatment is sometimes being implemented more intensely than program administrators understand it to be, an evaluator may mistakenly conclude that the treatment has a larger effect than it would have had it been implemented as intended. Thus, it is vital that the evaluator have a very thorough understanding of the program and exactly what the treatment entails and include measures that reflect the intensity of the treatment that participants received. Further, program management must provide a framework for the implementing staff that standardize the initiative—establishing standards as to exactly what the initiative entails, training staff on these standards, and having an accountability system that oversees the implementation of the initiative.

Fishing A trait of bad research is when a researcher goes "fishing" when doing quantitative data analysis. Fishing can be thought of as throwing all possible variables into an analysis and letting the statistical analyses (be the t-tests, chi-squared tests, regression analysis, and so on) reveal which variables show statistical significance. This is an atheoretical approach to research, as the analyst *post hoc* will create a hypothesis that explains the statistically significant relationship(s).

This approach to research is backwards. Statistical analyses should investigate the plausibility of the evaluator's hypotheses. The problem with fishing is that it increases the chance of Type I error—incorrectly concluding that the program is effective. The probability of committing Type I error is called the alpha level and is frequently set at .05. A lower alpha means that there is less than a 5 percent chance of Type I error. If a variable is deemed "statistically significant at the .05 level" then the evaluator interprets that there is less than a 5 percent chance that the statement that the independent and dependent variables covary is incorrect.

When an evaluator goes fishing, the evaluator tests the statistical significance of more variables than they have theorized *a priori* have a relationship with the outcome. If using a .05 alpha level, there is a 1 in 20 chance that a variable may be deemed statistically significant although the variable does not actually covary with the dependent variable. If using more than 20 variables, it is likely that one of the tests will lead to erroneous conclusions.

The antidote to fishing is to think clearly about why each variable is included in the analysis. The evaluator should have a rationale for each and every variable included in the analyses. If the evaluator does not have a rationale, then the variable should be omitted. The goal of an analysis is to discover the most parsimonious model that explains patterns found in the data. Including extraneous variables deters from this goal.

INTERNAL VALIDITY

Internal validity pertains to whether there is a causal relationship between two variables. Ultimately, evaluators would like to know whether the program caused the change. Whereas statistical conclusion validity pertains only to the presence or absence of a relationship, internal validity asks whether the relationship is causal. The following questions come under the purview of internal validity:

- Did the program cause the change?
- Without the program, would we have observed a change? Had the program not existed, what would have happened to participants' outcomes?
- What is the intensity of the intervention necessary for the change to occur?
- Do other factors help determine whether the causal process occurs?

As discussed in Chapter 4, determining the direction of causation depends on knowing a time sequence of events. Making false positive, and conversely, false negative conclusions is always a risk. Threats to internal validity are common and must be taken very seriously.

Threats to Internal Validity

History The threat of history occurs when an event that could affect the level of the outcome indicator, independent of the program's influence, occurs during the time between the start and the end of the program, or in the case of a lagged effect, between the program's start and when one would expect to see the effect.

Take the example of a mammogram awareness program that provides a community with information about the benefits of early detection of breast cancer. If, during the program's operation, a very prominent person announced that she was diagnosed with breast cancer and the diagnosis was detected in a mammogram, then women in the program's target population may have become more inclined to get mammograms, not because of the program, but because of the information conveyed in the media about the importance of mammograms.

The threat of history occurs when something that would independently exert an influence on the program's outcomes occurs during the program's operation, but outside of the program. The extent to which the outside occurrence influences the outcome measure is unknown, but clearly, the program cannot claim that all of the change in the outcome is due only to the program's activities. The mammogram awareness program cannot claim that all (or even any) of the increase in mammogram rates can be attributed to the program. If the program were replicated at another time (and if the public forgets about the celebrity's case), then evaluators would get a better handle on the extent to which this threat of history affected the program outcome.

Examples of the threat of history contaminating evaluation results abound. Many programs operating in 2020 and 2021 will need to consider how COVID-19 and the lockdown impacted their effectiveness. The threat of history can occur at a local level. It can also lead to overestimates or underestimates of a program's effectiveness, depending on the actual occurrence. For example, an overall labor shortage will make a job training program seem more effective than it actually is, while overall high unemployment will make a job training program seem less effective. Programs that encourage home ownership may seem less effective if operating in an environment of rapidly increasing mortgage interest rates.

When evaluating a program, changes in the program's context should be understood so one can assess whether the threat of history exists.

Maturation The threat of maturation pertains to the fact that some participants may have changed in the way that the program intends them to just because time passed. This threat is especially relevant when conducting evaluations of education programs, where one would expect children to become wiser and stronger as they age. Children are likely to improve their literacy and math skills, knowledge base, emotional capacities, and motor skills to some extent as they age, regardless of whether they participated in programs that stressed such skills.

An example of maturation as a threat would be examining a program that aimed to improve students' reading skills in second grade. If one simply examined the change in reading ability between second and third grade and showed that reading test scores improved, this would not be evidence that the program had any effect because of the threat of maturation. One would expect children to become better readers during this period, simply because time has passed. The evaluation should instead question whether their reading skills improved more than would have been expected.

The threat of maturation does not only appear in evaluations of programs that pertain to children (although when dealing with children, one should always be alert to this threat). In the case of a bereavement support program, an evaluator should be alert to the threat of maturation—some who lost loved ones may cope better simply because time has passed since the loved one's death. Also, in programs that aim to stave off the decline in the physical health of the elderly, a program that showed no change in the physical abilities of its clients may actually have been successful. In these cases, there is a trajectory over time that exists, and this trajectory in a sense represents "maturation."

One might also expect organizations to "mature" over time. Start-up businesses differ from businesses that have existed for at least five years. If one were examining a program that aimed to aid entrepreneurs starting new businesses, effectiveness would be assessed by asking whether the growth trajectory of their business differs from that of businesses that did not receive such assistance. Simply showing that the program participants' businesses grew would not be evidence of the program's effectiveness because of the threat of maturation.

Selection The threat of selection poses the most insidious threat to internal validity. One should be alert to this threat when evaluating any program in which participation is voluntary. When people can choose whether or not to participate in a program, it is likely that those who participate in the program differ in some way from those who do not participate.

Some argue that if we know the dimensions in which participants and nonparticipants differ, then we can statistically "control" those dimensions and continue to analyze the program's effectiveness. Stanley Lieberson, in his book *Making It Count* (1985), strongly argues that applying statistical controls for the known differences between participants and nonparticipants still does not address the essence of the selection issue. Participants will differ from nonparticipants in exactly the aspects that the program addresses. On the other hand, Nobel Economics Prize winner James Heckman devoted much of his career to developing econometric models to address the threat of selection.

Consider job training programs aimed at unemployed persons. If the program is voluntary, then one may suspect that the people who participate in the program tend to be the most motivated—those who perceive that they need job training services and have learned how and where to get them. On the one hand, nonparticipants may believe that they do not need the program or they may not be as concerned about their career prospects—they may be less forward looking and therefore less motivated to participate in the program. If participants were more motivated and invested in their careers than nonparticipants, one would expect that even without the program, the participants would have had better labor market outcomes than nonparticipants.

Another example is an MBA program at a prestigious university. The admissions process "creams" (takes the best of) the applicant pool. The threat of selection suggests that even if those accepted and rejected by the university attended the same MBA program, those accepted by the program would have better career outcomes than those who were rejected. Thus, when examining, for example, differences in wage rates between alumni of the prestigious university versus those of a less prestigious university, one should question what proportion of the difference in wage rates is accounted for by differences in the quality of education versus differences in the pool of people who attended the universities. Did the more prestigious university's program have any value-added?

Evaluations of the Supplemental Nutrition Assistance Program (SNAP)-- formerly known as the Food Stamp program-- provide another example of the threat of selection. When examining food security rates of SNAP participants while receiving SNAP versus comparably poor households that do not participate in SNAP, an evaluator sees that those who participate in the program (and thus are receiving benefits with which to purchase food) are less food secure than comparably poor people who do not participate in the program. It may be that people who decide to participate in the program are more concerned with food insecurity even before applying, and this aspect led them to participate in the program in the first place.

Another common example is of children whose parents enroll them in programs. For example, when examining the differences in education outcomes between children who attend a magnet school that their parents enrolled them in with children who attend the typical feeder public school for their area, the former will likely have better outcomes than the latter. The former group of students may also have parents that are more interested in their futures and thus researched school choices.

The threat of selection can interact with other threats. For example, the threat of *selection-maturation* appears when program participants and nonparticipants differ *a priori* with respect to their pace of growth or rate of change. Even if program participants and nonparticipants appeared identical at the time of entry into the program, differences in their rate of maturation suggest that they would have different post-program levels of the indicators of interest, even without the program's intervention.

Program evaluation is flooded with examples of the threat of selection. Antidotes to the threat of selection mostly focus on using random assignment to equalize treatment and control groups. Other antidotes are to use complex statistical techniques to account for selection. However, Lieberson would argue that the selection issue can never be fully accounted for without randomization because, ultimately, voluntary participants differ from nonparticipants in their propensity to achieve the desired outcome.

Mortality In the evaluation context, mortality refers to participants dropping out of a program. One can think of the threat of mortality as a special instance of selection. The threat of mortality occurs when those who stay in a program differ from those who drop out of the program. When evaluating a program, if the evaluator does not consider the threat of mortality, the evaluator may incorrectly estimate the program's impact.

For example, consider a program that has a big impact on a subset of participants in the first few sessions, but less of an impact on another subset. The former subset may drop out of the program after the first few sessions because of the initial sessions' success—these dropouts may feel that they do not need the remainder of the program. If an evaluator estimated the impact of the program by defining "participants" as only those who completed the program, then it is likely that she would *underestimate* the impact of the program.

Conversely, some may drop out because they felt that the program wasn't benefiting them, and indeed, they experienced less program success in the early stages than those who remained with the program. If participants are defined as only those who completed the program, then the evaluator would likely *overestimate* the program's impact.

An evaluator needs to carefully consider what participating in a program means—does it mean enrolling in the program, or does it mean completing the program? Upon which population should we consider the program's impact? A sizable dropout rate may indicate that the program is not working as intended or is ill-conceived. Examining data on dropouts—who they are, how they differ from those who complete the program, why they dropped out—can yield important insights into the program's operations and outcomes.

Testing Another important and common threat to internal validity is called testing, which can occur when participants are given the same test or asked the same questions multiple times. Respondents' test scores or responses may change not because of a real change in their knowledge base or in their situation, but because of the respondents' familiarity with the test or heightened awareness of their situation.

Preparatory courses for standardized tests provide students with information on the test. Students often are given practice questions aimed to increase test scores, not because experience with these questions will increase the students' knowledge of the subject area, but to familiarize them with the types and formats of questions likely to be asked. Preparatory courses also often simulate the test-taking experience, aimed to reduce anxiety during the real testing and thus raise test scores.

Another example involves when evaluators ask people about a situation, or their emotions, repeatedly. For example, the food security measure asks people questions involving their experiences with food shortages in the household and how they have coped with such shortages. The first time someone is asked such questions they may respond one way. But even if their situation has not changed, the second time the questions are asked they may respond differently because the initial interview sparked further thought about the issues.

The threat of testing can lead to a decrease in test scores when a new test is introduced. Between 2005 and 2006, third- through eighth-grade students in the state of New York experienced a precipitous drop in standardized test scores when a new (and reportedly more rigorous) test was introduced. Some of the decrease was because of the increased rigor of the test, but some was due to unfamiliarity with the new test among both students and teachers. Likewise, between 2006 and 2007, the state enjoyed a significant (approximately 10 percent) increase in test scores, some of which was due to familiarity with the test, but some may be due to a real improvement in students' knowledge.

Testing is a serious threat whenever an evaluator asks questions repeatedly on knowledge or attitudes. This threat emerges regularly in repeated surveys on education, the arts, and political attitudes. The antidote to the threat of testing is to avoid asking the same people the same questions more than once. Strategies include asking the questions first of one subset of individuals and then the same questions of a different subset of individuals. A weaker antidote is to change the way information is gleaned from the same respondents—that is, asking the questions differently. The next chapter discusses such strategies.

Statistical Regression The threat of statistical regression is a worry when a program is offered only to those who have been assessed as performing exceptionally well or exceptionally poorly. What occurs is that if services are provided to the extremes of performers (e.g., either the best or the worse on a single test), it is likely that on subsequent tests those who performed well will regress to the mean (see a decrease in their scores) and those who performed badly will also regress to the mean (see improvement in their scores).

This is particularly true when the measure used to identify people for a program is not a particularly good measure of their true status or abilities. Some of the people performed well on the test as a fluke—they were having a particularly good day, got lucky on answers that they guessed on, etc. Those who did well because of a fluke, when retested, would do less well.

The same is true for those who did poorly initially and were identified for the program because of their poor performance on a test. Perhaps they weren't feeling well the day that they took the test. When given the test again, after the program begins, they would do better on the test, not because the program is effective, but because they are having a better day.

The question becomes what proportion of the changes in the test scores is due to the program's impact versus the effect of the threat of statistical regression. If the threat of statistical regression is not accounted for, then the impact of programs aimed to improve the state of those at the positive tail may be underestimated, and conversely, the impact at the negative tail of the distribution may be overestimated.

For example, consider a tutoring program that is offered to children who score in the bottom 10 percent of a mathematics test. In any test score, there is an element of variation. A child may have scored badly because she was not feeling well, was under undue stress, or otherwise had a bad day. Scoring in the bottom 10 percent is atypical for some; the next time they are tested, some will score better simply because they are not having a bad day. If remedial services are offered to the bottom 10 percent, and one looks at the difference between the initial test score and a post-program test score as an evidence of the program's success, then one is likely to overestimate the impact of the remedial services simply because there would have been some regression to the mean even without services. That is, one cannot conclude that all (or any) of the difference between the pretest and the posttest is due to the program, as some children would have scored better in the absence of the program. If the evaluator does not account for the threat of statistical regression, she would overestimate the program's effectiveness.

The converse situation is also true. If gifted support is provided to children who do very well on a single test, one may underestimate the impact of such support if considering the difference between the initial test score and a subsequent test score, because some of the children identified as gifted had a high score on the pretest due to an exceptionally good day.

To address the threat of statistical regression, administrators should offer remedial or gifted services not on the basis of one test, but on the basis of a package of information about a student. This is more likely to assure that the student truly should be categorized in the tail of the distribution.

Instrumentation The threat of instrumentation appears when the means of data collection changes between a pre-intervention and a post-intervention observations and the change in means affects the level of the observation. For example, say I decided to examine aggression among students and I was able to observe classrooms through one-way mirrors. I am interested in whether a program teaching nonaggressive responses has an impact. Before the program, I observe the classroom, carefully noting the number of times that an aggressive situation has occurred. I poorly train an assistant to collect the post-program data, and she also notes the aggressive situations in the classroom (and misses many of them). The change in the observer, from me to my assistant, can be considered the threat of instrumentation.

Unless the assistant interpreted the situations identically as I would, then it is likely that we will both incorrectly estimate the program's impact.

A change in observers is not the only way that the threat of instrumentation appears. This is also relevant when the same observers become more experienced. The observers may become better at identifying and recording nuanced situations. Therefore, some of the differences between the pretest and posttest information should be attributed to the change in observers' experience level.

This can also happen with interviewers who are orally administering written questionnaires. The interviewers may become more experienced over time, and this may lead to surveys that are better and more quickly administered—ultimately resulting in higher response rates. In this case, the posttest sample may differ somewhat from the pretest sample.

The antidote to both of these situations—a change in the staff of interviewers or observers, and a change in the experience level of data collectors—is to thoroughly train all personnel who will collect data. They should be experienced before actual data collection begins, and their data collection techniques should be standardized. The more discretion given to the data collectors, the more likely that the threat of instrumentation will impact findings.

In surveys, the threat of instrumentation comes into play when the survey instrument changes between the pretest and posttest. To avoid the threat of testing, evaluators may be tempted to ask questions differently on the posttest than how they were asked on the pretest. It is important to be aware that the change in question format, or response format, may introduce the threat of instrumentation. To avoid any problems caused by a change in question wording or reordering of survey questions, surveys should be thoroughly pretested before they are used for data collection and their kinks worked out beforehand.

Diffusion of Treatments The diffusion of a treatment presents a threat to internal validity because it is not clear the extent to which the group identified to be the control group actually received no treatment. This may ultimately result in an incorrect conclusion that the treatment has no impact, when in fact, it does.

Diffusion of a treatment occurs when the treatment and the control groups overlap. For example, take a billboard campaign that occurred in a low-income neighborhood to encourage residents to take advantage of an energy assistance program. In this program, households in another low-income neighborhood in the same city are used as the control group. The evaluators planned to examine the impact of the billboard campaign by looking at the difference in the number of applications for a benefits program originating in the neighborhood where the billboards appeared versus the number from the other neighborhood. However, this design is valid only to the extent that those in the control neighborhood did not observe the billboards. If the billboards appeared on a main thoroughfare that residents from the control neighborhood would see, then the quasi-experimental design may not be valid because of the threat of the diffusion of treatment.

Another way that diffusion can occur is when the treatment group shares information with the control group. Sharing information is a possibility when the treatment provided is seen as clearly beneficial, as in the case of social service programs, programs that offer monetary benefits, or programs that offer something that is otherwise hard to get. If the control group receives all or part of the treatment unbeknownst to the evaluator, the program's impact is likely to be underestimated.

Compensatory Equalization of Treatments This threat is a special case of diffusion of treatments and can occur when subjects are randomly assigned to treatment or control groups. If implementers or administrators providing the treatment do not feel comfortable with withholding or not providing a treatment to the "control" group, they may provide the control group with either the actual treatment or some lesser version of it. In this sense, they are compensating for the "no treatment" state of subjects in the control group.

For example, consider an organization operating a program that aims to increase homeownership by walking potential applicants through the homebuying and mortgage processes. One way of determining the effectiveness of the program would be to randomly assign potential homebuyers to the program. However, organization staff may feel uncomfortable with the prospect of not helping other, equally needy people through the homebuying and mortgage process, and on an informal basis, they assist those who are not assigned to the program.

To address the possibility of compensatory equalization of treatments, those implementing the program must understand the research importance of withholding the treatment from the control group. Some staff may not feel comfortable withholding a treatment and may even feel that it is ethically wrong to do so. This is especially the case if the treatment is a desired good. To avoid this situation, there may be more buy-in to the quasi-experimental situation if the control group receives the treatment at a later date, rather than not at all.

Compensatory Rivalry and Resentful Demoralization These two threats—*compensatory rivalry by respondents receiving less desirable treatments* and *resentful demoralization of respondents receiving less desirable treatments*—occur when those in the control group resent being in the control group. They do one of two things. "Compensatory rivalry" occurs when the intended control group displays the "John Henry" effect, where the group behaves abnormally well to show that they are better than the treatment group. (This is called the "John Henry" effect in reference to the American folk tale about John Henry, the railroad steel-driver who, in a contest with a new steam-powered drill, worked himself to death.)

Conversely, if the control group knows that it isn't receiving the benefits that the treatment group is receiving, the group may perform abnormally worse than it would have had there been no program or if the group was not aware that it was not getting treatment. This is the threat of the resentful demoralization of respondents receiving a less desirable treatment.

In both cases, the control group performs abnormally, resulting in an inaccurate estimate of the impact of the treatment. If an evaluator were to estimate the impact of the treatment under these circumstances, the evaluator would either over- or underestimate the treatment's impact.

Summary

Showing that the intervention has the intended impact is the essence of internal validity (and of most evaluations). In addition to the above threats, it is important to consider the causal relationship being proposed and ask whether the evidence supports the proposition of the causal relationship. For the relationship to exist, the cause must come before the effect, and the type and form of the relationship should be considered. Even if an evaluation is not endangered by any of the above internal validity threats, the causal relationship between the program and outcomes may not exist.

More than one internal validity threat can operate in a given situation. The evaluator should consider the theoretical effects that each of the threats may have on the causal relationship (gross bias) and try to estimate the net bias that will result from the threats.

Depending on the severity of the threats to internal validity, the causal relationship inferred may or may not be valid. Therefore, evaluators should decide upon a quasi-experimental design that minimizes these threats.

CONSTRUCT VALIDITY

Construct validity pertains to whether theoretical constructs have been operationalized appropriately, the extent to which the relationships observed can be generalized to theoretical constructs, and the extent to which the measures used reflect theoretical constructs. Any relationship between two theoretical constructs ought to be robust, regardless of how the evaluator operationalizes and measures the constructs. Much can be learned from programs that deal with the same theoretical constructs, even if those constructs are not operationalized and measured the same way.

Generally, there are no common definitions of theoretical constructs. These definitions change from study to study, from researcher to researcher, and from context to context. For example, what one person may label an "employability" initiative, another might call a "human capital development" initiative. Evaluators may be hard-pressed when asked for the shared definition of "empowerment," although plenty of programs have the goal of empowerment. Therefore, it is important to be clear about how a construct is defined.

Examining the Theory of Change, one should be able to infer the relationship between constructs that program designers hypothesize. The ToC may have the construct-level relationships explicitly embedded in it, or the relationships may be implicitly embedded.

If one considers initiatives at the construct level, the universe of initiatives that operate in the same space becomes broader. If a construct-level causal relationship holds, then that relationship should exist for other initiatives that pertain to the same constructs. Thinking at the construct-level forces one to get to the essence of a program.

There exist five steps that the evaluator should consider when thinking about construct validity:

1. Think through a **construct's definition** and consider how others have defined the construct and how a layperson would interpret it.

2. Consider whether there are other, **possibly related constructs from which the construct at hand ought to be differentiated.** In these first two steps, the evaluator needs to be clear about what the construct is and equally important, what it is not.

3. Consider how one would **measure the now well-defined construct**, first considering measures that have been used by others. Recycling measures are wise for a number of reasons. Using a measure that others have used enhances the opportunity for direct comparison with other programs. If a measure has been used repeatedly, there may be research on its validity and reliability. For example, common measures, such as using self-reported health status as a measure of health status, have a research history. Evaluators should not waste time reinventing new measures. When possible and appropriate, use predeveloped measures.

4. If possible, **use more than one measure of a construct to assure that only the construct at hand is being measured.** I can't think of a construct that can be measured in one and only one way. For example, if the employment rate is used as the measure of "labor market success" for a program that intends to improve participants' employability, and this is the only measure used, then regardless of what happens with the employment rate, one cannot be sure whether what is being measured reflects participants' employability, or simply a change in labor market conditions. If measures such as skills test results and the ranking of clients to potential employers were added, then we would be more assured that the construct of "employability" rather than shifts in the economy was captured.

5. **Ensure that the measures of the construct used are robust to data collection approaches.** The measurement of the construct should be robust to whether data were collected using phone interviews versus internet surveys, observer information versus self-reported, administrative data versus self-reports.

Threats to Construct Validity

Mono-operation Bias The most serious and most common threat to construct validity is called mono-operation bias, which occurs when only one measure is used to reflect a theoretical construct. For example, the theoretical construct C can be operationalized in many different ways.

Consider micro-finance programs targeted at women, through which women are given credit and loans to assist in small business development. The goal of one such program was to improve the well-being of the family. The ToC is that if women are given small loans, they can develop small businesses, thus increasing the women's income and the family's income, ultimately improving the family's overall well-being. The construct of family well-being can be considered in many different ways—housing stock, health status of family members, access to clean water, education, and so on. If evaluators chose only one way of measuring family well-being—for example, disease rates of family members—they would not be sure that they were measuring family well-being or another construct, such as community health (which could be affected, for instance, by World Health Organization vaccination campaigns). But if they add more measures, such as whether children attend school and levels of domestic violence, they become more assured that they are actually measuring family well-being. Operationalizing the construct in all possible ways allows you to be assured that the construct of family well-being is being affected and not the construct of community health.

Mono-operation bias is more of a threat in program evaluation when examining cause rather than effect. When evaluating programs, the causal construct is usually operationalized one way—by the program itself. Therefore, the program's activities are the operationalization of the causal construct and thus the causal construct is usually operationalized in only one way.

There are usually opportunities to design the measurement of the effect construct so that it has strong construct validity. Many different aspects of this construct can be considered and incorporated into the design of measurement systems.

Mono-method Bias Another threat to construct validity, mono-method bias occurs when the various measurements are collected in the same way. For example, one may be considering different aspects of the construct in a survey and asking respondents to scale the degree to which they agree with a series of statements. Each statement considers different aspects of the construct, but the respondent is given a litany of statements. This type of survey has low construct validity because it is not certain that the respondent actually thought about the question, or whether an answer to one question affects answers to another.

Construct Validity and Literature Reviews Construct validity becomes important when deciding which literature to review. Evaluators review literature for many reasons, including to find support for the hypothesis of a causal relationship between theoretical constructs. If the literature review is restricted to only programs that are exactly like the program being evaluated, then there may be very little literature to review, particularly in the case of pilot programs (where a new idea or approach is being evaluated). However, the relevant literature isn't only studies that have considered similar programs—it is worthwhile to review the literature on the causal relationship between the theoretical constructs.

For example, consider a program that enhances participant's computer skills in order to improve participants' wages. At the operationalized level, the program's bare ToC is:

Computer skills ➜ Wages

At the construct level, the program exemplifies the relationship:

Increase in skills ➜ Labor market outcomes

There will be more literature to examine if one searches at the construct level. The program's focus on computer skills is one representation of increasing skills, and wages are one representation of labor market outcomes. The evaluator would review programs that provide training in other ways, such as programs that aim to increase workers' job retention by boosting their mechanical skills, because such a program pertains to both the causal and effect constructs of interest. Any study involving the theoretical constructs of interest should be reviewed to provide evidence that the theoretical relationship that the designers of the program believe exists has been found to exist in other situations. Whether those studies showing the theoretically posited relationship are likely to apply to the situation at hand is an issue of external validity.

Summary

The evaluator should be able to think at both the operationalized level and the construct level. An evaluator should ask what construct(s) the program represents and what construct is the program trying to affect. Then the evaluator should be able to show that the outcome measures decided upon are reasonable representations of the effect construct. To the extent possible, the ToC should be at construct level. The literature review should be guided by the relationship posited between the causal and effect constructs.

EXTERNAL VALIDITY

External validity deals with the appropriateness of generalizing findings from one study to other settings, places, times, and types of people. Even if a strong causal relationship was shown to exist between a program and outcomes in one instance, that does not mean that this relationship between the program and outcomes will exist if the program is replicated elsewhere. There are many reasons why findings from evaluations may not be generalizable.

Considerations for Determining the External Validity of Studies

Different Time Periods If a relationship is found at one point in time, the relationship may not be found at another point in time because of "period effects." Circumstances, beliefs, politics, culture, and social mores change with time. A study that found an identical program effective some time ago may have questionable external validity simply because of the passage of time.

It is impossible to determine how much time must pass for a study to become obsolete. Sometimes, things are slow to change, and at other times, rapid change can occur. For example, depending on the topic, an evaluator may feel comfortable applying the results from a study done 30 years ago if examining labor market outcomes and both periods were experiencing economic expansion. However, if the economic scene is important, then one might not want to use studies conducted during times of great prosperity if the current period is one of economic decline.

Different Places Studies on a program conducted in one locale may not apply to another locale because they present different challenges. A locale may have a unique history, which makes generalizing findings from it or to it inappropriate. When considering whether past studies on other locales apply to a specific program's locale, it is wise to consider whether the locales have a similar history and present similar challenges. For example, a program that works in an urban area may not be equally as effective in a suburban or rural area—population density may be needed for the program to be effective. Also, programs conducted in one country may show different rates of success in other countries.

When considering the history of a locale, evaluators should consider how systems have evolved over time, and even how the society tends to think about certain issues. For example,

New Englanders are famous for their sense of individualism, and Pittsburgh is known for playing a pivotal role in US labor history. Daponte and Bade conducted a study (2000) comparing the strength of the private food assistance network (such as food pantries and food banks) in Pittsburgh, Pennsylvania, and Bridgeport, Connecticut, concluding that the way in which each locale thought about the problem of domestic hunger and solutions to it influenced how each city's private food assistance network evolved. Pittsburgh's response to domestic hunger was much stronger than that found in Bridgeport. Thus, we would not expect studies on domestic hunger in Pittsburgh to apply equally well to Connecticut, and perhaps such differences would weaken the external validity of studies conducted on programs in areas that have a strong sense of class consciousness to any area where individualistic responses are paramount.

Different Populations Study populations can differ from a program's population in observable and unobservable ways. Observable differences can be demographic characteristics, such as age, gender, race or ethnicity, educational attainment, and socioeconomic status. Studies done on males may not apply equally well to females, and studies done on a population with low educational attainment may not apply equally well to a population with high educational attainment. Unobservable differences can include cultural differences and differences in motivation.

Summary

When reviewing literature and applying the results of studies to the program population at hand, evaluators should consider to what degree, if any, the findings from an evaluation can be generalized. The evaluator should reflect on these questions:

- Has a length of time passed that might make the study weak in external validity?
- Was the study done on a specific or a broad population?
- Were analyses done separately on subpopulations? If so, was the relationship found consistent among subpopulations?
- In what setting was the program operating? Is there a difference between that setting and the one currently being studied?
- Is there anything unique about the intervention being reviewed that might set it apart from other attempts at the same intervention? For example, the intervention may have had uniquely trained staff or headed by a director who had unique experience or community connections.

If the answer to these questions suggests that there is no reason, *a priori*, to suspect that the findings may not have external validity, then it could be reasonable to rely on prior results.

While conducting an evaluation, to increase its external validity, the evaluator would examine an intervention's impact not only on the entire population but on subpopulations.

For example, the evaluator could determine the extent to which the intervention has a similar impact on people of different educational levels, different ages, different ethnicities, different genders, and/or who live in different areas. If no differences appear by subcategory, then the evaluator would conclude that the intervention's effects are relatively robust across populations. If there appear to be differences, though, then the evaluator would doubt whether the results are externally valid across times, settings, and populations.

CONCLUSIONS

All four types of validity speak to the strength of studies and their theoretical usefulness. The best evaluations take into account threats to validity and are structured to minimize them. The next chapter discusses which quasi-experimental designs to use in order to maximize the validity of an evaluation.

KEY TERMS

- compensatory equalization
- compensatory rivalry
- construct validity
- diffusion of a treatment
- external validity
- fishing
- internal validity
- measurement error
- mono-method bias
- mono-operation bias
- negatively covary
- observable differences
- period effects
- positively covary
- resentful demoralization
- small sample size
- statistical conclusion validity
- threat of history
- threat of instrumentation
- threat of maturation
- threat of mortality
- threat of selection
- threat of statistical regression
- threat of testing
- threats to validity
- type I error
- type II error
- validity

DISCUSSION QUESTIONS

1. In general, why is internal validity the most important type in evaluation studies?
2. Select any completed evaluation and consider the four types of validity. Determine the degree to which the evaluation research has the four types of validity. What threats to validity did the authors address? Which remain unaddressed? Do you think that the intervention would have the same impact in other settings? If you do not have an evaluation in mind here are some evaluations to consider in the public health arena:

a. Hamra, Ghassan, Leah H. Schinasi, and D. Alex Quistberg. 2020. "Motor Vehicle Crashes Involving a Bicycle Before and After Introduction of a Bike Share Program in Philadelphia, Pennsylvania, 2010–2018." *American Journal of Public Health* 110, pp. 863–867.
b. Komisarow, Sarah and Emily L. Pakhtigian. 2021. "The Effect of Coal-Fired Power Plant Closures on Emergency Department Visits for Asthma-Related Conditions Among 0- to 4-Year-Old Children in Chicago, 2009–2017." *American Journal of Public Health* 111, pp. 881–889.
c. Cook, Amanda, Gregory Leung, and Rhet A. Smith. 2020. "Marijuana Decriminalization, Medical Marijuana Laws, and Fatal Traffic Crashes in US Cities, 2010–2017." *American Journal of Public Health* 110, pp. 363–369.

CHAPTER 6

ATTRIBUTING OUTCOMES TO THE PROGRAM: QUASI-EXPERIMENTAL DESIGN

LEARNING OBJECTIVES

After reading this chapter, you should be able to

- Understand the needs and limitations of different quasi-experimental designs
- Be able to diagram quasi-experimental designs
- Be able to determine and apply the most appropriate quasi-experimental design for the initiative being examined

Evaluation Essentials: Methods for Conducting Sound Evaluation Research, Second Edition.
Beth Osborne DaPonte.
© 2025 John Wiley & Sons, Inc. Published 2025 by John Wiley & Sons, Inc.

INTRODUCTION

The ultimate goal of a program or intervention is to cause positive change. How can we determine that it was the initiative that caused the change? Attributing changes to the intervention presents the ultimate challenge to evaluators.

A quasi-experimental design gives evaluators a framework to analyze the outcomes relevant to the initiative (from the Program Logic Model). The quasi-experimental design selected determines the timing and utility of the outcome observations collected for the attribution of change.

One should not confuse quasi-experimental design with the quantitative analysis of data, as even qualitative data analysis requires that the structure of data collection ultimately allows for causal attribution. Although one can use quantitative methods to statistically show the level and statistical significance of the change, quasi-experimental design is used to determine the timing and structure of data collection and analysis, thus should be used when collecting qualitative as well as quantitative data.

Quasi-experimental design informs the question of what we would have expected to occur in the treatment (also known as the program or intervention) group without the intervention. This chapter introduces and discusses a number of quasi-experimental designs that were put forth by Cook and Campbell (1979), starting with the simplest cases where causation cannot be shown to more complex and robust designs. The design implemented in evaluating a given intervention will be based on a decision that weighs the different types of validity and the different threats to each of the validity types. The design selected should make the best use of the situation at hand and minimize the most serious threats to validity.

QUASI-EXPERIMENTAL NOTATION

To display the quasi-experimental designs, we use Cook and Campbell's notation. "O" indicates an observation (or outcome measure) and "X" indicates the treatment (also known as intervention or program). Numerical subscripts indicate the first, second, third (and so on) observations, and lettered subscripts indicate a different type of observation or treatment. The design should be read from left to right, and rows separated by dotted lines indicate nonequivalent groups—groups from different populations that were not created by randomization. Observations can occur before treatment and/or after treatment.

Here, we continue Cook and Campbell's tradition of naming the designs, although, in practice, evaluators usually communicate about the designs by sketching out the design, not by the formal name of the design.

Sketching out the chosen design clarifies which design the evaluation will use as well as the threats to validity that the design does and does not address. Knowing the designs and their associated threats to validity are part of the set of tools evaluators bring to the table. Evaluators should be well versed in quasi-experimental design.

The observations of the quasi-experimental design are the outcomes specified in the PLM. The outcome measures inform what one will observe and keep track of, and the quasi-experimental design informs how the outcomes will be used to show that the change in the outcome is attributable to the program. The outcome measures should be operationalizations of the initiative's goals.

An evaluator may use more than one quasi-experimental design when evaluating a program, although often, the same design is used with different outcomes being examined. However, there can be situations where certain outcomes may be particularly vulnerable to a specific threat to validity. We start by considering designs that typically cannot be used to prove a causal relationship between the program and its outcomes.

FREQUENTLY USED DESIGNS THAT DO NOT SHOW CAUSATION

One-Group Posttest-Only

In this design (Cook and Campbell, 1979, p. 96), only the outcomes of the treatment group are examined and only at one point in time—after the program (see Figure 6.1). No pretreatment measure is used. Preprogram measures may be unavailable—they may not have been collected from participants and/or there are no archival data that would reflect pretreatment levels of the outcome measures. This design never examines the outcomes of nonparticipants.

With respect to conclusions that can be drawn from the design, no comment can be made on the change that occurred to the treatment group because pretreatment information about the group is unknown. Also, because the design lacks a comparison group, one cannot say that the treatment group had a posttreatment outcome level that differed from a no-treatment similar comparison group at the same point in time.

All threats to internal validity (except for testing) apply to this design. Causation cannot be shown because one cannot even say that a change in the outcome occurred. Even if the posttest shows that the treatment group had a "good outcome," one doesn't know whether the outcome changed over time or even the level of the "outcome" for a comparable group of people.

This design should never be used. No change can be shown to have occurred. Unfortunately, the use of this design is not uncommon. I have seen many programs use this design in situations where data collection was an afterthought. The programs believe that if they can show that their participants have "good" outcomes, then the programs must have been successful. This thinking is erroneous because not only does this design not indicate that any change occurred, it cannot show that the program caused the change to occur.

$$X \quad O_1$$

FIGURE 6.1. *One-Group Posttest-Only.*

Source: Cook and Campbell (1979) / Houghton Mifflin Harcourt Company

Posttest-Only with Nonequivalent Groups

A variation on the prior design (Figure 6.2) adds a control group which is technically known as a "nonequivalent" group. The control group is not drawn from the same population as the treatment group. The two groups differ in ways that are sometimes observable (e.g., demographic traits) and sometimes non-observable (such as motivation or willingness to participate in the program).

For example, take two people who look identical with respect to every observable characteristic imaginable—they live in the same neighborhood, are the same age, are of the same race and/or ethnicity, speak the same language, live in the same family structure, have the same number of children, same socioeconomic status, same education, and so on. These two people can still differ in their propensity to participate in the program; this difference is an unobservable characteristic. So, even when comparing the treatment and control groups, you are comparing two nonequivalent groups.

In this posttest-only design, illustrated in Cook and Campbell (p. 98), the evaluator does not know how these groups differed with respect to their pretreatment observation. Although nearly all threats to validity apply, selection presents the most severe threat to this design. The groups could have differed in terms of their outcome measures prior to the program's start or their rate of change in the outcome measure may have differed, but with this design, the evaluator would not have pretreatment outcome levels to determine the degree to which the groups differed *a priori* on the outcome measures.

Consider a program that provides incentives for low-income people to save for certain expenses, such as education and purchasing a first home. Those most likely to save may be more likely to participate in the program. Even if the outcome measure of the amount of money saved was shown to be higher among program participants than nonparticipants, the evaluator can't conclude that the program caused that change—because of the threat of selection. Those who participate in the program may have been more inclined to save in the first place. Therefore, a causal statement should not be made.

Sometimes, a variation of this design is used where, rather than considering one treatment group as compared to a control group, the treatment instead is provided in varying intensities (Figure 6.3). The design only makes sense when it is expected that different intensities of the treatment would yield proportionately different outcomes—the degree of change in the outcome measure would depend on the treatment's intensity. The subscripts in this case symbolize a different intensity of the intervention.

$$X \quad O_1$$
$$\text{-----------}$$
$$O_1$$

FIGURE 6.2. *Posttest Only with One Nonequivalent Group.*

Source: Cook and Campbell (1979) / Houghton Mifflin Harcourt Company

$$X_A \quad O_1$$
$$X_B \quad O_1$$
$$X_C \quad O_1$$
$$X_D \quad O_1$$

FIGURE 6.3. *Posttest Only with Many Nonequivalent Groups.*

Source: Cook and Campbell (1979) / Houghton Mifflin Harcourt Company

In this design, whether causation can be shown depends on how participants were assigned to each of the groups receiving varying intensities of treatment. If the participants themselves chose the intensity and the four groups were nonrandomly created, then causation cannot be shown because of the threat of selection.

However, if participants were entered into the program and then program administrators **randomly assigned** participants to one of the categories of intensity of treatment, then evaluators may be able to make a credible statement along the lines of "among people who desire the program, when the program is provided in a more intense manner, the participants experience a greater change in their outcomes than they do when the program is provided less intensely." For this statement to have any credibility, though, random assignment must have occurred after participants availed themselves of some form of the program. The design is not valid when participants can select the intensity of treatment.

Even without random assignment intentionally occurring, the design may be considered when a program is offered at many sites and the sites implement the program with different intensities. The different intensities could arise unintentionally but provide an evaluation opportunity. For example, take a program that offered both financial assistance and case management, intended to be provided in 10 meetings per client over a one-year period. One site implemented the program as intended. Another site had trouble recruiting case workers so offered only 4 sessions per client and met with them only quarterly. The outcomes could be examined because the two sites essentially offered the program with a different intensity. What occurred was the opportunity for a "natural experiment."

Participants' Pretest–Posttest

Another frequently used design that does not allow for causation to be deduced compares a single pretest (or pretreatment) measure with a single posttest (or posttreatment) measure of only the treatment group (Figure 6.4). There is no control group. Often, programs do not have access to a reasonable control group.

$$O_1 \quad X \quad O_2$$

FIGURE 6.4. *Only Participants, Pretest–Posttest.*

Source: Cook and Campbell (1979) / Houghton Mifflin Harcourt Company

In this design, the program records participants' outcome measure(s) at the time of entry into the program and again after the program's termination. If participants' outcome measures improved, then the program is assumed to have been successful and to have been the reason for the improvement.

This design is vulnerable to many internal validity threats. For example, the threat of maturation could exist—participants may have been on a trajectory where their outcomes would have improved given time, even without the intervention.

If the pretest and posttest measures used a "test" repeatedly, the design would be vulnerable to the threat of testing—scores changed because of familiarity with the test. The lack of a control group does not allow one to infer the degree to which the measure has increased because of testing.

The threat of history would pertain if an event occurred outside of the program that would have influenced the participants' outcome measures. The threat of statistical regression could appear with this design if the participants were chosen from either tail of a distribution and the regression toward the mean was considered an improvement.

DESIGNS THAT GENERALLY PERMIT CAUSAL INFERENCES

Untreated Control Group Design with Pretest and Posttest

The most basic design that permits causal inference includes both a treatment and a control group and two observations—one pretreatment and one posttreatment (Figure 6.5). The first observation, O_1, refers to the same point in time in both the treatment and control groups, and O_2 refers to a later date.

The first observation, which occurs before the treatment group receives the program's benefits or participates in the program, is recorded to determine the degree to which the treatment and control groups vary in the outcome even before starting the program. If the pretreatment measures are identical or nearly so, despite nonequivalence between the treatment and control groups, an evaluator would feel more comfortable using the "control group" as a control or counterfactual.

The timing of the second observation is critically important. Because the design only examines the observations at two points in time, there is scant evidence to prove causation. The challenge is to collect the second observation when the program has had its effect. But if the program produces a lagged effect and the second observation is collected too early to see an effect, the program will appear ineffective even if eventually it has a substantial impact on participants at a later point in time.

```
        O₁    X    O₂
        - - - - - - - -
        O₁         O₂
```

FIGURE 6.5. *Untreated Control Group with Pretest and Posttest.*

Source: Cook and Campbell (1979) / Houghton Mifflin Harcourt Company

The converse is also true. If the program's effects are only short-lived and dissipate over time, collecting the second observation too early will make the program seem effective, when in fact it is only temporarily effective and collecting it too late will lead one to conclude that the program had no effect, when the program actually only had a temporary effect.

For example, if one were examining weight-loss programs and the second observation was collected at the time of the program's completion, evaluators may find that program participants lost 10 percent of their body weight while nonparticipants did not lose any weight—and conclude that the program was effective. However, if the second observation was based on weight one year after the program's completion, evaluators may instead find no difference between participants and nonparticipants. That is, even though the program's true effect was temporary weight loss, collecting the data too early made the program look more effective than it was and collecting the data too late makes the program appear that it had neither a short-term nor a long-term effect on weight loss.

Or consider a program where a funder provided nonprofit organizations a "capitalization" grant that allowed the nonprofit to catch-up on debts and address structural financial issues. The program may seem effective in the short term if the outcomes involve examining the organizations' usage of their lines of credit. But in the long term, say that many of the organizations did not address their leadership issues and reverted back to their old ways of taking on too much debt. Depending on the timing of the second observation, one would come to different conclusions about the program's effectiveness.

Because the posttest is only a single data point, the evaluator cannot determine the function that the effect may take. Some effects may cause a sudden one-time change after which participants revert back to their typical growth pattern (a change in intercept). Another effect may be a change in the growth rate (a change in slope). With only two data points, the evaluator cannot distinguish which type of effect occurred—and also cannot comment on whether the effect is likely to persist (a continuous effect) or whether participants are likely to return to their pre-treatment levels (noncontinuous effect).

To some degree, how one interprets the change in outcomes from this design depends on the particular pattern of outcomes. There are four patterns to consider.

Pattern 1 (Figure 6.6). Consider a situation where the control group experienced no change between pretest and posttest in its outcome measures—that is, for the control group, $O_1 = O_2$. The treatment group shows an increase in its outcome, where $O_2 > O_1$.

If the control group is comparable to the treatment group, then you would assume that observing no change in the control group's outcome(s) supports the argument that the threats

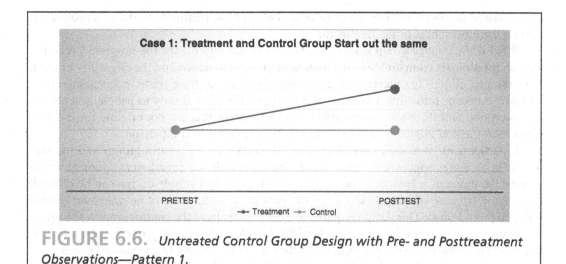

FIGURE 6.6. *Untreated Control Group Design with Pre- and Posttreatment Observations—Pattern 1.*

Source: Cook and Campbell (1979) / Houghton Mifflin Harcourt Company

of maturation and testing do not apply. You would interpret the stability of the control group's observations as evidence that natural growth would have caused no change in the treatment group's observations and also that repeating the test had no effect on test scores. With respect to maturation, you would really want to know more about the group's rate of growth prior to the treatment group's participation in the program, by examining more pretreatment observations of both groups.

If the observations were collected differently between the treatment and control groups, you would not be able to explain the change in the observations of the treatment as an effect of instrumentation because the control group's observations were also exposed to this threat. Also, if there was no unique "historical" event that would have contaminated either one of the groups, then the threat of history also would not apply. (If there was a "historical" event that might have caused a change, the event would have impacted both the treatment and control groups' observations.)

Selection could be a threat depending on exactly how the groups were created. If they were created voluntarily, then the treatment group presumably wanted the intervention more than the control group. The control group may have felt no need for the treatment or may have received the treatment elsewhere. The fundamental difference between the groups—their desire to receive the treatment—could correlate with the levels of the second observation.

On the other hand, the control group may have had no awareness of the treatment. If the members of the treatment group were aware of the treatment and the members of the control group were unaware of it, you need to consider whether the reasons that the two groups differ in their awareness could affect any difference in their outcomes. If treatment awareness is correlated with the outcome measure, then some of the differences of the posttreatment outcome measures may be attributable to the sorting of people into treatment and control groups based not only on the respective desirability of the treatment to the two groups but also on their awareness of the treatment.

What if the control group is composed of those not eligible for the program? Whether the control group is comparable to the treatment group will depend on the eligibility criteria. For example, eligibility criteria such as income are likely to have some independent effect on many outcome measures. However, if the program is offered only to people in a certain neighborhood and there are comparable geographic areas that are not eligible for the program, then the non-eligible control group may be a reasonable comparison.

If participants were randomly assigned to the treatment or control groups and the pretreatment measures appeared similar between the groups, then the random assignment would remove the threat of selection. Random assignment using this simple design can be difficult to structure because of ethical issues and the general unwillingness of an untreated control group to provide data. This design requires two data points from the control group—the group that never receives any of the program's benefits. People in the control group may be reluctant to provide information to the program when they are not receiving the potential benefits.

It may be unethical to withhold benefits from the control group and yet collect information from them. If the program is clearly beneficial or has a high likelihood of being so, ethical limitations may prevent evaluators from even having a control group. I have found that many nonprofits are understandably reluctant to form no-treatment control groups for evaluation purposes. The delayed treatment design, shown below, overcomes these ethical issues in most cases.

Pattern 2 In another pattern that can emerge, the treatment group has a higher pretest score than the control group, and the treatment group shows a greater increase in outcome between the first and second observations than the control group (Figure 6.7). The risk here is interpreting this pattern as evidence that the treatment was effective.

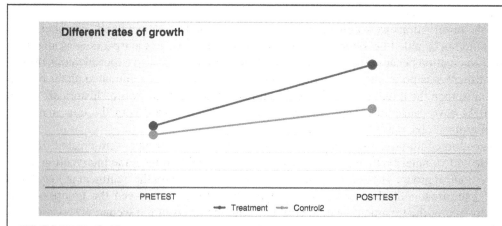

FIGURE 6.7. *Untreated Control Group Design with Pre- and Posttreatment Observations—Pattern 2.*

Source: Cook and Campbell (1979) / Houghton Mifflin Harcourt Company

This pattern is very common when people self-select the treatment group. The issue is the degree to which the groups were nonequivalent at the start in terms of their rates of growth or maturation. That is, a selection-maturation effect, where those who selected themselves for the program would have had a higher rate of growth even in the program's absence, may make it appear that the program is effective when it may not be.

One example of this could be when comparing the test scores of children going to magnet versus nonmagnet schools. It may seem that the magnet school is producing a steeper rise in knowledge. However, it may be that parents who are in the know about educational opportunities and take advantage of them have children who score better on tests, or who take education more seriously. It may be that the magnet school has no effect other than sorting children on the basis of parents' awareness of better educational opportunities for their children.

Consider a program that encourages people to save. Those who want the program may have saved just a small amount more than those who do not participate in the program. The program may have been the impetus to increase savings even more amongst those who would have saved anyway. The difference between the groups' second observations is an effect not only of the pre-treatment difference but also in the rates of growth of their savings. This design cannot determine the degree to which (if any) the program changed the rate of savings of the treatment group.

Pattern 3 Another pattern can occur when the control group's pretest score exceeds that of the treatment group, and the control group shows no change in scores between the two time periods although the treatment group experienced a positive increase in scores (Figure 6.8). This result is likely when there is an incentive for the treatment group's performance to improve. If such an incentive exists and is not part of the program, then the improvement should not be confused with true program effectiveness.

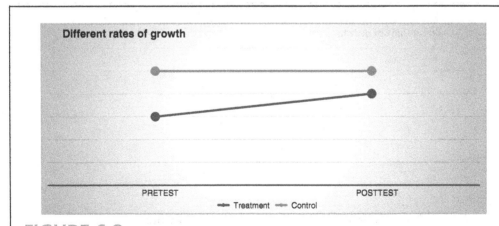

FIGURE 6.8. *Untreated Control Group Design with Pre- and Posttreatment Observations—Pattern 3.*

Source: Cook and Campbell (1979) / Houghton Mifflin Harcourt Company

Pattern 3 could also result when there is a "ceiling" on a test. It could be that the control group did not show an improvement on the test because it is not possible to show this based on the way the outcome is measured. For example, if the top income category is $100,000 and over, and the control group's mean income rose from $105,000 to $115,000 and the treatment group's income rose from $80,000 to $90,000, although there was a $10,000 real increase in both groups, the data would not show the control group's increase because of ceiling effects. The treatment group, with its lower income, would be able to show changes because most people in it had not yet reached the ceiling of the data collection instrument.

Statistical regression is another threat to internal validity to be considered when using this design. If the treatment group was composed of people who did particularly poorly on a pretest, it is likely that their scores would have regressed to the mean in any case. The possibility of statistical regression should be taken seriously. Programs are often only offered to those who appear in need of them, and identifying true need can be difficult. This is a serious threat, because often programs are offered only to those who appear in need of them, and some sort of pretest is used to determine that need.

However, in the absence of there being ceiling effects, this design rules out the threat of selection-maturation. Usually, people who score low on the pretest are likely to have slower outcome growth rates than those who have higher pretest scores. If between the first and second observations, the initially low-scoring treatment group shows a higher rate of growth than the higher-scoring control group, it is likely that the treatment was so successful that the treatment group overcame the expectation that it would have been even further behind the control group in the posttest.

Pattern 4 This pattern is similar to the third pattern, but at posttest, the treatment group scores even higher than the control group (Figure 6.9). This outcome is the most desirable.

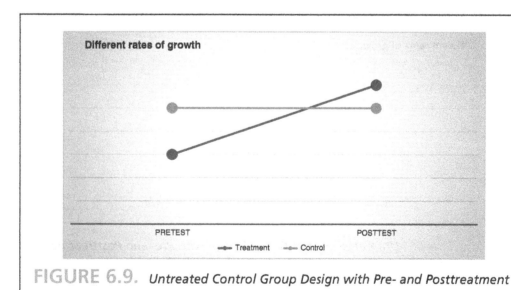

FIGURE 6.9. *Untreated Control Group Design with Pre- and Posttreatment Observations—Pattern 4.*

Source: Cook and Campbell (1979) / Houghton Mifflin Harcourt Company

In such a case, the program was offered to those who did not score as well in the pretest and then had better outcomes than the untreated control group.

Because the second observation is even higher than that of the control group, a ceiling effect would not apply. Although a ceiling effect can explain why a low-scoring pretest group could score as high as the higher-scoring group, it cannot explain the crossover in scores between the two groups.

Also, the threat of regression becomes less likely because of the crossover. This threat, even if very powerful, would cause the treatment group to have scores more similar to those of the control group. However, the threat of regression could not explain a treatment group scoring higher than the control group.

The crossover in the level of the outcome measure(s) also suggests that the threat of selection-maturation does not apply. It is unlikely that the initially low-scoring treatment group would suddenly develop a higher rate of improvement in outcomes than the treatment group.

If the design yields this crossover, the causal statements that derive may seem relatively robust. Using this design in the hopes of achieving this result is a risky strategy. The evaluator is better off using a stronger design when possible.

Delayed Treatment Control Group

I have found that the most useful, palatable, and parsimonious design is one where the control group eventually receives the treatment, but at a date later than the treatment group. This design (Figure 6.10) is sometimes known as the switching replications design. Because it is so informative, parsimonious, and equitable, this is my favorite design.

In this design, three data points are collected from the early treatment group and three from the control group, which is the delayed treatment group. If you consider only the O_1 and O_2 observations, then the design reduces down to the previous design. That is, O_2 of the delayed group provides information about what O_2 of the early group would have been had the group not received the treatment. Adding a third observation to the early treatment group provides some, albeit limited, information on how long-lasting the treatment's effects may be.

Between Times 2 and 3, the delayed group finally receives the treatment. That both groups receive the treatment allays some of the ethical concerns regarding no-treatment control groups. The availability of the delayed treatment makes this design palatable to Institutional Review Boards (IRBs) which are the committees in academic settings that

$$O_1 \quad X \quad O_2 \quad \quad O_3$$
$$\text{-----------------}$$
$$O_1 \quad \quad O_2 \quad X \quad O_3$$

FIGURE 6.10. *Delayed Treatment Control Group Design.*

review research designs for ethical issues. (In US universities, social science research usually needs IRB approval before it can proceed. Nonprofits and funders usually do not have formal IRBs, though they are equally concerned about potential ethical violations that research designs may present. There exist IRBs for hire that nonacademic organizations can use if they want the evaluation research to have such approval.)

With this design, everybody eventually receives the treatment. The only thing that is being withheld is the timing of the treatment, which may not be an issue at all if the program typically has a waiting list of people who desire the treatment.

The key here is how one allocates participants to the early versus the late treatment groups. If the allocation is done randomly, then the groups should be statistically equivalent. However, if the allocation is done on a first-come, first-serve basis, then the early and delayed treatment groups could differ in unobservable ways. That is, one might argue that the early treatment group is comprised of those more motivated to receive the treatment's benefits than participants in the delayed treatment group, and thus the groups' outcomes may be noncomparable.

The ideal way to carry out this design is for a program first to create a list of everyone interested in participating in the program. Neither group will start the program until this list is compiled. Typically, program administrators would saturate the target population with messages about the program's availability, and then give potential participants time to enroll in the program. When people first contact the program, the staff explains to them that the program will be offered at one of two times and assignment to groups is determined randomly. Data from potential participants are collected when the program screens potential participants using the program's eligibility criteria. Only those found eligible for the program are included on this list. The screening data of the eligible participants should comprise O_1. The outcome(s) of interest should be included in the screening.

Second, everyone on the entire list is divided randomly into two groups—the early and the delayed treatment groups, and each group is informed when it will receive the treatment. The early treatment group goes through the program. When their posttreatment outcome is first measured (O_2), the second pretreatment outcome is measured for the delayed treatment group (O_2). The evaluator should note if there are people who decline to be measured or dropout of the delayed treatment group because they no longer need the program. If possible, the evaluator should try to collect second and third observations from people who dropped out of the program. Such cases are important because they may suggest that the program was not necessary for participants to experience a change in outcome.

The third data point represents, for the early group, a second posttreatment data point and, for the delayed group, the first posttreatment data point. The O_2–O_3 change for the delayed group may mimic the early group's O_1–O_2 change. If it does, then you would place more credence on the causal statement that the program produced the effect, because the same relationship was observed in both groups at two different time periods. Thus, the threat of history seems unlikely. Figure 6.11 demonstrates possible results from the design.

In this fictional example, the early treatment group saw its outcome increase from 1 to 4 between the screening and the first posttreatment measure. During that period, the delayed-treatment control group saw the outcome increase from 1 to 1.25. One might

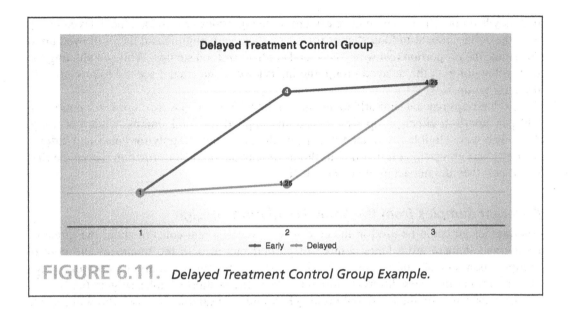

FIGURE 6.11. *Delayed Treatment Control Group Example.*

conclude that going through the program accounted for 2.75-point increase in the outcome measures. The delayed treatment group sees its outcome increase from 1.25 to 4.25 when it experiences the program. However, during the second and third observations, the early group's outcome measure increased by .25. Thus, for the delayed treatment group, 2.75 points of the increase was associated with the program, while .25 points of the increase was not associated with the increase—would have occurred anyway. Both groups experienced an increase in the outcome of .25 in each period.

This design was used by Daponte, Sanders, and Taylor (1999) in an experiment conducted on whether informing people of the exact dollar amount for which they are eligible in food stamp benefits affects their food stamp participation rates. To summarize, they examined enrollment in the SNAP/food stamp program who were comparably poor and lived in the Pittsburgh, Pennsylvania, metropolitan area, were not using SNAP/food stamps in the fall of 1993, and were given information about the program. The researchers randomly divided the sample into two treatment groups—early and delayed. The early group was contacted between January and March 1994 and asked whether they would be willing to be screened for food stamp eligibility if the researchers gave them a grocery store credit. Nearly all persons contacted agreed to be in this quasi-experiment. The interviewer screened the participant for food stamp eligibility and informed the participant of the exact dollar amount they would receive in benefits if they enrolled in the program. Six weeks later, in March, the participants were contacted again for follow-up and asked whether they applied for benefits and if not, why not.

When the follow-up of the early group occurred, the delayed group was screened to determine whether they had started to receive food stamp benefits since the fall, and all said that they had not. Then, as with the early group, the interviewer provided the delayed group with the dollar amount in food stamps for which they were eligible and then followed up to determine the proportion that went ahead and applied for food stamps. While conducting the first follow-up with the delayed group, the interviewer conducted a second follow-up with the early group.

Both groups reacted similarly to the information. Those who were eligible for more than $40 per month in either group went ahead and applied for food stamps, while generally, those who were eligible for under $40 per month tended not to apply for benefits. Findings from the first group suggest that if households did not act on the information within the first six weeks, they did not act on it at a later date.

Different Samples from the Same Populations Design

Another design could be used in the case when there is a real concern about the threat of testing and if there are a large number of participants in both the treatment and control groups. Then, one should consider drawing from the treatment group and control groups pretest samples that have different individuals from the posttest samples (Figure 6.12).

Considering only the treatment group, O_1 would be a sample of those who will receive the treatment. O_2 would be a different sample, and anyone who was in the first sample would be ineligible to be in the second sample. In statistical terms, this is called sampling without replacement. A similar process would be used to draw the two samples for the control group.

The vertical line after the first observation represents that the samples of the first and second observations are drawn from the same population (treatment or control) but are from different units.

For example, perhaps you want to learn whether an advertising blitz changes people's perceptions of a political candidate. The fear is that once people have been asked about the candidate, their perceptions of the candidate might change by the second time they are asked, simply because they became more aware of the candidate after the first observation (the threat of testing). So, rather than follow the same people over time, you would instead derive the observations from independent samples.

For the treatment group, the first observation derives from responses from a randomly chosen sample of people who will be targets of the advertising campaign. The second observation, collected after the completion of the advertising blitz, derives from a sample of people

$$O_1 \mid X \quad O_2$$
$$O_1 \mid \quad\quad O_2$$

FIGURE 6.12. *Different Samples from Same Populations Design.*

Source: Cook and Campbell (1979) / Houghton Mifflin Harcourt Company

who were targets but did not provide data for the first observation. Similarly, for the control group, the first observation derives from survey responses from a population that the blitz will not target (perhaps because they do not reside in the geographic area that the blitz focused upon), and the second observation occurs after the blitz, but from a different sample of non-targeted people. By structuring observations in this way, this design addresses the threat of testing. An individual can only provide information for exactly one of the responses; no one is asked the same set of questions twice.

This design is particularly useful when simply asking the questions is likely to influence the outcome. Thus, it is particularly applicable to the arts. For example, evaluators might expect a museum exhibit to change one's thoughts on an issue. To show this, you would derive the pre-exhibit observation from a randomly drawn sample of people and a post-exhibit observation from a different sample. These samples represent the population from which they are drawn, within statistical sampling error.

If you only had these two data points, even if the exhibit visitors showed a change, the statement would be limited to "People who see the exhibit change their perspective on this issue more than those who have not seen the exhibit." This statement is quite limited because of selection issues—a select group has seen the exhibit. Those who intended to see the exhibit might have been more open to changing their perspective on the issue (selection). Further, this finding may have little generalizability because of the unique character of the treatment group. That is, although the design addresses the threat of testing, it does not address the threat of selection or the likelihood of low external validity in this example, depending on the population sampled.

When testing poses a serious threat to internal validity, this design can strengthen the evaluation research, depending on the sample size. However, this design does not address the threat of selection.

Nonequivalent Observations Drawn from One Group

A less common design used when a control group may not be possible to obtain is a design that uses the same units for the treatment group *and* the control group (Figure 6.13). The essence of this design is that it conducts measurements on only a single group of persons (note that there is no dashed line between the treatment and control groups). The pretest

$$O_{1A} \quad X \quad O_{2A}$$
$$O_{1B} \quad \quad O_{2B}$$

FIGURE 6.13. *Nonequivalent Observations Drawn from One Group Design.*

Source: Cook and Campbell (1979) / Houghton Mifflin Harcourt Company

measures are of two different but related constructs. The intervention is intended to affect only one of the constructs.

In this design, the intervention is intended to affect only the indicator of the A construct and not the indicator of the B construct. The change in B observations acts as the control. However, if A and B are related, because of spillover effects within the same units, it is difficult to imagine an intervention that affects only A and not B. This aspect of the design makes it quite weak.

This design might be used for a tutoring program intended to teach people one subject, but not the other. For example, consider a mathematics tutoring program. O_{1A} might be mathematics preprogram test scores and O_{1B} might represent verbal preprogram test scores. If the program is effective, one would expect an increase in the mathematics scores but not the verbal scores. But if the tutoring program taught students studying skills while teaching them math, then the program could have substantial spillover effects. The change in the A observations would reflect the contribution of tutoring math as well as increased studying skills, while the change in the B observations would only reflect the change in studying skills. For example, say that a group of students increased their math scores from the 30th percentile to the 45th percentile, but the language arts skills increased from the 35th percentile to the 40th percentile. The math tutoring program itself may be responsible for a 10 percentage point increase in the percentile of the student's math performance and the other 5 percentage point increase could be due to the improvement in general study skills.

The strength of this design comes from its use of the same people in both the treatment and control groups. Its weakness derives from the challenge of conceptualizing two observations that are closely related—but the intervention would only affect one of the measures.

Equivalent Groups Using Switched Measures

Related to the previous two designs is the one that exploits the existence of two measures that both sufficiently measure the outcome construct. The benefit of this design is that both groups receive the treatment concurrently and that it avoids the threat of testing.

This design divides the total group of people who receive the treatment into two subgroups (I and II). Figure 6.14 shows that because all observations come from the treated group, the design's schematic does not have a dashed line between the groups. The first observation of subgroup I is the outcome measure A, and the first subgroup's second

$$O_{1A} \quad X \quad O_{2B}$$

$$O_{1B} \quad X \quad O_{2A}$$

FIGURE 6.14. *Equivalent Groups Using Switched Measures Design.*

TABLE 6.1. Yad Vashem Holocaust Museum Evaluation Design.

Grand survey	Survey I	Survey II
Demographic and background questions	Demographic and background questions	Demographic and background questions
Holocaust knowledge and views questions, set A	Holocaust knowledge and views questions, set A	
Holocaust knowledge and views questions, set B		Holocaust knowledge and views questions, set B

Source: Bickman and Hamner. 1998.

observation is of the outcome measure B. For the second group, B is the first measure and A is the second.

For this design to be useful, the two subgroups must be statistically similar. If people are randomly assigned to one of the two subgroups, then this assumption is valid. Also, one must assume that the A measures are reasonable proxies for the B measures. Another assumption is that the pretreatment measures of A and B would not have changed without the treatment. If these assumptions are valid, then the design reduces to two applications of the pretest–posttest design, but with the testing threat largely avoided.

Bickman and Hamner (1998) used this design to study the impact of Yad Vashem Holocaust Museum on visitors. They designed a survey with three parts (Table 6.1). One section of the survey measured a respondent's demographics and background information. The second and third sections contain a series of questions that asked sets of questions about one's knowledge and views of the Holocaust.

Those questions were divided into two parts. Part A measured knowledge and views, as did Part B. However, Part B did not contain any of the questions from Part A of the survey. That is, from the grand survey, two different surveys were created that ostensibly measured the same construct—one's knowledge and views of the Holocaust.

Testing was a very real concern. The authors feared that if respondents were asked identical questions twice, their knowledge and views about the exact issues could have changed because having seen the questions the first time would have influenced their response if asked the same questions again.

Before entering the museum, a person randomly received either survey I or II. Upon exit from the museum, the respondent is given the other survey. Using this design, responses from both surveys from both groups are used to measure the short-term impact of the museum on visitors.

If evaluating the impact of any intervention where asking pretest questions could alert people to what they should pay attention to, then this design should be considered. This is especially the case for museums, concerts, expeditions, and other experiences.

Cohort Designs

A **cohort** is defined as a group that experienced the same event at the same time. One example is birth cohorts, whose members were all born within the same time period (such as within a given year). Alternatively, a cohort could be a group of people who enter a graduate program at the same time. These people are likely to have been born in different years, and perhaps in different decades, yet they all experienced the beginning of their graduate education simultaneously. One could also think of a cohort of organizations that formed in the same year. The concept of cohorts can also apply to program participants, where a cohort can be a group of people who enter a program at the same time.

The concept of a cohort can be used for evaluation purposes. It is often reasonable to assume that a cohort differs only in minor ways from cohorts that immediately precede or follow the cohort. When a treatment is provided to one cohort, assuming that contiguous cohorts would otherwise appear similar, the treatment's effects can be inferred by examining the differences in outcomes between the contiguous cohorts. Figure 6.15 shows the most basic of cohort designs. Key with this design is that the pretest and posttest measures of the different cohorts are collected at different dates. A solid, squiggly line distinguishes the two cohorts.

For example, a school district started a new mathematics program, starting with the second grade, in 2018. Considering children who entered the second grade in the school district in 2018, it is likely that in the aggregate, they differed in minor ways, if at all, from children in the district who entered second grade in 2017 and 2019. However, because of the effects of the COVID-19 lockdown in 2020–21, the cohort that entered second grade in 2018 may differ from the group that entered second grade in 2021. In thinking about the comparability of contiguous cohorts, one should consider whether there have been any events that may make one question the similarity of cohorts.

If in 2018 the second graders were introduced to a new mathematics curriculum, assuming that proficiency in math would have otherwise been similar between the 2017 and 2018 cohorts, any differences that appear may be inferred to have been caused by the new curriculum.

Applying the basic cohort design to this example (shown in Figure 6.16), the math proficiency of children entering second grade in 2018 is compared with math proficiency of children entering second grade in 2017. The first observations between the two cohorts should be similar, within a margin of error. If the new curriculum is effective, the second

Treatment Cohort	O_1	X	O_2
No-treatment Cohort	O_1		O_2

FIGURE 6.15. Basic Cohort Design.

Attributing Outcomes to the Program: Quasi-Experimental Design

```
Students in 2nd grade in 2018    O 2nd grade, Sept 2018    X New math curriculum    O 3rd grade, Sept 2019
- - - - - - - - - - - - - - - - - - - - - - - - - - - - - - - - - - - - - - - - - - -
Students in 2nd grade in 2017    O 2nd grade, Sept 2017                             O 3rd grade, Sept 2018
```

FIGURE 6.16. *Application of Basic Cohort Design.*

```
Students in 2nd grade in 2018   O 1st grade, Sept 2017   O 2nd grade, Sept 2018   X New math curriculum   O 3rd grade, Sept 2019   O 4th grade, Sept 2020
- - - - - - - - - - - - - - - - - - - - - - - - - - - - - - - - - - - - - - - - - - - - - - - - - - - - - - - - - -
Students in 2nd grade in 2017   O 1st grade, Sept 2016   O 2nd grade, Sept 2017                           O 3rd grade, Sept 2018   O 4th grade, Sept 2019
```

FIGURE 6.17. *Application of Extended Cohort Design.*

observation of the 2018 cohort should be greater than the second observation of the 2017 cohort. In fact, the utility of the first observation of each cohort is minimal—the effect of the program could be inferred by the difference between the second observations. The first observations are useful, though, to make the argument that the two cohorts were similar preprogram and thus the difference between the second observations is attributable to the program and not to pre-existing differences with respect to the outcome that may have existed between the cohorts.

If there was a concern that the cohorts had preexisting differences, one could also examine their first-grade scores. Considering the first-grade score would also strengthen the design because it would show that the two cohorts had similar patterns of growth before the treatment (change in the curriculum). Further, adding another posttest observation would reveal whether the change in test scores is long lasting, or whether there is a lagged effect.

In the example illustrated by Figure 6.17, these observations have been added. One concern, though, is that the fourth-grade observation for the 2018 cohort is from a fall 2020 observation. One might suspect that that observation may have been affected by many schools closing during the 2020 COVID-19 pandemic, thus not a good measure of the long-lasting effects of the new curriculum under more normal circumstances. This is a good example of the issue of period effects influencing measures. The longer the time frame that one uses to determine a program's effect, the greater the likelihood that other occurrences may have impacted the outcome measure (e.g., threat of history).

Cohort designs tend to rely on archival data. The designs are most useful when there is a clear point at which the cohorts were provided with different treatments. The design has obvious applications in school settings, where there is a steady stream of cohorts. However, the design can be applied in any number of settings, for example, to human resource practices in companies, where the cohorts are defined as a group of employees who start with a company within a given period, and the treatment could be changes in orientation procedures or changes in benefits packages offered. It can also be naturally applied to age groups, in terms of a treatment or intervention that occurred that affected people according to their age.

The key feature of the design is that the observations for the cohorts actually occur at different time periods. The evaluator must keep clear when the intervention occurred and whether the contiguous cohorts are actually comparable groups. If done correctly, quasi-experimental designs that rely on cohort differences can be quite powerful. But the threat of history could be serious if events occurred outside of the program that would have affected the assumption of comparability between the cohorts.

Time Series Designs

Time series follow the same "unit"—people, households, neighborhoods, and so on—over time. Such data are called ***longitudinal data.*** The key feature of longitudinal data is that the same unit is followed over consecutive periods. In the simplest pretest and posttest design with a control group, the units of analysis are followed for two time periods, and in the delayed treatment design, they are followed for three. In time series designs, the same units are followed for multiple time periods, both before and after the treatment. We start with the simplest time series design, which does not have a control group (Figure 6.18).

This design does not have a control group because the pretreatment measures should establish a pattern that would suggest that in the absence of the treatment, the pattern would have continued. The design is illustrated arbitrarily with ten observations. There is no fixed number on the number of observations needed to establish a time series. The number of observations should be large enough to establish a pattern both before and after the treatment.

Sometimes, longitudinal observations reflect seasonal effects, where there is a predictable change in the level of the observation at particular times. For example, in a school setting, "summer slide," where students lose some degree of competency over long breaks from school, would be a seasonal effect. In the world of retail, one expects higher sales in November and December.

A change in the slope, intercept, or functional form of the pattern would suggest that the treatment had an impact. The threat of history curtails the evaluator's ability to draw causal conclusions from the data. The evaluator would want to consider whether other concurrent treatments could have produced the effect rather than the treatment or could have contributed to at least a portion of the change. Further, there could have been countervailing forces that would have upset the pretreatment pattern even if the treatment had not occurred.

$O_1 \quad O_2 \quad O_3 \quad O_4 \quad O_{5...} \quad X \quad O_6 \quad O_7 \quad O_8 \quad O_9 \,...$

FIGURE 6.18. *Simple Interrupted Time-Series Design.*

Source: Cook and Campbell (1979) / Houghton Mifflin Harcourt Company

If a treatment has immediate effects, then the evaluator can limit the examination of the threat of history to the time period immediately surrounding the treatment. However, if the treatment has lagged effects, then one would need to consider any other events that could have affected the observations for an even greater length of time.

Imagine a program designed to provide seasonal construction workers with employment opportunities during the winter months. Such a program is intended to disrupt the seasonal pattern. A summer reading program is intended to decrease "summer slide" among schoolchildren. The program has years of data showing that children's reading abilities increase during the school year but after summer break, their reading abilities were below what they were in the previous June. The program is intended to change this pattern. In this case, there is no reason to expect a lag in the program's effects and there is probably no need for a control group. A control group would strengthen the causal argument, but the pretreatment time series may be sufficient to convince most who consider the program's effects.

The time series with a control group (Figure 6.19) allows evaluators to better consider whether the threat of history has impacted the posttreatment level and pattern of the outcome(s). Of course, in this design, if the treatment has an effect, one would expect to see it only in the treatment group.

Another time-series pattern to consider is the treatment–removed treatment pattern (Figure 6.20). Here, the treatment is applied and then later removed, with the expectation that after the treatment's application, an effect would exist, and when the treatment was removed, the effect would cease. Although some treatments may have such a mechanical cause-and-effect relationship, many treatments do not. Some treatments have long-lasting effects, and their effects can continue beyond the application of the treatment. That is, some treatments—particularly those that build the capacities of people, or relay information—produce irreversible effects.

The removed treatment design is most useful in the policy arena, where public policies may be implemented for finite time spans, and then stopped. Or, alternate public policies

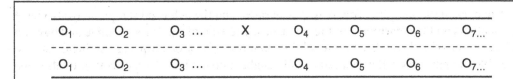

FIGURE 6.19. *Interrupted Time Series with a No-Treatment Control Group Design.*

Source: Cook and Campbell (1979) / Houghton Mifflin Harcourt Company

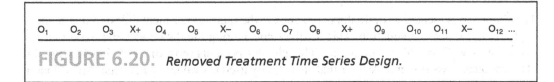

FIGURE 6.20. *Removed Treatment Time Series Design.*

could exist over time. The design essentially assumes that any introduction or removal of the treatment would impact the observations. If the effect is lagged, then the design can become very difficult to interpret.

Archival Data Time series designs often depend on archival or historical data. You should be careful when using archival data for two reasons—the threat of mono-operation bias and the threat of instrumentation.

The threat of mono-operation bias appears because typically there will be only one way that the treatment and effect were historically operationalized. An evaluator is often constrained by having to work with the data and operationalizations that have been used over the time period, even if they are not perfect or even good measures of the constructs of current interest. Thus, the evaluation research becomes quite constrained by data collected in the past. The questions that the current evaluation activities are investigating may not even have been issues in the past, and the data collected may not be a very good fit with the current evaluation questions.

When using historical data, you must be acutely aware of whether or the degree to which the data collection systems and/or the definitions of the indicators changed over time. There could have been subtle changes that affected the level or pattern of an indicator. For example, if examining a time series of statistics in the United States broken down by race/ethnicity, you should be aware of any changes in the way that race data has been collected—changes in wording of questions, categories, and options to choose more than one category.

The threat of instrumentation derives not only from the possibility of changed definitions over time but also from changes in the data collection processes that may have occurred. For example, if relying on survey data, you must inquire exactly how the data were collected over the period of the data being used. If at one time data collection relied on a mail-back survey design, and then the data collection transitioned to a telephone survey design, the change in the collection approach could have ramifications on the quality of the data and the achieved sample.

Changes in the sampling frame, response rates, and the achieved sample may also have ramifications on the measures. For these reasons, you should carefully examine and have an understanding of archival data before relying on it for evaluation purposes. Archival data are inflexible. If appropriate, the data can reveal insights into the long-term effects of treatments. However, one should be cautious about using such data when indicators do not closely align with the constructs of interest, or when changes have occurred in the definitions or data collection systems.

SUMMARY

The challenge presented to evaluators is to choose the quasi-experimental design that is most appropriate for a given situation. This involves considering the data collection opportunities that exist as well as ethical limitations. This chapter presents most of Cook and Campbell's classical quasi-experimental designs that are actually used in evaluation research. An evaluator may create a new design, mixing favorable elements of the above designs.

KEY TERMS

archival data
cohort
delayed treatment control group design
different samples design
longitudinal data
nonequivalent groups using switched measures
nonequivalent observations design drawn from one group
one-group posttest-only design
one-group pretest-posttest design
posttest-only design with nonequivalent groups
quasi-experimental design
quasi-experimental notation
time series
untreated control group design with pretest and posttest

DISCUSSION QUESTIONS

1. Explain how a clear understanding of the threats to validity impacts the quasi-experimental design chosen to evaluate a program.

2. What are the benefits and concerns of using control groups?

3. The program you are evaluating has a wealth of archival data collected under three different program leaders over a 12-year period. What concerns might you have about the usefulness of this data to your evaluation? What questions would you ask about the data?

CHAPTER 7

COLLECTING DATA

LEARNING OBJECTIVES

After reading this chapter, you should be able to

- Decide what the best data collection approach will be for the evaluation questions that need primary data collection
- Develop protocol for collecting data
- Decide upon the target population and sampling approach for primary data collection

Evaluation Essentials: Methods for Conducting Sound Evaluation Research, Second Edition.
Beth Osborne DaPonte.
© 2025 John Wiley & Sons, Inc. Published 2025 by John Wiley & Sons, Inc.

An evaluator can take a variety of approaches to collecting relevant data. This chapter outlines various approaches to collecting data, starting with informal interviews and finishing with archival data. Regardless of the approach used to collect data, an evaluator should proceed with a well-thought-out data collection plan which will ultimately result in data that will produce the outcome measures that will be used in the chosen quasi-experimental design and answer the evaluation questions.

INTRODUCTION

Thus far, we have discussed the more theoretical aspects of evaluating an initiative—describing it thoroughly, conducting literature reviews, and proposing quasi-experimental designs that could be applied. An evaluation needs data upon which to base findings, conclusions, and recommendations. The form that data collection will take is a balance between wanting to have data on every aspect of each evaluation question, the resources available for data collection, the timeframe of the evaluation, the availability and willingness of persons with knowledge to reveal information, and the availability, reliability, and credibility of archival data and data that an organization may have already collected.

In deciding whether to collect new, primary data, the evaluator should first exhaust all existing data sources. It is less expensive to analyze existing data sources than to collect new data. Collecting data is expensive and should be undertaken only when alternative pre-existing data sources that provide the same information do not exist.

Before collecting any new data, the evaluator should have a data collection plan that describes in detail the means of data collection, how the data collected will relate to the evaluation questions, how the data will be used in reporting, and how the evaluator will assure that the data collected is unbiased, credible, and reliable. The evaluator should first consider why each data element is needed. The data collected should be the smallest, most parsimonious set that is necessary to answer the evaluation questions that the literature review does not already answer. The literature review may answer some of the evaluation questions, but more information will be needed to answer others. While this chapter is written with an evaluation in mind, the data collection issues and approaches also apply to creating a monitoring system for an initiative.

When thinking about data, issues of bias, validity, and reliability should be forefront. To remind, **bias** refers to the extent to which the data misrepresent the actual status of the population and present a skewed vision of the population. Sources of bias include sampling a subset that overrepresents one end of a spectrum, asking questions in a way that responses will overemphasize one end of a spectrum, and using measures where all units cannot be fairly represented. **Validity** refers to the extent to which the measure or question captures the construct of interest. **Reliability** refers to the extent to which the measures would garner the same result if data collection is repeated. Unreliable measures make it difficult to detect program effects, since they will have larger measurement error.

When considering data collection, ask whether data are needed to discover the *existence* of issues as opposed to knowing the *preponderance* of issues. If the former, then informal interviews, focus groups, and document and database review (depending on what data has already been recorded) would suffice. If one needs to know preponderance or frequency of issues, data sources become surveys, census data, and databases (depending on what data have been recorded).

Both focus groups and informal interviews can be a way to discover areas of inquiry that could be included in a formal survey, and in that sense become a means to an end. They should be conducted before the start of designing a survey instrument. We start by considering informal interviews.

INFORMAL AND LOOSELY STRUCTURED INTERVIEWS

As discussed in Chapter 2, informal interviews with the stakeholders must be done initially to develop an understanding of the program. The interviews are more or less conversations, and though they can provide useful insights into the subject matter, they cannot lead to statements regarding the frequency of issues. The interviews conducted to understand the program at the outset differ from interviews conducted as part of a data collection plan.

Beyond helping to develop an understanding of the program, informal interviews can be used to understand issues surrounding the need for the program and its possible success. They can also highlight the stories of individual cases, especially useful for telling the experiences of program participants. These informal interviews are useful in uncovering issues.

When conducting informal interviews with program developers and implementers, the interviewer can base the interview on the Theory of Change (ToC) and Program Logic Model (PLM) and ask questions and follow-up questions regarding these models. Questions to ask abound and include:

- Does the ToC seem reasonable? In what ways, does it seem uncertain to occur?

- What assumptions does the initiative make in the PLM that are not reasonable or that do not have supporting evidence?

- How does the initiative reach its target population? How well does it reach its target population? Are the right people enrolling? How might it improve outreach?

- Are people sticking with the program or is dropping out an issue? Why might people not complete the program?

- To what degree does the target population need what the program offers? Are there better ways to address the target population's needs?

- Regarding resources, does the program have enough funding to reliably operate in the way intended? Has it needed to cut back to save money? Are partners providing to the program what was expected?

- Is the initiative attracting the volunteers it had hoped for?

- To what degree is the program having the intended effects on participants?

- How do we know that the program caused the effects? Was there something else that happened that may have caused the effects?

- How efficient is the program? How could it become more efficient?

If interviewing program staff, examine where they land on the organizational chart and what aspects of the program they would be expected to have expertise. Naturally, ask the staff about those aspects of the program. While informal interviews usually include only the evaluator or an evaluation team of two persons and one interviewee, at times it may make sense to interview two persons who have the same or similar function concurrently. For example, if interviewing about the recruitment processes for the initiative, the evaluator may want to include two persons who have this function or a small group who deal with different aspects of the recruitment function.

If interviewing program participants, the interviewer would ask about how they became aware of the program, their personal expectations for the program, the degree to which their expectations have been met, how the program serves them, challenges with the program, and recommendations for modifications.

A data collection plan that includes informal interviews should include the sampling plan for interviewees and interview protocol. The sampling plan would show who the evaluator hopes to interview (and why). For example, the sampling plan may refer to interviewing specific people who hold specific positions from the program's organizational chart, particular partners, and types of program participants. The interview protocol should outline the set of questions each interviewee would be asked. The questions will be open-ended, allowing for the interviewee to explain processes and impacts of the program.

I have conducted (or have led teams of evaluators that have conducted) evaluations that relied heavily on informal interviews. In such cases, a 360° view of the initiative was gathered by interviewing staff at various levels, a heterogeneous group of participants/clients, partners, beneficiaries, funders, government officials, and persons who work in the same "sphere" as the initiative. The number of interviews for such an evaluation usually ranges from 30 to 60 (though I was once a team member on an evaluation that interviewed approximately 200 people, clearly, an outlier). In addition, documents on the initiative are reviewed as well as any quantitative data that the initiative has already collected.

When conducting the informal interviews, take copious notes on each interview. My style is to type quickly as people speak which results in nearly verbatim notes. (Some people electronically record interviews, but doing so could double the amount of time it takes to conduct and create notes on the interview. Another alternative is to use automated voice transcription, which could provide a reasonable first draft of notes, but which would again require careful review, which would again increase the amount of time spent on creating interview notes.)

I personally believe that taking notes during the interview is the most efficient approach (see Box on creating a Word file), given the speed at which one can type/write. More than one person can take notes at the time of the interview, and immediately after those notes rectified to produce one document that reflects the interview.

> **Organizing interview notes in Microsoft Word**
>
> I create one Word file for each set of evaluation interviews and structure the file so that it becomes organized not by date of interview, but by the hierarchical structure of interviewees.
>
> For each interview, include on a new page the name of the person being interviewed, their position (e.g., title, or client) with respect to the initiative, place of interview, and date of interview.
>
> Using Word's Heading function and navigation view, one can move the interview to the place in the file's structure where the interview best fits. The file with interview notes can easily grow to one hundred pages (or more).
>
> Using the Headings and Table of Contents functions in Word to structure the information being gleaned from the interviews, one might assign a Level 1 Heading for the Executive Director, Level 2 Heading for Directors of Departments, and so on. Doing so allows for easy organization of the notes.
>
> The search function allows one to easily identify how interviewees responded to themes that arose and count the number of interviewees who provided such information or feedback. One could also use the Index function in Word to create an index of issues that appear, and then analyze the data that appear in the index.

When analyzing the data from interviews, one could, if already aware of themes that emerged, search the file to determine who gave feedback and the substance of the feedback given on the issue. Another way of analyzing the qualitative data is to use computer software, with NVivo being the most popular. Any qualitative software requires coding of interview notes. If interviews were conducted by multiple people (as opposed to one team carrying out all interviews) and there was a large number of interviews, then the interviews should be coded, with the team agreeing on the codes to develop, and software used for analysis.

The findings that result from interviews usually pertain to the existence of an issue and not the issue's propensity, though one could make statements such as "among those interviewed, X% indicated. . .". The recommendations that result usually pertain to the relevance of the initiative, its processes, and efficiency. Using interviews solely as the means of data collection is reasonable when the evaluation is being conducted before one would expect to see results from an initiative. Thus, in mid-term evaluations, one might limit data collection to informal interviews, perhaps combined with focus groups.

FOCUS GROUPS

Focus groups are similar to informal interviews in that they provide insights but cannot reveal the propensity of an occurrence in the population. A focus group consists of people who are willing to share their thoughts, attitudes, and experiences. Think of a focus group as a dinner party with a leader. In this case, the leader is the evaluator who uses open-ended questions, when needed, to stimulate conversation.

A focus group differs from an informal interview in that in the latter, the interaction is limited to that between the interviewer and interviewee. In a focus group, the group dynamics can lead to a topic of conversation that is totally unanticipated by the evaluator. Personal experience shows that focus groups are more likely to provide insights into unanticipated issues than are informal interviews. One person's perspective can trigger another person to respond with a related, unexpected perspective or experience, thus opening up a new line of inquiry.

Focus groups can be used as a source of information when designing a survey and be a means to an end. Alternatively, one may decide to collect data only through focus groups. Used in this way, the focus groups are not a means to designing a survey but an end in and of themselves. For example, a series of focus groups with different types of program participants may be conducted, and they may reveal different experiences that participants have had with the program. If interested in the perspective of service providers, then focus groups would be held with only the providers to better understand the system and the issues with which providers are concerned.

Evaluators have different styles in conducting focus groups, and a review of social science and marketing methodology texts reveal varying approaches. The style I advocate has evolved from conducting focus groups with many types of stakeholders.

Focus Group Size The size of a focus group should be limited to between five and nine people, with a strong preference for six to eight—the size of an intimate dinner party. To get that many attendees, you may need to invite more. Usually, some invitees don't show up for the focus group (regardless of reminders sent).

Duration With respect to the length of the focus group session, 90 minutes is usually appropriate. Exceeding 90 minutes tires participants and could jeopardize the quality of discussion. It usually takes approximately 30 minutes at the beginning of the session for people in the group to feel comfortable with each other and the setting. Allow time at the end of the session, perhaps about 10–15 minutes, for participants to make last-minute observations. In a 90 minute session, that leaves only 45 minutes for high-quality interactions.

Number of Focus Groups Plan to conduct several focus groups, though the right number can't be determined in advance (however, budget and planning considerations may force one to set a number). Collecting information via focus groups should continue until no new issues or perspectives are revealed. For simple issues with a homogeneous client population, the number of groups conducted could be as low as two or three, but for more complex issues where a variety of perspectives are needed, 8–12 groups may be convened.

Composition Groups must be carefully composed and their composition depends on the issues they will discuss. Carefully consider what is wanted out of the group and how its composition could promote or impede that goal. Consider any power imbalances that may exist between focus group participants, since power imbalances can impede frank conversation.

For example, one group may include only people who participate in the program. If the program has different effects on subpopulations, then multiple groups could be run, stratified by characteristics—for example, having a group with people who are members of families with school-aged children, have another group with persons 50–64 years of age, etc. With multisite programs, at least one group may be held with each site.

When holding a focus group with program staff, you may want to assure that people at different levels of the organization are not in the same group since persons at lower levels of the hierarchy may be inhibited from expressing their frank thoughts in the presence of persons at upper levels.

Another way of composing groups is to consider the program's processes involved. The group's composition would be built around how people are affected by or participate in a process, possibly resulting in a group including different people at various levels of an organization, or a mixture of very different types of clients. For example, a focus group may include persons who ask partner organizations for referrals, representatives of partnering organizations, and program personnel who receive the referrals. Do not include funders and representatives from grantee organizations in the same group, since the grantees typically will defer to the funders.

Recruitment and Compensation There are three distinct approaches to recruitment: (1) passively asking for people to participate in a group, (2) actively asking for volunteers, and (3) purposely recruiting particular types of participants.

- With *passive recruitment* (such as flyers that advertise the study or using mass media to recruit volunteers), the onus is on the potential participant to decide to join the focus group and take the initiative to enroll. A passive approach could yield a very select group of participants—those who are abnormally interested in the discussion.

- An *active recruitment* approach targets particular individuals for participation and helps them overcome barriers to participating—for example, by sending a letter to everybody in a neighborhood informing them of the need for participants and following up on the letter with a telephone call. Active approaches make it easier for participants to join, thus resulting in a more representative sample.

- *Purposive recruitment* targets certain individuals and does whatever it can to make sure that those individuals will attend. For example, the date and time of the focus groups may be formed around the targeted persons' schedules. This approach will yield participants who are most representative of the population of interest.

Compensation Paying or otherwise compensating people to participate incentivizes participation. Compensation can help ensure that the group includes desired people. Compensation usually is not provided to staff or program partners, since the program is part of their job or their organization's mission. In practice, without compensating participants, an aberrant sample is likely to result—only those abnormally interested in the issue will want to participate in a focus group and ultimately evaluators will not be able to generalize findings because the participants do not represent any known population. To attract both those who are moderately interested and those who are abnormally interested in the subject of the focus group, you must compensate participants for their time. The same strategy pertains to the target population of surveys.

With passive recruitment, unless the level of compensation for participating in the group is high enough that everybody would want to be a part of the group, it is likely that those who volunteer for the group differ from those who do not volunteer with respect to their experience with the issue or program. Volunteers may be more likely to have had either an exceptionally good or bad experience with the program. If the focus group aims to learn about the possible range of experiences with the program, then no compensation may be necessary. But, if the focus group is aimed to learn about the experiences of all, to decrease selection bias, you should offer compensation sufficient enough to overcome a potential participant's reluctance to participate. Exactly what the level of compensation might be depends on who you want to be in the focus group. The compensation should be large enough so that most people will agree to participate in the group. In one study, low-income participants were given 30-dollar coupons to a local grocery store, and this level seemed to induce cooperation. However, that level of compensation may not be great enough to induce participation of a higher-income population. If a focus group is held during a mealtime, the organizers should provide the meal.

It is not uncommon for studies to offer childcare to parents while they are participating in a focus group, thinking that such an offer will reduce barriers to parents' participation. Offering childcare may seem to reduce a barrier, but, in practice, many parents are not comfortable leaving their children in an unfamiliar situation; thus, the barrier would remain. The barrier could be more effectively reduced if parents were reimbursed for childcare costs.

Recording Focus Groups Some researchers advocate the use of electronic equipment to record a focus group, believing that it will provide a more accurate record of what transpired. This approach certainly allows the researchers to review the exact content of the group. However, participants may not feel free to discuss a topic if they believe that they are being recorded making statements. If you envision that sensitive issues could arise during the course of a focus group, then alternative approaches should be used.

An approach that works well is to run the session with a research team consisting of a group leader-facilitator and an assistant/notetaker. The leader interacts with the participants and the assistant takes detailed notes, either by hand or on a laptop. When the leader explains to participants that they will only be identified by a number and a general description (usually limited to gender, age, and perhaps race) participants generally feel more at ease with this approach. The increase in their comfort level allows participants to speak freely and ultimately yields higher-quality information.

Immediately after each focus group ends, the leader and assistant should review the notes, filling in where necessary from their recollections. A draft of the report on the group should be written on the same day, if possible. In this day of electronic recording, some may be skeptical of going back to this "old school" way of taking notes on the focus group's conversation. However, I have found that the increased recording capacity offered by electronically recording the groups does not outweigh its inhibiting impact. When I conduct focus groups, it is with an assistant (who takes handwritten notes) and we type up the notes together, immediately after the group ends. This yields very high-quality notes of the focus group without having to go back and listen to all 90 minutes of the group.

Venue Rather than conduct the group face-to-face in a physical setting, another approach is to ask participants to be part of a virtual meeting or conference call. This approach has advantages and disadvantages. The cost and convenience of conducting a focus group virtually make doing so attractive. However, some interactions, and, I would offer, some of the joy, are sacrificed. Since the reason to use focus groups is to exploit the information that results from interactions, using a venue that decreases interactions can be counterproductive.

If possible, hold the focus groups in a comfortable, private room. The room could be at a program site, public libraries, church basements, etc. Provide transportation to the venue for participants (or compensate them for transportation).

Possible topics/questions to promote conversation for a focus group of program participants:

- How did you become aware of the program?
- What circumstances brought you to the program?
- What do you hope the program will do for you/ your household/ your family?
- What better approaches do you think could exist to address what brought you to the program?
- What would you have done if this program didn't exist?
- What do you like about the program? What do you dislike?
- What suggestions do you have for the program to improve?

Leading the Focus Group The leader should prepare for the focus group by creating a list (of 5–10) open-ended questions that should stimulate conversation. Closed-ended, yes or no questions and those that have predetermined categories of responses are conversation ending, not conversation starting. The leader should be flexible about the timing of asking the questions and understand that valuable conversation could mean that there is not enough time to ask all of the planned questions in one group. The conversation may lead to an unanticipated area or participants may delve into an issue in more depth than was anticipated.

The leader should be very careful about intervening in the conversation and should intervene only when the conversation goes astray for a long period, lags, or is dominated by one or more participants to the extent that others cannot participate. It is natural for conversation to go astray for short periods of time—in fact, that is often the purpose of running the session. However, if the conversation seems to be leading to a direction that is not the topic of the focus group, then the leader should intervene to bring the conversation back to the topic at hand.

Sometimes, one participant can dominate the conversation. The leader's obligation is to assure that the group's environment is such that all participants feel that their participation is valuable. The leader should take care to elicit input from all. This can be delicate, though, because some people are naturally quieter than others, and the leader certainly does not want to alienate or draw too much attention to these participants. Some participants may in fact be quiet because they are reflecting on their own experiences and views and will speak up when they feel it is appropriate.

Using Focus Groups as the Basis for Survey Design If the groups are being used to design a survey, notes from each session should be reviewed to determine whether any new issues or new responses have emerged. If new issues surface, then the survey designer needs to determine whether the issue is significant enough to be included on the survey. Likewise, if there are new responses to issues that were already included, then the survey designer needs to determine whether the propensity of that response will be large, or whether the response is important enough to be included on the survey instrument.

To give an example, in the early 1990s, the Food Distribution Research Project in Pittsburgh was contracted to design a survey on the use of food pantries in the United States. It was the first large survey on this topic. Focus groups were used to discover the issues and possible responses to questions for inclusion on the survey. A number of focus groups had already been conducted where participants were asked why they started using the private food assistance network (food pantries and food banks). In one of the final focus groups, one woman spoke up and said that medical bills incurred from childbirth were the catalyst for her using a food pantry. Because of her experience, the response of "medical bills" or "medical debts" to a question on reasons why a household used a food pantry was added to a subsequent survey. Although the research team was uncertain of how many others might have been driven to rely on a food pantry for this reason, the response seemed important enough in a policy context to include on the survey. The survey results consequently showed a substantial number who were driven to use a food pantry because of medical bills.

After becoming aware of the existence of issues through interviews and/or focus groups, to learn about the **propensity of issues**, conduct a **formal survey instrument**.

EXAMPLE OF FOCUS GROUP PROTOCOL

Living on the Edge: Housing and Income Challenges

Participants: Persons who provide services to persons and households that face budgetary challenges.
Place: Stratford Public Library, Lovell Room, 3000 Main Street, Stratford, CT
Time: September 20, 2–3:30 PM

Prompting questions:

- In the last decade, what changes have you observed with respect to the number of persons facing severe budgetary challenges? In what ways, if any, has the composition of persons facing budgeting challenges changed?
- In what ways are you seeing that household budgets have changed in the past decade?
- What are the implications of increasing housing prices that you are seeing? What challenges do increasing housing prices bring?
- How are people with tight budgets managing? What strategies are being used?
- To what extent are forms of assistance (not housing assistance) freeing up money to use for housing expenses?
- How strong is the safety net for those unable to make ends meet?
- What could we be doing better at the local level to better support those at risk of being unable to make ends meet?

SURVEYS

Surveys are used to discover the frequency of issues and views—the evaluator knows the issues to inquire about, has a good idea of the possible universe of responses, and wants to know the frequency of the response categories. There are three aspects of conducting a survey:

- designing the survey instrument (questionnaire),
- determining and accessing the survey's target population, and
- implementing the survey instrument.

Survey Instrument Design

A well-designed survey consists of the shortest set of valid and reliable questions that are structured to maximize the response rate. **Question validity** refers to the extent that a given response reflects what a survey designer intends and expects the response to mean. **Question reliability** refers to the extent to which people in comparable situations will respond to questions in similar ways. Reliability also refers to the extent that the same respondent in unchanged circumstances will respond to the same questions in the same way. With a highly reliable survey, if a respondent was surveyed at two points in time and the respondent's circumstances or views had not changed, the respondent would provide identical responses at the two points in time. Measurement error derives from the extent that a question is unreliable.

In informal interviews and focus groups, the questions should be open-ended questions. In a well-designed survey, the survey designer has done the homework of knowing how to best ask the questions and the possible responses to the questions. Therefore, all but the last question on a survey ("Is there anything else you would like to tell us about the program?") should be closed-ended questions, meaning that there are predetermined possibilities of responses. A well-designed survey asks questions identically to all respondents and all respondents bear the same burden of providing a response.

General Rules for Designing a Survey Instrument *Keep the survey as short as possible.* Each question added decreases the probability that the respondent will complete the survey or will agree to being surveyed at all. There is a trade-off between short surveys that provide a snapshot of an issue, and longer ones that may delve into one issue's interaction with another. Evaluators want quality data that yield insight into a problem, but they should carefully consider the burden on respondents when adding each and every question. For this reason, each question on a survey should be there for a reason. Before a survey is implemented, the evaluator should already have a plan as to how the responses to each survey question will be used in the evaluation report.

Know how others have asked questions on the topic. There is usually a history of asking questions on a topic. The literature review should inform as to whether the topic has been included in previous surveys. If it has been, try to locate the actual surveys that included the questions. Consider whether those questions would suffice for the questions you were considering asking. Those questions have presumably been pretested. Further, adopting those questions would allow for easy comparison with studies or data sets that have included those questions. In considering questions written by others, definitely examine how governmental entities have asked those questions for inclusion in your survey since those questions are not copyrighted. Only create new questions if the literature does not provide a precedent of the topic being asked about that would suit the evaluation. Be purposeful and thoughtful when creating new questions.

Vary the format of questions throughout the survey. The goal is to get respondents to think about the responses they provide. Faced with a long list of questions asked in the same way, respondents are tempted to go down a list quickly and provide the same response, without thinking through each question. This is especially common in written or computer surveys, but it also occurs in interviewer-administered surveys. Often, this happens when people are asked to "rate" a series of items, perhaps how much the respondents like something. Just as respondents wouldn't want to have a conversation that was monotonous, the survey instrument should not be monotonous, or it will yield poor-quality data. Vary questions using multiple choice, ratings where one can move a scale, drop-down menus, etc.

Order survey questions so their progression flows like a conversation. After the set of questions has been designed, move the questions so there is a natural flow to them. I recommend starting the survey with demographic questions, then moving to questions that may have a natural flow (perhaps leading the respondent through a program process—e.g., recruitment, interactions with staff, impacts), and then concluding with an open-ended question along the lines of "Is there anything else that you would like to offer about the program?" That would be the only open-ended question on the survey and is meant to allow the respondent to vent. Often, responses to such questions can be very positive and remark on particular staff.

Make the "look" of the survey user-friendly. Use large type, spacing, and color to make the survey easy for respondents to understand and complete. Small type discourages completion of a survey.

Use the best, least expensive survey software that will meet the survey's needs. Most surveys today are done electronically, using survey software. In my opinion, Qualtrics is the best survey software. It has a number of functions that allow the respondent to take the shortest survey possible, based on responses to earlier questions. It also allows for great flexibility in creating a certain look and feel, depending on what the designer wants. Qualtrics allows for the same questions to be asked in various languages, with the respondent only seeing the language that they indicated in a screening question they would like the survey presented. However, Qualtrics can be very expensive.

Survey Monkey is a less expensive alternative (though it does not seem to offer the same flexibility). Other packages abound. When considering which software to use, take into account whether your survey has skip patterns (questions that should only appear based on the answers to previous questions) or piping (the wording of a question will include the response from a previous question). Some packages suggest how to ask questions and offer question banks—examples of questions on the same topic that have been asked in the past. As of 2024, one difference between Qualtrics and Survey Monkey is that Qualtrics allows for questions to be skipped, whereas Survey Monkey allows only for pages to be skipped. If the survey have many skip patterns, using Survey Monkey can be challenging.

When selecting software, consider the analysis capabilities of the software. This isn't a consideration if you plan to download the survey results and input them into a statistical software package or a spreadsheet. But some survey software takes results and automatically offers analysis and the sophistication of possible analysis varies between survey platforms.

Avoid "yes bias." Research shows that respondents prefer to answer "yes" more than "no"—people like to agree. Word questions in a way that would prevent this bias. For example, rather than ask "Do you like the weather today?" use the question "What, if anything, do you like about the weather today?" with various categories of responses, including "nothing" (which would substitute for a "no" response).

Steps to Designing the Survey Instrument

1. **Decide how the survey will be administered.** Will it be a survey that is emailed to people? Will it be a paper survey that people complete by writing? Will it be an interview-administered survey? Telephone survey?

2. **Determine the topics the survey will include.** Not all evaluation questions require survey results. Limit the topics to include on the survey to only the necessary areas of inquiry—either there is no other data source for the answer to the evaluation question or survey data is needed to triangulate the other data source.

3. **Develop an outline of the survey.** Organize the topics in a way that will allow the survey to flow like a conversation. The Theory of Change could help guide the placement of topics.

4. **Decide the wording of questions.** This decision will be informed by the literature review (which should be done prior to creating a survey) that may have revealed surveys conducted by others. In deciding the wording, one should also consider whether the survey will be presented in one language or in multiple languages.

5. **Organize the questions within each topic.** Within each topic, the survey should flow like a conversation.

6. **Build transitions between topics.** Transitions are words in the survey that lead the respondent through the topics. For example, "Now, we would like to ask you about your interactions with program staff."

7. **Pretest the draft survey instrument.** There are many ways to pretest a survey instrument. Psychological pretesting has the respondent talk through, while taking the survey, how they are thinking about the questions. This approach is not commonly used. A more usual approach is to administer the survey to individuals under conditions similar to those in which the survey will ultimately be administered, and then informally interview the respondents immediately after they complete it to make sure that the data collected were what the designer intended and to uncover any glitches in the process.

After pretests, the designer will revise the survey instrument accordingly and the new survey instrument will also need to be pretested. Pretesting and revising should continue until all kinks are addressed. If the survey is revised substantially or if a significant amount of time has passed between the pretest and the time that all other respondents complete their surveys, the data collected from respondents in the pretest cannot be used in the final data set.

Concurrently, one should determine who the survey will be going to and how people will be asked to complete the survey.

Open-Ended versus Closed-Ended Questions An open-ended question offers no response categories and instead asks the respondent to write-in or verbalize a response. Responses can be difficult to get and difficult to analyze. Open-ended questions should be avoided because they yield unreliable responses. In open-ended questions, respondents bear the burden of providing an appropriate response. Responses between respondents can vary because of differences in their willingness or ability to provide thorough answers to questions and not because they have different situations. For example, the open-ended question asked in an interview or focus group could be "Why did you enroll in this program?" and the interviewee could give any response. The response provided will be a function of how the interviewee understands the question, their willingness to provide information, and what they think would be an appropriate response. Responses can range from one word to paragraphs.

Information gleaned from focus groups and informal interviews helps to design closed-ended questions, as these sessions will reveal the bulk of possible responses to questions. Thus, if the survey designer knows that the survey will include an issue but does not know what the possible responses may be, the focus groups should bear out that information. It is wise, though, to leave a category for closed-ended questions—such as "other, please explain"—providing space for respondents to give a response that was not included as an option.

However, analyzing data from open-ended questions and the "other, please explain" category of responses can be extremely burdensome. When respondents provide an "other" response, the analyst should read through each response and determine if there are enough of the same type of response to manually create a new response category, post-survey. Determining appropriate categories by which to organize the data and fitting each open-ended response into a category post-survey requires thought and manpower. It is far more efficient to have thought through the appropriate categories of responses and included them on the survey from the beginning, instead of having to go back and retrofit the responses to open-ended questions.

Collecting Demographic Information Because evaluators might analyze responses by demographic characteristics, it is usually important for a survey to collect demographic information. Certainly, if conducting a survey in the United States, you would want to become familiar with how the US Census Bureau asks demographic questions on its most recent census (see www.census.gov). Even if evaluators disagree with how the US Census Bureau has asked demographic questions, they will probably want to compare the survey population's demographic characteristics with the US population's or a US subpopulation. If a survey asks demographic questions differently from the US Census Bureau's practices, then one has forfeited the opportunity to make direct comparisons with census and census-derived data.

For example, if a program serves the population in a municipality, one would probably want to compare the program's and municipality's populations, as reflected in Census Bureau products (including the American Community Survey). If evaluators do not collect demographic characteristics in the same way as the Census Bureau collects them, then making the comparison could be problematic. As the government's questions are not copyrighted, they can be used on an evaluation's survey.

Survey designers differ in their opinions of where demographic questions should appear on a survey. Some place demographic questions at the end of a survey, the rationale being that these questions tend to be alienating and having them at the beginning could lower the survey's response rate. Others prefer placing the questions at the very beginning of the survey, for two reasons. First, if people are reluctant to provide such basic information, they may be reluctant to provide topical information, and second, if respondents do not complete the survey, one would want to know how their demographics differ from those who complete the entire survey. I fall into this second camp.

Other Considerations in Designing Survey Questions In an effort to make a survey as short as possible for respondents, the survey should have built into it skip patterns so that no respondents see any question that is not relevant to their situation. Each question added to a survey decreases the probability that the respondent will complete the survey, even if the respondent is instructed to "skip" the question if it doesn't apply to their situation.

Likewise, every word on a survey lengthens the survey. Any extraneous word, in the questions, responses, transitions, and instructions lengthens the survey. Keep the word count of the survey as low as possible.

There are generally six types of survey questions:

- Mutually exclusive multiple choice. The respondent can choose only one of the possible response categories, and the response categories cover the universe of all possible responses. Yes/no questions are a special type of these questions.

- Checkboxes. In these questions, the respondent can "check all that apply." The major problem with these questions is that one cannot distinguish between "no" from having skipped the entire question or having skipped a possible response category. For this reason, I avoid using checkboxes.

- Rating scales. These questions ask the respondents to rate how they feel about something. The rating is on a scale. The scale could be 1–10, 0–100, two thumbs down to two thumbs up, etc. The key with rating scales is to have a scale that will elicit responses that vary. The scale should be large enough to detect differences between responses. Rating scales can be a way to get valuable information and respondents often feel "heard" using such scales. They can also provide a way to vary how the survey asks questions and may make the survey a more interactive experience for respondents. Often, survey designers will allow only an even number of categories for rating (e.g., four categories—strongly disagree, somewhat disagree, somewhat agree, and strongly agree), believing that the even number forces the respondent to ultimately choose between positive and negative. An odd number of categories often allows respondents to provide a neutral response (strongly disagree, somewhat disagree, neutral, somewhat agree, strongly agree). Being wary of the risk of respondents stopping a survey, I will include a neutral category.

- Ranking. Such questions where respondents are asked to put a list in a rank order can have high respondent burden. If the list is short (say, three categories), then the respondent may be able to rank the categories quickly. But four or more categories may increase the time to take the survey substantially and decrease interest in other questions.

- Choices. With these questions, the respondent picks one, two, or three of the possible options. This essentially is a form of ranking, but with less respondent burden. It does require the respondent to read through all of the options and weigh them, thus can increase respondent burden.
- Asking the respondent to fill in a number or date. Here, there is no set of options given. The respondent must provide the information in a numerical or date form. These questions have issues of rounding error. If asking for dates, people tend to "heap" on the first of the month and years ending in 0 or 5. If asking for a number (e.g., income, rental payment), people tend to provide a rounded number.

Example of a choice question versus a matrixed multiple choice question:

Choice question:

Which of the following was the most important reason you enrolled in the program? *please select one of the following:*

___ An alternative program did not have space for me
___ The times of the program were convenient for me
___ I was referred to this program
___ The location was most convenient for me
___ This program seemed to take an approach that would work best for me
___ This program has an excellent reputation
___ Other (please give the reason)
_____
_____

Matrixed multiple choice question

Which of the following were reasons you enrolled in the program? *Please enter a response for each reason below:*

Yes No
___ ___ An alternative program did not have space for me
___ ___ The times of the program were convenient for me
___ ___ I was referred to this program
___ ___ The location was most convenient for me
___ ___ This program seemed to take an approach that would work best for me
___ ___ This program has an excellent reputation

Note a few things about the structure of these two close-ended questions. In the first, the respondent is being asked to consider one of alternative responses. This requires the respondent to weigh alternatives, and then give a response. The weighing could be burdensome (depending on the number of possible categories) and could lead a respondent to skip the question or give an unreliable response. In the second question, the respondent can say "yes" to all of the reasons, regardless of whether the reason had a major or minor impact on enrollment. In the first question, "other" is a possible response, to be used if the offered reasons do not capturing the respondent's sentiments. If the designer has done homework, the "other" response will be rarely used.

The structure that isn't proposed is "check all that apply." That question structure is problematic because in analyzing the survey data, one cannot distinguish between people who inherently responded "no" and those who skipped the question or category. The "check all that apply" question structure should be avoided.

Anonymity and Confidentiality Survey designers often like to promise respondents that their responses to the survey will be kept "anonymous" and "confidential." Anonymity means that exactly who participated in a survey is unknown.

The survey's target population is known, but the evaluator does not know who in the target population responded to the survey. Usually, responses do not become truly anonymous until after all follow-up of units is complete, since the survey director needs to know who in the sample has or has not completed the survey in order to follow up only with those who have not completed the survey.

To uphold anonymity, after the data collection phase is over, the managers remove the names and identifying information from a respondent's record and give each respondent's record an identification number, which has no meaning other than being the case number for the purpose of the study. The ID number should not be a social security number, passport number, or any other sort of number that could identify an individual (I advise against collecting or storing any such information, since a data breach could have serious ramifications if it included such information).

Confidentiality means that the data will be held in confidence and used appropriately. Responses will never be presented at a level of detail that would allow anyone to identify the respondent. In practice, to accomplish confidentiality, in addition to not being able to release individual-level data, the evaluator cannot release information at such a small level that would allow an inquisitive person to figure out who was likely to have provided the response. For example, evaluators may not be able to present data comparing statistics in a local area on a small number of minority children with majority children, because one may be able to deduce exactly to whom the statistics on the minority group refer. If the evaluator promises confidentiality on the survey, then statistics can only be released in the aggregate. The evaluator may be restricted in releasing anecdotes, or telling the "stories," from the data that appear at the individual level.

The traditional school of thought is that the promise of anonymity and confidentiality increases response rates and entices respondents to reveal things that they would not if confidentiality were not promised. Confidentiality and anonymity are often promised, but one should carefully consider whether it is appropriate to do so. For example, a project had the purpose of surveying food programs in rural areas. Its ultimate goal was to provide the funder with a map of exactly where each program existed and the nature of each program. The survey could not promise anonymity and confidentiality for questions involving the name and location of a particular food program, as that information was certain to be shared. Also, if maps reflecting the type of program (such as number of users, amount of food distributed, and number of volunteers used) were created, the project could not promise confidentiality for those questions either. Even releasing the names of the sites that provided responses would have violated the promise of anonymity. The evaluators determined that the project would have to present information at a level detailed enough to enable an inquisitive reader to deduce a particular program, so ultimately they decided not to promise confidentiality or anonymity. Given the survey's high response rate, it is not clear that not promising confidentiality and anonymity had any effect in this particular situation. However, if one is collecting sensitive information or information on individuals rather than public institutions, one may need to promise both anonymity and confidentiality to elicit responses.

Boilerplate Introduction to a Survey and Request for Participation

BOILERPLATE INTRODUCTION TO A SURVEY

[NAME OF ORGANIZATION OR PROGRAM] is evaluating its impact and has contracted with an independent evaluation firm—[NAME OF FIRM CONDUCTING SURVEY]- to carry out the evaluation. Because [REASON WHY YOU HAVE ASKED THIS PARTICULAR PERSON TO RESPOND TO SURVEY], you are requested to complete this survey which will be a data source utilized for the evaluation.

[FIRM OR ENTITY CONDUCTING SURVEY] will keep all survey responses confidential. Responses will be presented in the aggregate and no identifying information will be included in any evaluation reports. Should you have any questions about the survey, please feel free to contact [NAME OF SURVEY DIRECTOR] at [EMAIL OF CONTACT PERSON] or [PHONE NUMBER OF CONTACT PERSON].

The survey is estimated to take approximately [NUMBER] minutes to complete.

Please complete the survey before [DATE]. Thank you for your cooperation and response.

Example:

The Main Street Food Pantry is evaluating its impact and has contracted with an independent evaluation firm-- Social Science Consultants, LLC-- to carry out the evaluation. Because you or someone in your household received food from The Main Street Food Pantry, you are requested to complete this survey which will be a data source utilized for the evaluation.

Social Science Consultants, LLC will keep all survey responses confidential. *Responses will be presented in the aggregate and no identifying information will be presented to the foundation or to your organization. Should you have any questions about the survey, please feel free to contact Beth DaPonte, Ph.D. at daponte@socialscienceconsultants.com or 1-999-999-9999.*

The survey is estimated to take approximately 8 minutes to complete.

Please complete the survey before November 1ˢᵗ. Thank you for your cooperation and response.

I use the boilerplate above in the survey's introduction. This text comes before any respondent has seen any questions. This text would be revised for your exact situation.

Note that the introduction includes why the survey is being conducted, who is conducting the survey, a statement of confidentiality, contact information for a person, the estimated time it will take to complete the survey, and when the survey will be closed. It also informs as to how the data will be used.

Structure of a Survey Typically, the overall structure of a survey instrument is as follows:

I. Introduction includes the boilerplate language above

II. Demographic questions

III. Questions on topics

   a. Topic 1

   b. Topic 2

IV. Conclusions—Open-ended question and statement of thanks

Between the sections, there should be statements indicating to the respondent that a new line of inquiry on a different topic will be asked.

TARGET POPULATIONS AND SAMPLING

The other aspect of primary data collection is determining exactly from who data is needed. If conducting a survey, the evaluator needs to decide who will be asked to complete the survey and how they will be surveyed. This section provides only a very broad overview of various sampling approaches and issues.

Every data collection approach requires a **target population**. If conducting a survey, the target population consists of the people who belong to the group who will be asked to complete the survey. The target population is the group that the evaluator wants to know about. Since a survey is used to determine the propensity of an issue in a population, the target population should be a known, defined population. Examples of target populations include:

- Program participants.
- Nonprofit organizations that refer people to the program.
- Persons in a town the program operates in between the ages of 25 and 49 that have incomes below 200% of the federal poverty line.

The evaluator must be clear about the characteristics of the population who the survey is intended to reach. Sometimes, a survey requires a small set of screening questions that are asked for the purpose of determining or verifying that the surveyed person is a member of the target population. If a respondent's answers to the screening questions indicate that they are not in the target population, then the survey ends.

In determining the target population, the following questions should be considered:

- What is the unit of analysis? For example, does the person surveyed represent individuals, or is the person providing data on the household that they live in? Will results be representative of individuals or households?

- What characteristics define the target population? Characteristics to consider are typically demographic characteristics, members of defined communities, and experience with the program.

- How feasible is it to reach the persons in the target population? What information does the survey director have that will allow the survey to reach the target population? Is there a list of persons in the target population? Can a list be developed? Is there a list of emails, phone numbers, and/or addresses? Is there a place where the target population goes where the survey could be distributed?

After the target population is described, the evaluator must decide on a sampling plan for the target population. Will information be needed from everybody in the target population, or could data from a subset of people in the target population be obtained and used to generalize to the entire target population?

In a **census,** data is (ostensibly) collected from 100 percent of the units in the target population. The US Census is a survey that purports to collect data on person who reside in the United States as of April 1 of years ending with a zero. (While 100 percent is the goal, it is never exactly reached.)

Depending on the size of the target population, one may not want to go through the effort (and expense) of collecting data from everybody in the target population. If surveying and the target population is program participants, so all program participants feel valued, it may be important to offer a survey to everybody in the target population.

Rather than conduct a census of the population, one can **sample** from the target population.

Different approaches can be taken to developing a sample. There are many ways of achieving a sample of the population. **Informal sampling** does not ensure that all in the target population have the same (or even any) probability of being sampled. The critical aspect of a **formal sample** is that all in the universe must have some probability of having been selected into the sample.

Informal Sampling Approaches

A **convenience sample** is an informal sampling approach. The persons who are asked to be interviewed or to take a survey are easy to reach for some reason, or volunteer to take the survey. For example, a senior center that wants information from the participants in all of its programs may decide to offer the survey only to people who come for its lunch service on a particular date. The target population (all who use any service) differs from the survey population (persons who receive lunch on a date), but the survey population was easy to reach. People who use services other than lunch will not be represented in the survey population.

A convenience sampling approach is also used when one advertises a program's survey to an unknown population and only those people interested in the survey respond. This approach is likely to include those who are abnormally interested in the program—typically, people who are very pleased, or abnormally displeased with the program. An example of such an approach taken is with community assessments, where the survey is advertised using flyers (that contain a QR code to the survey) and/or social media posts (with links to the survey). There is no additional effort to entice those who have typical feelings about the program to participate in the survey. The same issues pertain to interview or focus group recruitment.

Similarly, a **"snowball" sample** is not a purposeful sample. Snowball samples occur when after identifying someone in the target population and that person participates in data collection, the data collector asks the person for references to other similar cases. In a human rights example, a snowball sample would be created when the first person who experienced human rights abuses refers data collectors to another person (who was likely also a victim of human rights abuses) and who would become the next case in the sample. The sample grows because of referrals from people already in the sample, hence, the term "snowball."

A snowball sample cannot yield population estimates of the incidence of an event or characteristic because evaluators do not know the degree to which people who were not included in the sample experienced the event. A per capita rate of the occurrence of an event in a population is calculated by dividing the total number of times the event occurred by the number of people in the population. Even if some people who were entered into the snowball sample did not have their human rights abused, it is likely that the sample that results does not represent the population as a whole. Everybody in the population did not have a known probability of being included in the survey sample.

Formal Sampling Approaches

The most basic formal sample is a **simple random sample.** The key to developing a simple random sample is that there must be a list from which to draw sampled units. The list is known as the **sampling frame**. Starting with a list of every unit in the target population, one would determine the sample size needed from the number in the target population to obtain statistics that derive from the survey within a desired **margin of error**.

In a simple random sample, every unit on the list has the same chance of being entered into the sample. Thus, if the target population has 500 people in the desired sample size of 125, then each person would have a 25% chance of being randomly selected for the sample. To determine which 125 people to select, use a random number generator. (Do not take the first 125 on the list because the order of appearance may not yield good representation of the entire target population.)

If using a spreadsheet, first list all of the units in the target population in a column. In the next column, assign to each unit using the spreadsheet's random number function a number.

Then, sort all of the units by random number (e.g., by smallest to largest of the random number) and then select the first 125 cases for the sample. This procedure will yield a random sample of 125, where all units had the same probability of being selected.

To determine the needed sample size for a particular margin of error, consider that the mathematical relationship between sample size and the margin of error at the 95% confidence interval is:

$$1.96 * \sqrt{(p(1-p)/n)} = \text{Margin of error}$$

P is the proportion of responses to a question in a category. Solving this equation assuming a 50 percent chance of a particular response (which is the scenario that would yield the largest sample size) and that a 4 percent margin of error is acceptable for statistics that derive from the survey, one gets $1.96 * \sqrt{((.5*.5)/n)} = .04$ and the needed sample size, n, is 600.

Another approach to sampling is **stratified random sampling.** A simple random sample, as shown above, allows each unit in the universe to have the same probability of being selected. However, there are times when the evaluator may want to design a sample that guarantees that the sample includes enough units in various categories so that statistics can be calculated for minority as well as majority units.

When using a stratified random sampling approach, evaluators should consult with a statistician on the drawing of the sample, the weighing of the data, and how to calculate population statistics on the basis of the sample. In general, while a stratified random sample approach can allow one to create estimates of subpopulations, the overall sample size needed will exceed that of a simple random sample. Getting more specific information on subpopulations comes at a cost.

Best Practices in Administering Surveys to a Purposive Sample

If administering an electronic survey through a survey platform, best practices follow:

The sample should be informed that they will be receiving a survey shortly. A letter, email, text, or phone call should be sent by someone associated with the program being evaluation (e.g., Executive Director and Program Director) informing persons in the survey sample to expect the survey and asking them to respond to the survey.

The survey should be sent out and the invitations should be followed-up on. The evaluator should set up the survey platform to send the link to all in the sample simultaneously. If the request is by email or text message, about 3 days after the link is sent, the evaluator should send only to nonrespondents a reminder email. This should continue about every 3 days until approximately 5 reminders are sent. Again, only nonrespondents should be sent reminders. After each reminder, many people will respond within 24 hours, and then after that, responses will decrease to a trickle.

Follow-up for Nonresponse

Nearly any data collection method will have "nonresponse"— not all persons in the target population will respond when asked for information. Nonresponse can happen with any of the above data collection methods. Some people who are asked to be interviewed will not make themselves available for an interview, some asked to participate in a focus group will not attend, and in surveys, those asked to complete the survey (or census) will not do so. With surveys, nonresponse can take the form of not taking the survey (survey nonresponse) or refusing to answer particular questions on the survey (question nonresponse).

The issue with nonrespondents is whether nonrespondents are a random subset of the target population, or are nonrespondents a selective subset. In a survey, if the nonrespondents differ from respondents in how they react to the program or would respond to questions, then the results from an achieved survey population are not generalizable to the survey's target population. Estimates derived from a survey have a margin of error that pertains to the sample derived. The margin of error does not incorporate the issue of the degree to which respondents and nonrespondents differ with respect to their answers to questions asked.

To determine whether respondents and nonrespondents differ, a smaller sample for nonresponse follow-up (SNRFU) can be created. That is, the evaluator would take from a list of survey nonrespondents and entice the nonrespondents to respond to the survey, perhaps by offering additional compensation and/or having intense outreach to the sample. The evaluator would then compare the survey responses from this smaller sample of nonrespondents and determine whether their responses fall within the margin of error of the estimates derived from the answers of respondents.

SECONDARY DATA SOURCES

Evaluators frequently use pre-existing data sources, either in combination with new data that they will collect, or, sometimes as the sole data source for the evaluation. Pre-existing data may be structured in a way that can provide meaningful information. Consider the following pre-existing sources:

- Organizational and initiative-level budget plans
- Organizational and initiative-level expenditures
- Annual reports of organizations
- IRS Form 990, which every nonprofit organization in the USA must submit and is easily found online
- Minutes of meetings
- Attendance at meetings

- School records
- Voting records at the level of a geographic unit
- Records on the frequency and value of benefits a program participant received, as recorded by a program

Each of these data sources (and the list above is not exhaustive) can be mined for valuable information.

When using data that others have collected, the evaluator must be certain of the definitions that are being used for indicators, and exactly how the indicators have been calculated. The evaluator should check to see if, in creating a time series of data from secondary sources, definitions or calculations of indicators and the nuances of data collection (e.g., change in sampling or how issues have been recorded) have changed over time.

SUMMARY

This chapter provides an introduction to the many approaches used to collect data. For many small programs, even a new evaluator will be able to conduct informal interviews, run focus groups, and even develop, pretest, and administer a survey. For small programs, sampling may not be an issue because the universe of program participants is not large enough to warrant a sample, so a census of participants will be conducted. For larger programs, the novice evaluator should develop ties with local statisticians to discuss the sampling plan and possibly assist with data analysis.

It is helpful, even before collecting data, to map out exactly how the information from each question will be used in a report. This exercise saves time and money in the end, because all involved in the evaluation will be better able to see which data will be useful and whether there are questions that evaluators were going to include that ultimately have no place in the report.

Collecting and analyzing data require time and resources and it is easy to underestimate resources needed. Collecting data should be done thoughtfully, with a well-detailed plan of how data collection will proceed, a realistic budget, and a realistic timeline. It may be worthwhile to explore whether any academic centers in your community offer data collection services. An experienced center may ultimately provide an economical approach to collecting the data.

KEY TERMS

census
confidentiality
convenience sample
focus group
formal survey instrument
informal interviews
question reliability

question validity
sample
sampling error
simple random sample
snowball sample
stratified random sample
target population

DISCUSSION QUESTIONS

1. If you are the leader of a focus group, why should you *not* be concerned if you don't get through all of your questions?
2. Why is it important to offer open-ended questions to a focus group, but not in a survey?
3. Discuss the benefits and drawbacks of offering confidentiality to survey respondents.

CHAPTER 8

CONCLUSIONS

LEARNING OBJECTIVES

After reading this chapter, you should be able to

- Explain how evaluation tools can be used to sharpen grant proposals
- Write a Scope of Services or Terms of Reference used to contract with evaluation consultants/firms
- Write recommendations

Evaluation Essentials: Methods for Conducting Sound Evaluation Research, Second Edition.
Beth Osborne DaPonte.
© 2025 John Wiley & Sons, Inc. Published 2025 by John Wiley & Sons, Inc.

USING EVALUATION TOOLS TO WRITE GRANT PROPOSALS

An evaluation approach will strengthen grant proposals. Increasingly, funders want from prospective grantees details on how they think about their work and exactly what they will be doing with the funds if awarded. A concise and respected way to present the program to funders is to present them with a well-thought-out Theory of Change (ToC) and Program Logic Model (PLM). If a literature review supports the approach being proposed and if there is space within the word limit of a grant proposal, the grant proposal should include an abbreviated literature review.

Most funders have constituencies to whom they must share the impact of their support. When potential grantees show that they have a plan for evaluating the impact of the potential support, potential grantees strengthen their applications. Potential grantees should provide in their grant application the likely high-priority evaluation questions. It serves potential grantees well to also show that they have included a budget for evaluation that is reasonable considering the budget for the overall initiative—typically approximately 1–3% of the total amount being requested for initiatives that are not pilots, and up to 10% for pilot programs.

HIRING EVALUATION CONSULTANTS

While I do not expect everybody who has read this book or taken a course in Program Evaluation to become evaluators or conduct evaluations themselves, I hope that this text has provided enough background so you can critically read the evaluation literature, determine the characteristics of a high-quality evaluation consultant, and be able to structure the work of and contract with or hire an evaluator.

If hiring an evaluator, either to join the staff of an organization or as a consultant, one should expect the candidates to possess skills including being able to adeptly describe programs using a ToC and PLM, survey design, data analysis, knowledge of quasi-experimental design, ability to conduct literature reviews—but also and perhaps most importantly, an ability to think creatively. Perhaps the best way to judge potential evaluators is to ask them to show a portfolio of past evaluations and ask them which evaluation(s) they are most proud of. Evaluators at the beginning of their careers should be able to show through their classwork that they have the competencies to either be a valuable evaluation team member or that they could carry out more limited evaluation engagements.

If hiring an evaluation consultant, an organization should create a Terms of Reference, also known as a Scope of Services or Request for Proposals (RFPs). The Terms of Reference (TOR) should include a description of the initiatives' background and history, its organizational structure and budget, the evaluation questions (if they have been determined), the methodology expected (if it has been agreed on), the audience for the evaluation products, dates that evaluation products are due, and the maximum budget for the evaluation. The TOR should be widely circulated (e.g., posted on the American Evaluation Association's website, ImpactPool). Evaluation consultants and firms would submit bids in response. The more detailed the TOR/RFP, the more likely that the submissions the entity receives from evaluators will be on point (see Box for the outline of a TOR/RFP).

> **Outline of Terms of Reference/Request for Proposals**
>
> I. **Introduction**
>   Description/history of program, reason for evaluation activities, audience for evaluation activities
> II. **Structure of evaluation activities**
>   To whom the evaluator(s) will report
>   Intellectual property considerations
> III. **Evaluation questions**
> IV. **Anticipated methodology/approach**
> V. **Expected activities and due dates**
>   a. Inception report
>   Evaluator will describe in detail the approach that will be taken throughout the evaluation (typically due within 1 month of signing contract for evaluation).
>   b. Data collection: time period
>   c. Reporting
>   i. Evaluator will present preliminary results: due date
>   ii. Evaluation will submit first draft of evaluation: due date
>   iii. Final report: due date
> VI. **Payments**
>   a. Total maximum sum available for evaluation activities
>   b. Schedule of payments
>   i. Tie to evaluation products and steps in the evaluation process
>   ii. Clarify how travel costs will be covered
>   iii. Clarify whether evaluation proposals should include payments to interview and focus group participants and survey respondents

By creating and circulating a detailed TOR/RFP, the organization controls how evaluation activities will be conducted. Sometimes, organizations will instead create a very broad TOR and ask evaluators to determine the methodology and cost. This approach is inefficient for a number of reasons, the most important being that it leaves the evaluation activities up to the evaluators who submit bids. Also, there is no assurance that the cost of the submissions will fit into the budget set aside for the activities.

A detailed TOR/RFP allows potential evaluators to decide whether they can meet the organization's evaluation expectations within the maximum budget. If they cannot, then they will not submit proposals, which could save everybody time and effort—the organization does not need to review proposals for work that it cannot afford.

Sometimes, organizations will release TORs/RFPs that are poorly written. I have seen organizations put out very broad TORs/RFPs with a loose description of what is wanted and with a total budget that they clearly have not thought through. Such TORs/RFPs have come from small nonprofits as well as large, international organizations.

Four typical problems appear with poorly written TORs/RFPs. First, the TORs/RFPs may have in them **unrealistically short timelines for the workplan.** A good evaluator could not possibly conduct the evaluation within the allotted time. Even if the organization decides later that the timelines could be extended, the damage has already been done—the best evaluators may not submit proposals because they know that they cannot possibly accomplish the required work by the deadlines. Unrealistically short timelines in TORs/RFPs can also indicate that the organization has delayed the evaluation work and that the work is an afterthought. I have seen TORs/RFPs with timelines for complete evaluations as short as 3 weeks.

Second, poorly written TORs/RFPs may **lack clarity on what the evaluator should include in their budgetary submission.** They may have included the total budget for the evaluation, but when evaluators are creating their budget submission, it is sometimes impossible to estimate the cost of needed travel and the cost of compensating people for their participation in interviews, focus groups, or completing surveys. Knowing how much travel and data collection will cost becomes more apparent after an evaluator has developed the evaluation plan. In my opinion, if the hiring organization can, it should develop the evaluation plan, and then evaluators/firms will be hired to execute the plan.

Once, based on a proposal submitted in response to an RFP, a firm was being considered to conduct a final evaluation of a program. The hiring organization did not put in the RFP that the program was a multisite program and that the organization expected the evaluator to conduct in-person data collection at each site. The sites were about 300 miles apart. The organization also wanted the applicant firm to hire specific local data collectors. They also believed that meals would need to be offered at focus group sites. All of this could have been put into the RFP. The applicant firm would have never submitted a proposal if this information was in the RFP because the organization had an unrealistic budget and expectations. The organization had set aside for evaluation only 0.25% of the program's budget. As a result, both the applicant firm and organization wasted time and effort.

Third, poorly constructed TORs/RFPs have **unclear lines of communication and/or include an organizational structure that will not allow the evaluator to have independence.** Organizations issuing the TOR/RFP have not considered how the proposed organizational structure of the evaluation activities will impede the evaluator's independence.

Fourth, some TORs/RFPs are written in a way that raise suspicions that **the evaluator has essentially already been selected.** Proposals are being requested so it seems that there is a competitive process occurring, when, in fact, there is not. Such TORs/RFPs include unneeded requirements. For example, the TOR/RFP may list as a requirement previous experience conducting evaluations for exactly the same sort of program or exact client, or include geographic experience that is unnecessary, and/or demographic characteristics of consultants that are unrelated to producing a high-quality evaluation. I have seen TORs/RFPs that required a certain number of evaluations on the same or similar programs in a short period of time (e.g., must have conducted 4 evaluations on light rail transportation initiatives in the city in the last 3 years).

In order to attract high-quality evaluation consultants, organizations must put the time and effort into writing high-quality TORs/RFPs. They could hire an evaluation consultant (who would be ineligible to apply for the contract) to write the TOR/RFP.

WRITING RECOMMENDATIONS

Every evaluation should end with recommendations. In writing recommendations, evaluators should consider who needs to act, the time period that the recommendation should be implemented in, what the actions are, and the resources needed to carry out the recommendation.

For example, participants in a program reported that they were not reimbursed for travel quickly and that threatened their participation. A well-written recommendation could be that:

The Chief Financial Officer should ensure that participants receive reimbursements for their travel within one week of travel occurring.

A poorly written recommendation would be:

The program should pay its participants for travel faster.

In a program that trained negotiators, participants noted that some of the trainers seemed not to have deep experience with the topic that they were teaching. Indeed, the entity administering the program reported that they had no set criteria for selecting the trainers, although, in the field, it was common for trainers to have certification. Rather than recommending "All trainers should be certified," the evaluation recommended that:

The Human Resource Director should assure that all persons hired as trainers hold the negotiator certification and have worked for at least three years as a negotiator.

Recommendations can be classified as to whether they are critical, important, or opportunities for improvement. Critical recommendations are those actions where if not remedied or taken, put the entire program or organization at risk. They can involve funding or reputational risks. They are existential. Important recommendations will have a large effect on the program, but if not implemented, the program will continue to operate (albeit very inefficiently and/or with compromised impact). Opportunities for improvement are actions that the program could take for improvement. Often, these are managerial recommendations and include ways to better access/attract the target population, address funding issues, and/or staffing. If the evaluator has no critical recommendations to make, that should be noted in the recommendations section.

For recommendations to be impactful, there should be a mechanism to follow-up on their implementation. If an organization has a large number of evaluations occurring and recommendations being made by evaluators, then it could have a central office that oversees the implementation of recommendations. In the United Nations, this office is the Office of Internal Oversight Services. The OIOS issues reports to the General Assembly that informs on the implementation of recommendations.

The Tone of Evaluation Reports

In writing an evaluation report, it is easy for an evaluator to get into the mindset that they know best. Such reports become very negative toward the program, highlighting its deficiencies and ways that it could be improved. Such reports often get little traction.

Evaluators must appreciate that program implementers and funders generally come to the initiative with the best of intentions and have often worked hard in getting the initiative to be impactful. They have sometimes engaged an evaluator to help them think hard about the initiative and provide honest, unbiased, and useful information about the initiative. It is critically important for an evaluation report to acknowledge the good work that has been done. There is a fine line between an evaluation report and a vanity paper. I am not suggesting that the evaluation exists only to point out the program's "good" aspects and where it has been impactful. But where there are wins to be addressed, the evaluator should include those in the report. Any evaluation report should be a balance between the good and not so good. By celebrating the areas that can be celebrated, the evaluation report will become more appreciated and recommendations from the report will more likely be endorsed and acted upon.

Finalization Process of Evaluation Reports

"No one likes surprises." The issuance of an evaluation should not be the first time that the Evaluation Reference Group (ERG) and evaluand learn of the evaluation's findings and recommendations. The finalization process is a vital step in issuing an evaluation report. The evaluator, after having analyzed the data, determined the findings of the evaluation, and having drafted recommendations should share with the ERG the evaluation's tentative results. I typically share a PowerPoint presentation that includes all aspects of the evaluation report. This will serve as the outline of the evaluation report. But before the evaluation team actually writes the report, the evaluation team should meet with the ERG (for about 1.5–2 hours) to review the entire outline of the report. The ERG can comment on the findings, clarify, correct, and share perspectives. The ERG can react to the proposed recommendations in the meeting. The evaluation team will find this meeting extremely useful since it will clarify where there is acknowledgment and acceptance and where there could be "pushback." The meeting will help the team draft the evaluation report.

The second stage of the finalization process is when the evaluator provides the ERG with the draft report. The evaluator would have written the draft report keeping in mind the feedback from the meeting. The evaluator and ERG will determine how widely the draft will be disseminated (e.g., only the ERG? The ERG and senior management?) and when the evaluator should expect written comments on the draft. A three-week period of review could be a reasonable period for review.

The evaluator should not be surprised if the comments received will push the report to be more positive towards the program than the draft report was. If the evaluator has independence, the evaluator will decide how to deal with comments and suggested changes to the draft report.

In areas where there is pushback, the evaluator must decide whether the issue should be kept in the report, or whether bringing the issue to the attention of the ERG and the program's management is sufficient to seeing improvements occur. Some findings from an evaluation could prompt managerial-level recommendations that are not critical to the program's success but represent opportunities for improvement. Sometimes, bringing the issues to the evaluand's attention is sufficient for change to occur, and there is no need for a finalized, possibly public report to include the issue. These decisions must be made on a case-by-case basis, since the report should not be needlessly critical but also not be a whitewash. Remember, the purpose of evaluation reports is not to be needlessly critical, but to bring about positive change. When the finalized report is issued, there are no surprises.

Typically, the finalization process results in a higher-quality report. In developing a timeline for an evaluation report, the finalization process, which could take up to two months, should be considered.

CONCLUSIONS

The field of evaluation is dynamic and incredibly interesting. But for it to be effective, evaluators must not only possess high competence in a number of areas but also have independence. Evaluators must report not to program implementers, but to boards of organizations and to funders of initiatives. Boards of organizations should be aware of the recommendations that evaluators have made.

The combination of evaluators being highly skilled and independent is potent. This combination will allow evaluators to recommend improvements to initiatives, and ultimately, for organizations and initiatives to achieve their missions and have greater positive impact.

DISCUSSION QUESTIONS

1. Describe the parallels between the evaluation report and a grant proposal.

2. Practice writing actionable recommendations.

GLOSSARY

activities. What a program actually does, activities the public may witness and those that occur behind the scenes; often includes how clients are recruited, how staff is trained, how the program reaches the target population, and how the program interacts with its clients.

anonymity. The link between an individual's responses and the individual's name will be broken.

archival data. Data collected in the past; also called historical data.

assumptions. How a program perceives the environment in which it operates.

categorical data. Data collected in terms of categories.

CATI system. Computer Assisted Telephone Interview system; an interviewer reads questions from a computer screen and enters responses directly into the computer, which typically creates a database of responses.

causation. To bring about change.

census. Data collection from 100 percent of the units in the universe.

cohort. A group which experienced the same event at the same time.

compensatory equalization. When the control group receives either the actual treatment or some version of it.

compensatory rivalry. The control group behaves abnormally well to show they are better than the treatment group.

confidentiality. Data will be held in confidence and used appropriately.

construct validity. Degree to which the theoretical constructs have been well-specified and both the cause and effect constructs have been appropriately operationalized.

continuous data. Raw, non-categorical data; allows for the most flexibility in data analysis.

continuous effects. Effects that last forever.

convenience sample. Created at the convenience of the data collectors; not a formal sampling approach.

delayed treatment control group design. Where the control group eventually receives the treatment, but at a later date than the "treatment" group; sometimes known as "switching replications design."

different samples design. Also called sampling without replacement; drawing pretest samples from the treatment and control groups that have different individuals than posttest samples.

diffusion of a treatment. Treatment and control groups overlap or share information.

discontinuous effects. Short-lived effects; impacts that wear off with time.

evaluation. Done to examine whether a program or policy causes a change; assists with continuous programmatic improvement and introspection.

Evaluation Essentials: Methods for Conducting Sound Evaluation Research, Second Edition.
Beth Osborne DaPonte.
© 2025 John Wiley & Sons, Inc. Published 2025 by John Wiley & Sons, Inc.

evaluation plan. Consists of what the central questions of evaluation activities will be, how processes will be examined, what sort of outputs and outcomes are expected, and how the program intends to show that changes in outcomes are attributable to the program.

evaluation report. After research is done on an intervention, a report is written and disseminated to relevant stakeholders.

evaluator. The person who performs or studies evaluations.

external evaluator. Evaluator hired on a contractual basis; has the appearance of impartiality.

external validity. The generalizability of the relationship found in one evaluation or study to other people, places, and contexts.

false negative conclusion. False conclusion that a causal relationship does not exist when, in fact, there is a causal relationship.

false positive conclusion. False conclusion that a causal relationship does exist, when, in fact, there is not a causal relationship.

fishing. Throwing all possible variables into an analysis and letting the statistical analysis reveal what variables show statistical significance.

focus group. A group of people who can reveal their thoughts, attitudes, and experiences about an issue. Used to discover the issues that exist and range of circumstances and views.

formal survey instrument. Used to discover the frequency of issues and views.

formative evaluation. Produces information that is fed back to decision makers who can use it to continuously improve the program; often referred to as "evaluatory activities."

goals. Change(s) that the program anticipates will result from the intervention's activities.

high stakes evaluations. Outcome-based evaluations used as the basis for making important decisions about the survival of a program.

high stakes testing. Occurs when test results are used to make decisions that have large ramifications; can lead to a weak evaluation and distort behavior around the test.

informal interview. Conversation with stakeholders done initially to understand the program.

inputs. What it takes to operate the program, including monetary funding, in-kind contributions, physical space, characteristics and qualifications of staff, and particular expertise of staff.

internal evaluator. Usually on the staff of the program's organization; has familiarity with the organization, sometimes the particular program being evaluated; may have an understanding of the personalities within the organization.

internal validity. The degree to which the study has shown that a causal relationship exists.

intervening variable. Factors other than cause and effect whose presence or absence can cloud the true relationship a program has with outcomes.

interviewer-administered survey. Conducted in person in a face-to-face interview or over the phone.

iterative process. Multiple rounds of examining and crafting before the final.

lagged effect. Delay before effect appears, not immediate; the time delay makes the effects difficult to attribute to the intervention.

longitudinal data. Data from the same unit over consecutive periods of time.

measurement error. The degree of imprecision in measures.

mono-method bias. Only one measure is used to reflect a theoretical construct.

mono-operation bias. Various measurements are presented in the same way.

necessary. The only way the desired outcome could occur is if the intervention caused it to occur.

necessary and sufficient. The outcome can only be produced by the program or intervention, and if one went through the program the outcome would always be produced.

negatively covary. Increase in the causes would be associated with an observed decrease in the effect, and vice versa.

nonequivalent groups using switched measures. Total group of people who receive the treatment are divided into two subgroups; the first observation of one subgroup is the outcome measure A, and the first subgroup's second observation is of the outcome measure B; for the second group, B is the first measure and A the second.

nonequivalent observations design drawn from one group. Uses the same people in the treatment group as the control group; conducts measurements on only a single group of persons.

observable differences. Differences in demographic characteristics.

one-group posttest-only design. Quasi-experimental design where only the outcomes of the participant group are examined at only one time—after the program.

one-group pretest-posttest design. Quasi-experimental design where the treatment group is measured with a single pretest and a single posttest.

operationalize. Brings a theoretical concept down to the practical realm.

outcome evaluation. Emphasizes the change in clients or participants that resulted from the program's activities.

outcome measures. Quantitatively reflects the measures, counts, rates, or indicators used to operationalize articulated outcomes.

outcomes. The desired impact of the program using words, not numbers; usually relate to the program's goals.

outputs. Measures that show the program is actually operating.

parsimony. The smallest set that will deliver the most bang for the buck.

period effects. The passage of time affects the identical program in two different time periods.

permanency of effect. The length of time an effect is present, long-lasting vs. short-lived.

positively covary. Increase in the cause would be associated with an increase in the effect.

posttest-only design with nonequivalent groups. Quasi-experimental design where the outcomes of two groups, the participant group and the control group, are examined only after the program.

primary goals. Primary reasons for the program's existence; goals the program must achieve.

process evaluation. Focuses on program processes—the "how" of program delivery processes.

program implementation model. Reflects the sequence of a program's activities, akin to a flow chart.

program logic model (PLM). Models the operation of the program and the logic behind it; details how the program is operating, with what resources, whom it targets, what it intends to accomplish; consists of eight columns: (1) goals, (2) assumptions, (3) target population, (4) inputs, (5) activities, (6) outputs, (7) outcomes, (8) outcome measures.

program theory. A diagram of the theory behind the program, sometimes called theory of change.

psychological pretesting. The respondent talks about how s/he is thinking about the questions as s/he is taking the survey.

publication bias. Evaluations that show that programs have impacts are more likely to be published than those that show programs have no effect, are poorly implemented, or show conflicting results.

quasi-experimental design. A way to examine qualitative data in a structured way.

quasi-experimental notation. A way to display the quasi-experimental design where "O" indicates an observation and "X" indicates an intervention or treatment [introduced by Cook & Campbell (1979)].

question reliability. The extent to which people in comparable situations will respond to questions in similar ways; also the extent to which the same respondent in unchanged circumstances will respond to the same questions in the same way.

question validity. The extent to which a given response reflects what the survey designer intends and expects the response to mean.

resentful demoralization. The control group behaves abnormally poorly.

sample. A collection of data from less than 100 percent of the units in the universe.

sampling error. The extent to which the sample estimate varies from the population estimate.

secondary goals. Goals a program has but which are not the primary reason for the program's existence.

simple random sample. There must be a list from which to draw sampled units; every unit on the list has the same chance of being entered into the sample; units are selected by chance to be in the sample.

small sample size. Sample size of less than fifty units; conclusions from small sample sizes can be unreliable.

snowball sample. The sample grows because of referrals from people already in the sample.

spectacular causes. In a tipping point situation, a large dose of the cause (program or intervention) produces small effects.

spectacular effects. In a tipping point situation, a small dose of the cause (program or intervention) produces very large effects.

stakeholders. People who have an interest in the program, such as program administrators, funders, boards of directors, clients, staff, advocates, and alumni.

statistical conclusion validity. The appropriateness of the statistical techniques used for the analysis.

stratified random sample. Separating the sample and assigning different probabilities of being selected.

sufficient. The program will absolutely procedure the intended outcome.

summative evaluation. A "report card" evaluation; information produced is used to determine the extent of the program's effectiveness; often takes the form of evaluation reports.

target population. The units of analysis or population that the program or intervention intends to impact.

targets or benchmarks. Measurements by which program success is defined.

Theory of Change. A schematic that shows how program designers believe that the activities will lead to the goals of the initiative being achieved.

threat of history. An event that could affect the level of the outcome indicator, independent of the program's influence; occurs during the time between the start and end of the program when something that would independently exert an influence on the program's outcomes occurs during the program's operation but outside of the program.

threat of instrumentation. Means of data collection changes between pre-intervention and post-intervention observations, and this change affects the quantification of the observation.

threat of maturation. Some participants may have changed in the way that the program intends them to just because time passed.

threat of mortality. Those who dropped out of the program differ from those who stayed in and completed the program.

threat of selection. When participation is voluntary, it is likely that those who participate in the program differ in some way from those who do not participate.

threat of statistical regression. A program is offered only to those who have performed exceptionally well or poorly on a pretest, and their posttest observation is likely to be closer to the mean of all units who were pretested.

threat of testing. Responses on a test change as familiarity with the test increases.

threats to validity. Events or circumstances that have the potential to make conclusions based on the research invalid in a certain respect.

time series. Follow the same "unit" over time.

type I error. Evaluator concludes the outcomes of various treatment groups differ, when in reality they do not.

type II error. Evaluator concludes the outcomes of the various treatment groups do not differ, when in reality they do.

unit of analysis. What the program aims to affect; the "thing" to which the outcome measure applies.

untreated control group design with pretest and posttest. Quasi-experimental design that includes both a participant and control group and two observations—one pre-treatment and one post-treatment.

validity. Extent to which there has been an approximation of truth.

INDEX

A

Activities (program logic model)
  Child Stunting and Child Wasting Initiative, 46–47*t*
  Comprehensive Charity, 52–53*t*
  description and importance of, 27*t*, 32
  Funder's Nonprofit Capitalization Initiative, 60–61*t*
  Health Care to Unsheltered Homeless Provision Program, 58–59*t*
  Housing Recovery Program, 60–61
  Labor Union Capacity-Building Initiative, 42–43*t*
American Evaluation Association, 75–76, 177
Americans with Disabilities Act (ADA), 64
Anonymity issue, 167–168
Archival (historical) data, 128
Assumptions (program logic model)
  Child Stunting and Child Wasting Initiative, 46–47*t*
  Comprehensive Charity, 52–53*t*, 58–59*t*
  description and importance of, 26, 27*t*, 29
  Funder's Nonprofit Capitalization Initiative, 60–61*t*
  Housing Recovery Program, 60–61
  Labor Union Capacity-Building Initiative, 42–43*t*
  program failure from faulty assumptions, 64–65
  Rehabilitating Housing Program, 64–65

B

Bade, S., 123
Bias
  mono-method, 121
  mono-operation, 120–121
  "yes", 162
Bickman, L, 143

C

Campbell, D., 104, 106, 127, 128, 129
Caulkins, J., 81
Causation
  intervening variables, 95–97
  multiple threats to causal relationship validity, 118–119
  necessary and sufficient variables, 88–91
  quasi-experimental design permitting, 127–149
  types of effects, 97–100
Census, 30, 164, 170
Child Advocacy Coalition (CAC), 62
Children's Health Insurance Outreach Program, 62–66
Cohort designs
  archival data used in, 128
  description of, 144–146
Compensatory equalization, 118
Compensatory rivalry, 118
Comprehensive Charity Services, 54–62
Confidentiality issue, 80–81, 167–168
Construct validity
  definition of, 104, 119
  issues related, 105
  literature reviews, 121
  mono-method bias threat to, 121
  mono-operation bias threat to, 120–121
  priority given to, 105
  questions as to, 105
Contribution analysis, 20–21
Control groups
  definition of, 129
  delayed treatment, 137–140
  untreated design with pretest and post-test, 131–137
Convenience sample, 170–171
Cook, T., 104, 106, 127, 128, 129

D

Daponte, B. O., 123
Data analysis
  methodology, 84
  planning process of, 7
  quasi-experimental design, 127
  validity of, 110
Data collection
  best practices, 173
  computer-based technology used for, 154, 161
  developing plan for, 7

Evaluation Essentials: Methods for Conducting Sound Evaluation Research, Second Edition.
Beth Osborne DaPonte.
© 2025 John Wiley & Sons, Inc. Published 2025 by John Wiley & Sons, Inc.

focus group interviews used for, 154–160
follow-up for nonresponse, 173–174
formal sampling approaches, 171–173
informal and loosely structured interviews, 152–154
informal sampling approaches, 170–171
secondary data sources, 174–175
stakeholder interviews used for, 72–73, 152
surveys used for, 160–169
on target population, 169–174
Delayed treatment control group, 137–140
Dembosky, J, 81
Different samples design, 140–141
Diffusion of treatments threat, 117–118

E

Early Childhood Initiative (Evaluation Policy), 81
Ethical issues, 134, 138
Evaluation *See also* programs
  approaches to, 69–71
  building knowledge base from, 110
  confidentiality and ownership issues of, 80–81
  contribution analysis, 20–21
  endorsement of, and action on recommendations of, 81–82
  high stakes, 74–75
  insincere reasons for, 74
  parsimonious approach to, 12–13
  policy, 82–83
  program description component of, 11–14
  summative and formative, 69
Evaluation framework
  carry out the evaluation plan, 8
  conduct a literature review around the theory of change and to learn about similar initiatives, 6
  determine the audience and accountability structure for the evaluation activities, 5
  determine the universe of possible evaluation questions, 5
  develop the evaluation plan, 7
  endorsement of, and implementation of, recommendations, 8
  finalize the evaluation report, 8
  report on draft evaluation findings and recommendations, 8
  revisit and narrow the universe of evaluation questions, 6–7
  rigorously describe the program, 5
  summary of steps, 6
Evaluation plan (inception report)
  carrying out of, 7
  creation of, 5
  developing the, 7

Evaluation questions *See also* Respondents
  determining possible, 5
  evaluation report's presentation of, 84
  framing of, 71–74
  for Opera Trunk Program, 24
  program theory used to narrow, 6–7
  revisiting and narrowing, 6–7
  survey instrument (questionnaire), 163
  validity threatened by inappropriate, 85
Evaluation-related activities, 18
Evaluation reports
  finalization of, 181–182
  outline, 83–85
  tone of, 180–181
Evaluation tools
  grant proposal development using, 177
  PLM (program logic model), 5, 12, 25–36, 41–44, 41–66, 45–48, 84
  Theory of Change (ToC) (program theory), 5, 12, 20–21, 23–24, 40
Evaluators
  background, skills, and training of, 4
  external evaluators, 76–78
  external or internal, 79–80
  hiring external consultant, 177–178
  independence of, 78–79
  internal evaluators, 78
  mistakes of, 16–17
  persons in role of, 75–76
  primary job, and secondary job of, 2
  program description by, 12–13
  questions asked by, 2
External evaluators
  description of, 76–78
  external or internal evaluators, 79–80
  hiring external consultant, 177–178
External validity
  definition of, 105, 122
  different places issue, 122–123
  different populations issue, 123
  different time periods issue, 122
  "period effects" and, 122
  priority given to, 105
  questions as to, 123–124

F

"Fishing", 110–111
Focus groups
  data collection using, 154–160
  surveys compared to, 160
Food Distribution Research Project survey (1990s), 159
Food stamp program, 113–114, 139

Formal survey instrument, 171–173
Formative evaluation, 51t, 69–70, 81
Functional form of impact, 99–100
Funder's Nonprofit Capitalization Initiative, 48–54

G
Gill, B., 81
Goals (program logic model)
  Child Stunting and Child Wasting Initiative, 46–47t
  Comprehensive Charity, 52–53t
  description and importance of, 26–27
  Funder's Nonprofit Capitalization Initiative, 60–61t
  Health Care to Unsheltered Homeless Provision Program, 58–59t
  Labor Union Capacity-Building Initiative, 42–43t
Grant proposals, 177

H
Hamner, K., 143
Heckman, J., 113
Heinz Endowment, 81
High stakes evaluation, 74–75
Historical (archival) data, 128
Housing Recovery program, 60–61t, 64

I
"If" statements, 19
Inputs (program logic model)
  Child Stunting and Child Wasting Initiative, 46–47t
  description and importance of, 27–28t
  Health Care to Unsheltered Homeless Provision Program, 58–59t
  Housing Recovery Program, 60–61t
  Labor Union Capacity-Building Initiative, 42–43t
Instrumentation threat to validity, 116–117
Internal evaluators, 78
Internal validity
  compensatory equalization of treatments threat to, 118
  compensatory rivalry and resentful demoralization threat to, 118
  definition of, 104
  diffusion of treatment threat to, 117–118
  history threat to, 111–112
  instrumentation threat to, 116–117
  issues related to, 111
  maturation threat to, 112–113
  mortality threat to, 114–115
  multiple threats to causal relationship validity, 118–119
  priority given to, 105
  questions as to, 111
  selection threat to, 113–114
  statistical regression threat to, 115–116
  testing threat to, 115
Interviews
  focus groups, 154–160
  stakeholders, 72–73, 152
  surveys compared to, 160

J
"John Henry" effect, 118

K
Knowledge base, 110, 112, 115

L
Labor Union, 37–44
Lagged effects, 98
Lieberson, S., 113, 114
Literature reviews, 6, 21–22, 25, 121

M
Making It Count (Lieberson), 113
Mammogram awareness program, 112
Maturation threat to validity, 112–113
Measurement error, 33, 109–110, 151, 161
Mono-method bias, 121
Mono-operation bias, 120–121
Mortality threat to validity, 114–115

N
Necessary program variable, 88
NGOs (nongovernmental organizations), 3
"A Noble Bet" (Gill, Dembosky, and Caulkins), 81
Nonequivalent observations design drawn from one group, 141–142

O
One-group post-test-only design, 128–129
One-group pretest-post-test design, 130–131
Opera Trunk Program, 23–25
Outcome measures (program logic model), 33–34
Outcomes
  attribution of, 127–149
  necessary and sufficient variables and 88–91, 91t
  PLM (program logic model) component of, 27–28t

Outcomes (program logic model)
　Child Stunting and Child Wasting Initiative, 46–47*t*
　Comprehensive Charity, 52–53*t*
　description and importance of, 32–33
　Funder's Nonprofit Capitalization Initiative, 50–51*t*
　Health Care to Unsheltered Homeless Provision Program, 58–59*t*
　Housing Recovery Program, 60–61*t*
　Labor Union Capacity-Building Initiative, 42–43*t*
Outputs (program logic model), 143
Ownership of evaluation, 81–82

P

Parsimonious program models, 12–13
Participants *See also* Respondents
　confidentiality and anonymity of, 109, 167–169
　focus group, 154–160
　pretest-post-test of, 130–131
　randomly assigned, 130
Patton, M. Q., 4
Permanency of effects, 98–99
Post testing
　pattern, 1 design using, 132–134
　pattern, 2 design using, 134–135
　pattern, 3 design using, 135–136
　pattern, 4 design using, 136–137
　untreated control group design with, 132*fig*
Post-test-only design with non-equivalent groups, 129–130
Prenatal care program example
　background information on, 65–66
　program theory application to, 66*fig*
Pretesting
　pattern, 1 design using, 132–134
　pattern, 2 design using, 134–135
　pattern, 3 design using, 135–136
　pattern, 4 design using, 136–137
　survey instrument (or questionnaire), 110
　untreated control group design with, 132*fig*
Private food assistance network, 123, 159
Program description
　common mistakes made in, 16–18
　conducting initial informal interviews for, 72, 115, 152
　dynamic nature of, 18–19
　examples of, 37–67
　logistics of, 14–19
　models for, 12–13, 36, 45, 152–153
　motivation behind, 13–14
　pitfalls in, 65
Program description examples
　Children's Health Insurance Outreach Program, 62–66
　Comprehensive Charity Services, 54–62
　Funder's Nonprofit Capitalization Initiative, 48–54
　Labor Union, 37–44
　Program to Reduce Child Stunting and Wasting in a Developing Country, 44–48
Program description models
　PLM (program logic model), 5, 25–36
　program theory, 23–25
Program description update
　challenges of multiple sites for, 35–36
　as continuous process, 18–19
　program implementation model used for, 36
　program logic model used for, 26–34
　program theory used for, 19–25
Program implementation model, 36
Program logic model columns
　activities, 32
　assumptions, 29–30
　goals, 26–28
　inputs, 31
　outcome measures, 33–34
　outcomes, 32–33
　outputs, 32
　summary of, 25–26
　target population, 30
Program logic model (PLM)
　analysis of, 34–35
　description and evaluation use of, 5, 12, 25–34
　eight columns of, 26, 28–33, 41, 44, 65
　examples of program descriptions, 37–67
　motivations behind development of, 12
　multisite programs, 35–36
　program implementation model, 36–37
　of W.K. Kellogg Foundation, 26
Program logic model (PLM) examples
　Funder's Nonprofit Capitalization Initiative, 49–54
　Labor Union, 41–44
　Program to Reduce Child Stunting and Wasting in a Developing Country, 45–48
Program staff
　creating shared vision with, 13
　summative evaluation reservations by, 70
Program theory examples
　Funder's Nonprofit Capitalization Initiative, 49–54
　Labor Union, 41–44
　Program to Reduce Child Stunting and Wasting in a Developing Country, 45–48
Program theory (theory of change)
　applied to program description update, 12, 19–25
　contribution analysis, 20–21
　description and evaluation use of, 5, 12
　diagramming, 5, 20–21
　literature reviews and, 6, 21–22, 25
　motivations behind development of, 13–14

Program theory (theory of change) (cont'd)
  used to narrow evaluation question, 6–7
  Opera Trunk Program example of, 23–25
  unit of analysis of changes component of, 20–21
Program to Reduce Child Stunting and Wasting in a Developing Country, 44–48
Programs *See also* Evaluation
  building knowledge base from evaluation of, 110
  description of, 12–36
  necessary and sufficient, 88–91
  target population reached by, 2
  types of effects of, 97–101
  understanding different perspectives of stakeholders on *See* Evaluation
Propensity of issues, 160

Q

Quasi-experimental design
  archival or historical data included in, 128, 145, 148
  cohort, 144–146
  data analysis, 127
  delayed treatment control group, 137–140
  description of, 7, 127
  different samples, 140–141
  equivalent groups using switched measures, 142–144
  non-equivalent observations drawn from one group, 141–142
  not showing causation, 128–131
  notation to display, 127–128
  one-group post-test-only, 128–129
  participants' pretest-post-test, 130–131
  permitting causal inferences, 131–148
  post-test-only with non-equivalent groups, 129–130
  time series designs, 146–148
  untreated control group design with pretest and post-test, 131–137
Quasi-Experimentation: Design and Analysis Issues for Field Settings (Cook and Campbell), 104–106, 127–129
Question reliability, 110, 161
Question validity, 85

R

Randomly assigned participants, 130
Reliability (question), 110, 161
Researcher "fishing", 110–111
Resentful demoralization, 118
Respondents *See also* Evaluation questions; Participants
  compensatory rivalry and resentful demoralization of, 118
  confidentiality and anonymity of, 80–81, 167–168
  response to unclear questions by, 108
RFP (Request for Proposals), 76, 177

S

Samples
  convenience, 170–171
  definition of, 170–171
  simple random, 171–173
  "snowball", 171
Sampling
  small sample size, 107–109
  survey design, 161–169
Sampling error, 141
Selection threat to validity, 113–114
Self-administered surveys, 163
Simple random sample, 171–173
Small sample sizes, 107–109
"Snowball" sample, 171
Staff, 70
  creating shared vision with, 13
  summative evaluation reservations by, 70
Stakeholders
  creating shared vision with, 13
  different perspectives held by, 12
  informal interviews done with, 72–73, 152
  outcome measures that are meaningful to, 33–34
Statistical conclusion validity
  biased responses threat to, 109
  definition of, 105
  measurement error threat to, 109–110
  priority given to, 105
  questions at heart of, 106
  research "fishing" threat to, 110–111
  small sample sizes threat to, 107–109
  Type, 1 and Type 2 errors 106–107, 110–111
  unclear questions/bias responses threat to, 108
  unreliable treatment implementation threat to, 110
Statistical regression threat to validity, 115–116
Sufficient program variable
  connections between variables, 95
  cut points of variables, 93
  description of, 88
  variables of necessary and, 88–90
Summative evaluation, 69
Survey design, 161–169
Surveys
  anonymity and confidentiality issues of, 167–168
  compared to focus groups and interviews, 160
  data collection using, 160–169
  open-ended questions used in, 161
  telephone, 148, 163

T

Target population
  gathering data on, 169–174
  Housing Recovery Program, 60–61*t*, 64
  program logic model component of, 30
  program reaching intended, 2
Telephone surveys, 148, 163
Testing threat to validity, 115
Theory of Change. *See* Program theory (theory of change)
Threat of history, 111–112
Threat of instrumentation, 116–117
Threat of maturation, 112–113
Threat of selection, 113–114
Threat of statistical regression, 115–116
Threat of testing, 115
Time series designs, 146–148
Treatments
  diffusion as threat to validity, 117–118
  threat of compensatory equalization of, 118
Type I error, 106–107, 111
Type II error, 106–107, 109, 110
Types of effects, 97–1000

U

Unit of analysis, 20–21
Unreliable treatment implementation, 110

Untreated control group design with pretest and post-test, 131–137
U.S. Census Bureau, 30, 164, 170

V

Validity
  construct, 104, 119–122
  data analysis, 110
  external, 105, 122–124
  general issues related to, 104–105
  internal, 104, 111–119
  question, 117
  statistical conclusion, 105, 105–111
  threats to, 107–122
  types of, 104–105

W

W.K. Kellogg Foundation, 26

Y

Yad Vashem Holocaust Museum, 143*t*
Yes bias, 162